WE MET IN MEMPHIS

we were born
with eyes that looked
and saw, recorded, interpreted, expressed
through hearts and hands and minds
speaking with a confidence only born through
endless pracice, failures, and successes
silent conversations of no and yes or maybe
delivered to juries to be received with joy,
understanding or confusion

we kept drawing, paint ing, writing, expressing
we kept being in conversation with ourselves
until we understood
the meaning or question
we discovered

we had an urgency within
we discovered we had important things to say
the conversations were usually one-sided

we went to the place with other people
who had this insatiable
curiosity and language

we learned to speak louder and more clearly
because we found others with whom to speak

WE MET IN MEMPHIS

First published in North America in 2020 by C.S. Hubble

Produced, edited, and designed at C.S. Hubble,
Paducah, Kentucky

Text and consultant editor: Billie Dean Shoemate III

Contributing editors: Margaret Takei, Sue Brown, and Sandra Stuart

Cover design: C.S. Hubble

ISBN 978-1-934740-99-6

Library of Congress Control Number:
2020904141

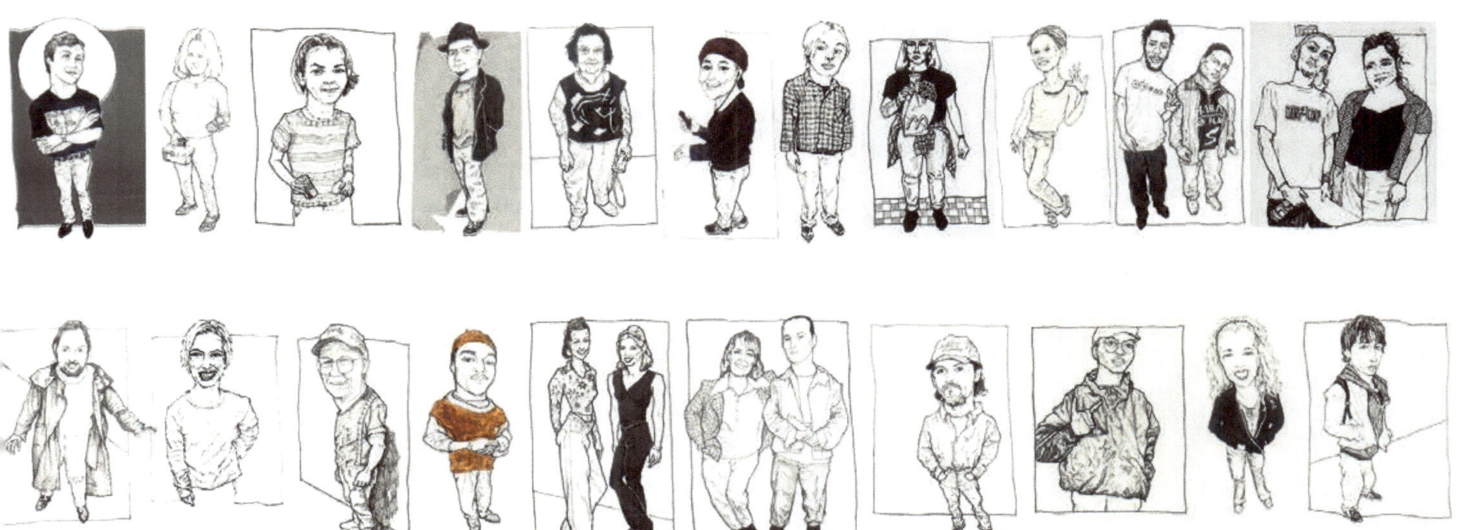

WE MET IN MEMPHIS

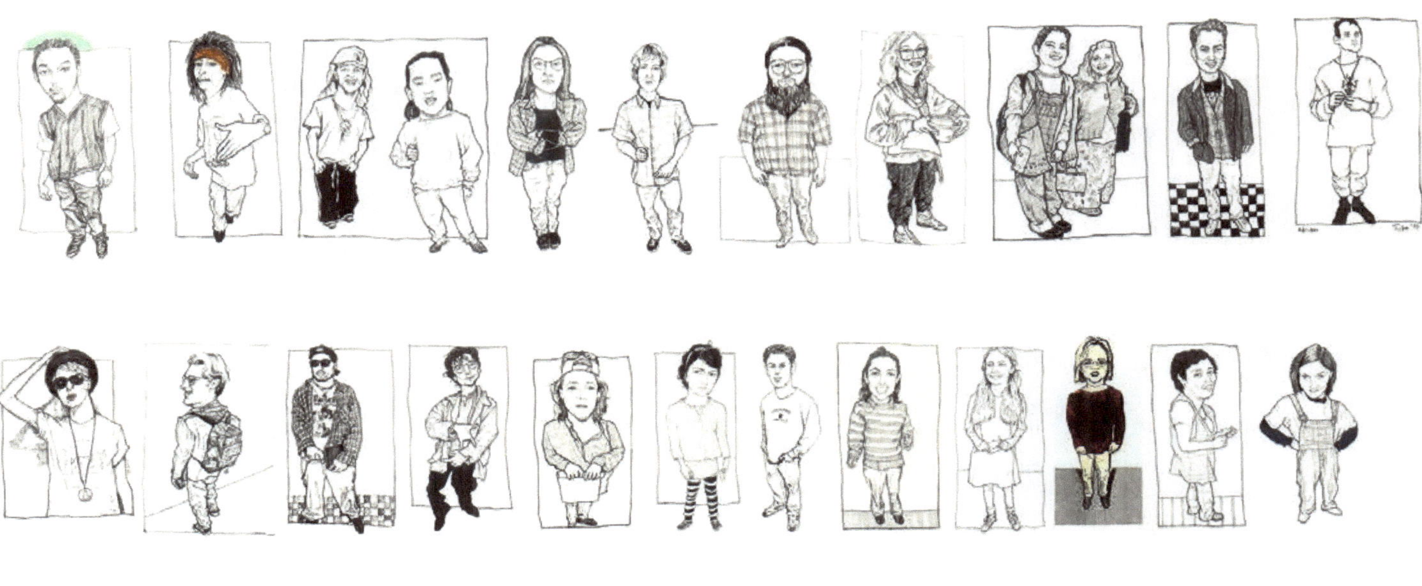

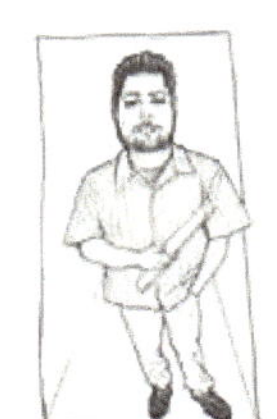
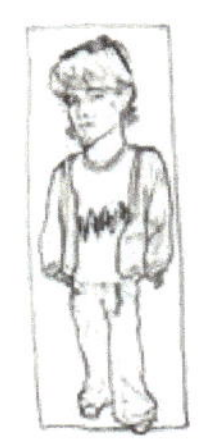
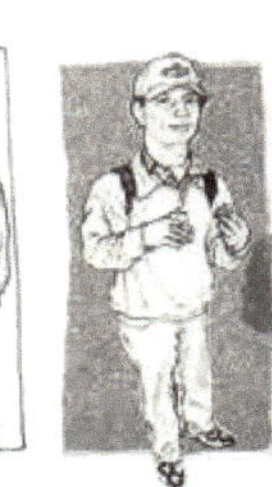
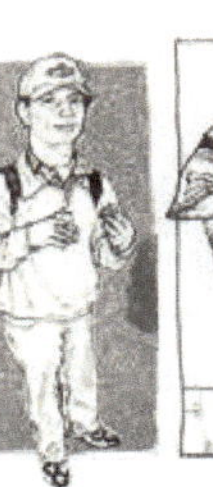
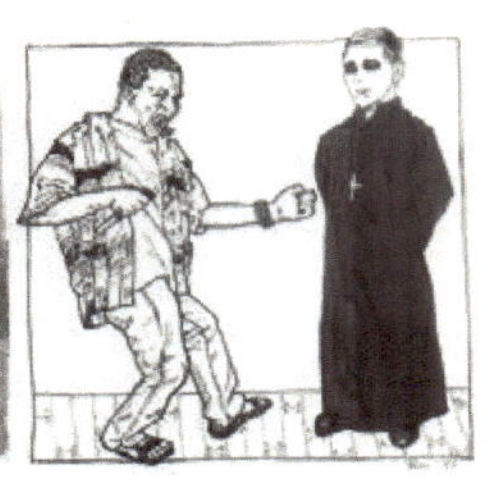
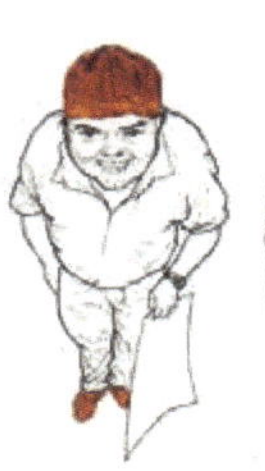
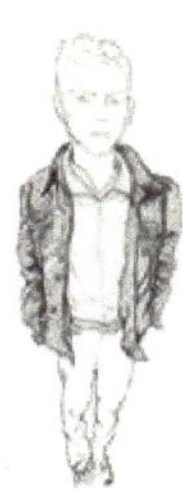
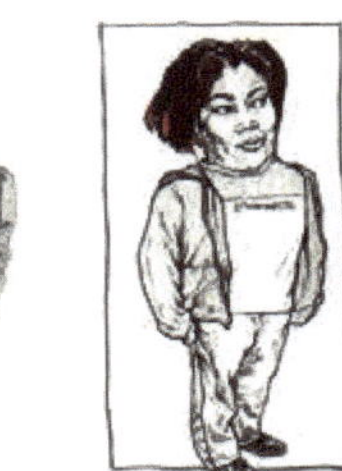
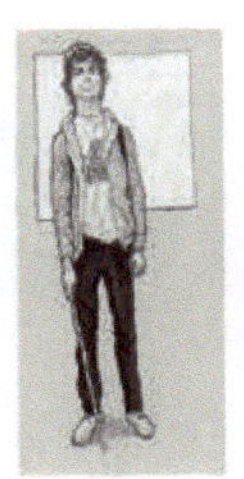
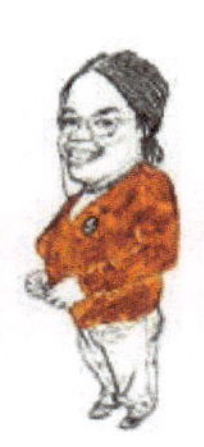
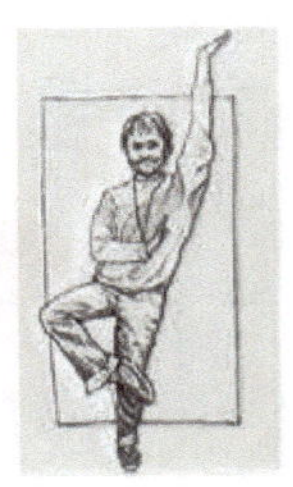

SPECIAL THANKS TO LISA TRIBO FOR THE USE OF HER SKETCHES

ADAM HAWK.com

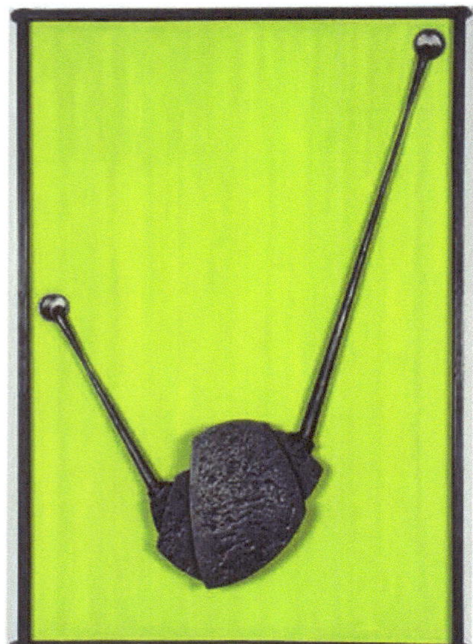

"Black on Green", Forged and Fabricated Steel, Acrylic Paint, 36" x 24", 2008

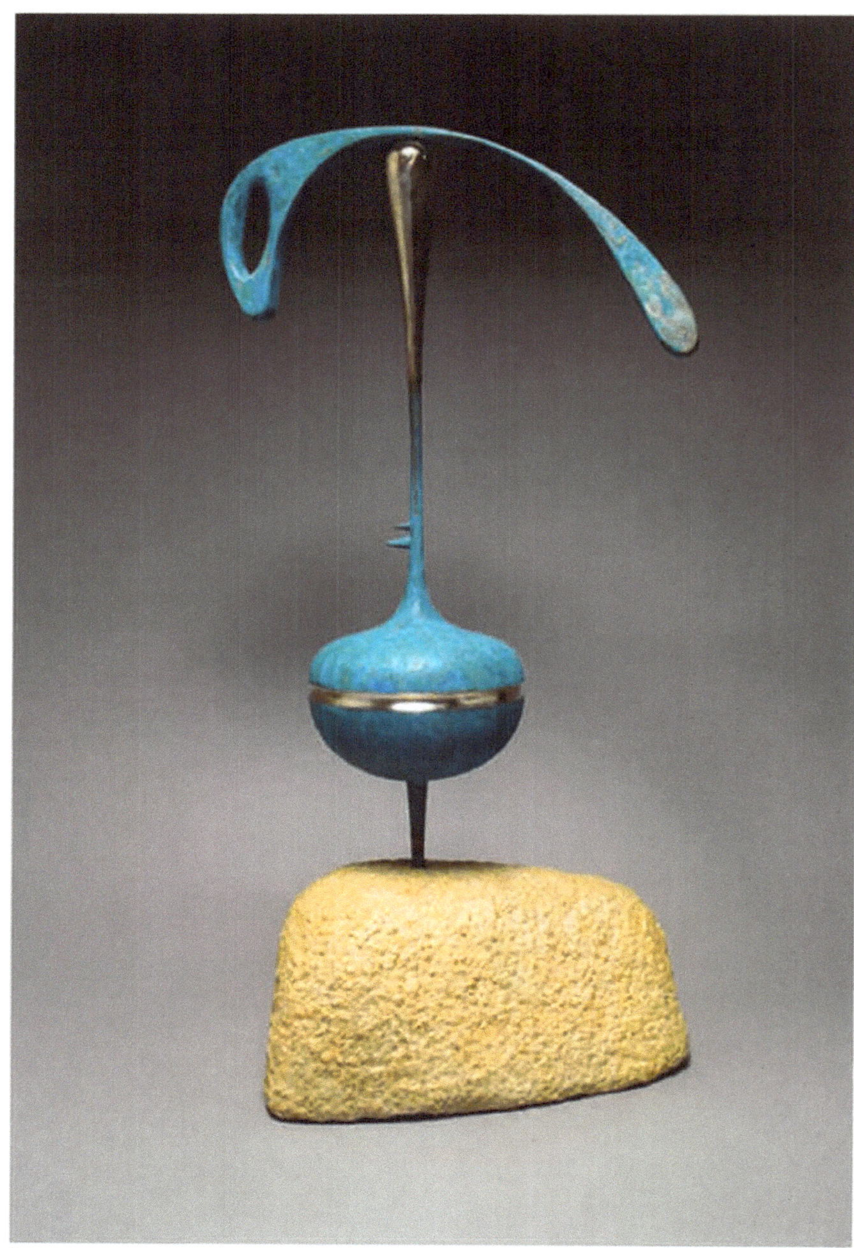

"Bronze Cast from 3D Print", Limestone, 24" x 12" x 4", 2016

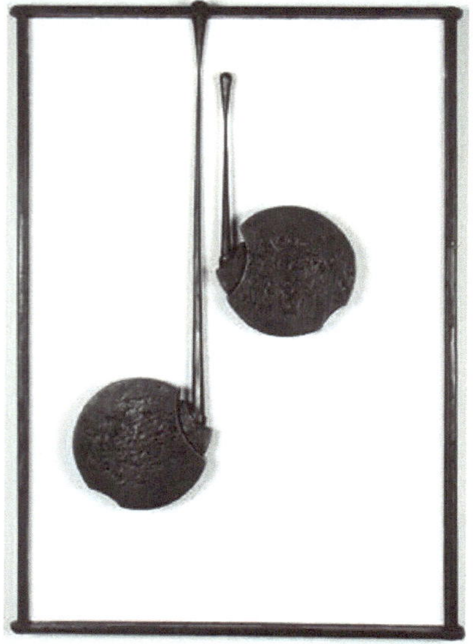

"Black on White", Forged and Fabricated Steel, Acrylic Paint, 36" x 24", 2008

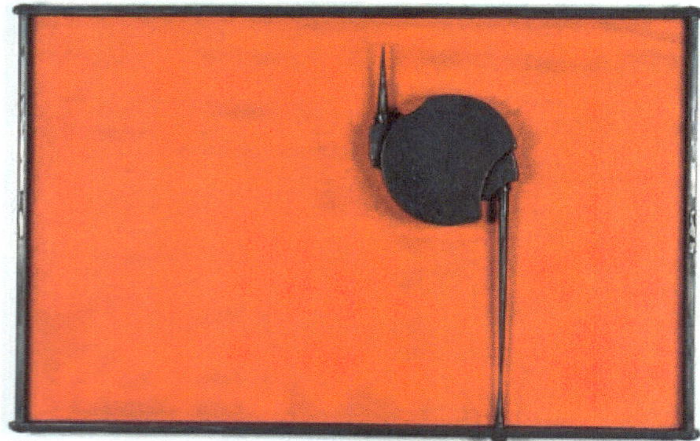

"Black on Orange", Forged and Fabricated Steel, Acrylic Paint, 24" x 36", 2008

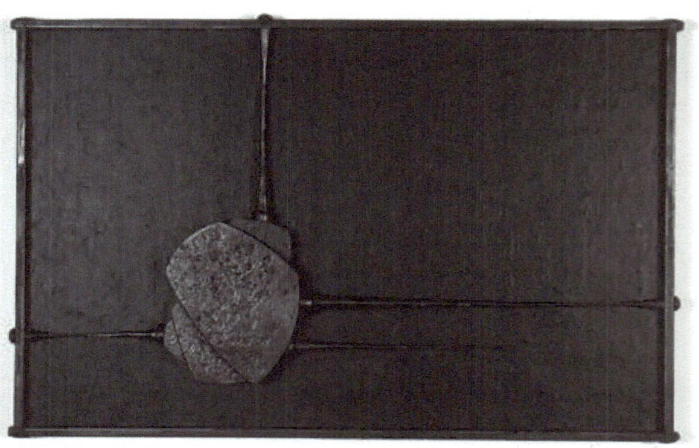

"Black on Black", Forged and Fabricated Steel, Acrylic Paint, 24" x 36", 2008

ADAM HAWK

Instagram: adamhawk_

Adam Hawk is a studio artist and Visiting Assistant Professor at the University of Wisconsin-Milwaukee. Hawk earned his MFA in metalsmithing /blacksmithing from Southern Illinois University Carbondale and BFA in sculpture and computer fine arts from Memphis College of Art. Previously, Hawk has served as an assistant professor at Memphis College of Art and worked as a blacksmith at the National Ornamental Metal Museum. His work has been exhibited at the National Ornamental Metal Museum, Leigh Yawkey Woodson Art Museum, Walter Anderson Museum, the Fuller Craft Museum, Arrowmont School of Arts and Crafts, the HOW art museum in Shanghai, China, The Villa Braghieri in Italy, and the LA Joaillerie par Mazio in Paris, France. Most recently, Hawk was included in an exhibition at the National Metal Museum titled 40 Under 40, which "explores the next generation of influential American metal artists."

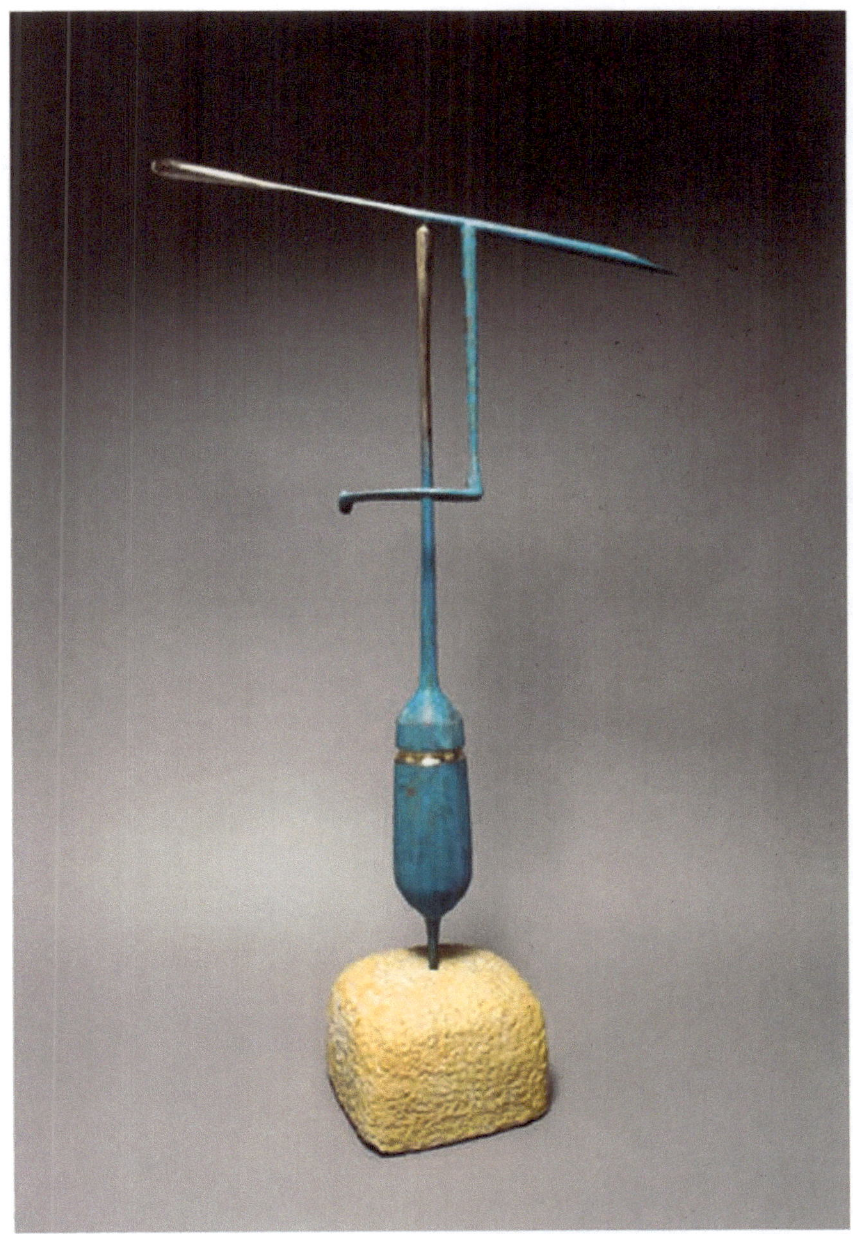

"3DP5", Bronze Cast from 3D Print, Limestone, 26" x 16" x 4", 2016

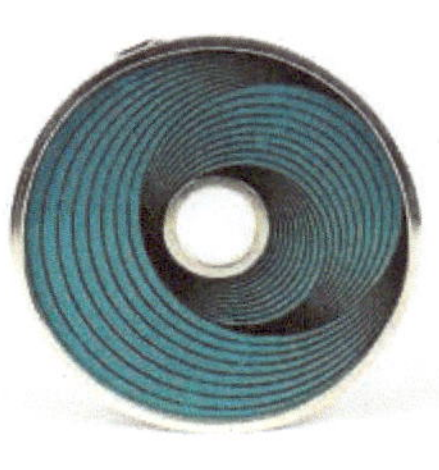

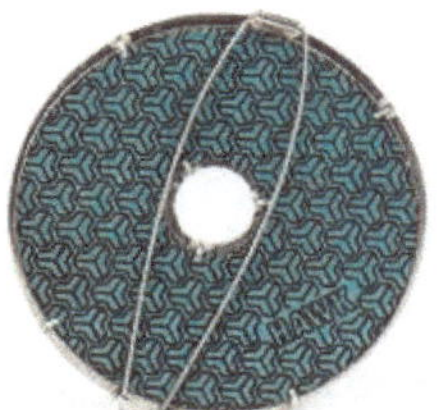

"Ellipse", Enamel, Copper, Sterling Silver, 2.5" x 2.5", 2018

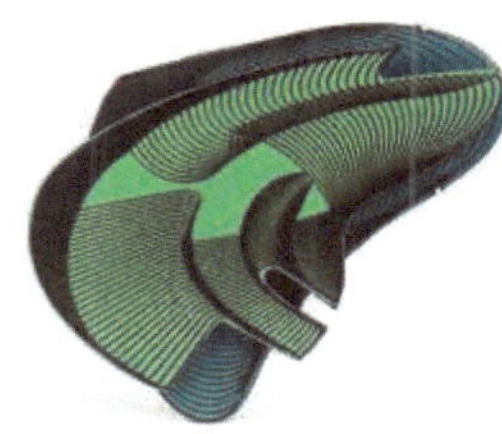

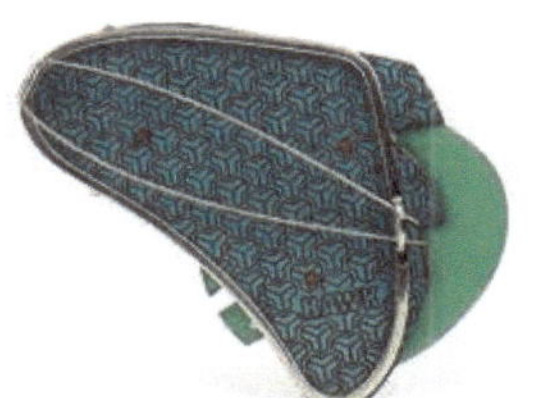

"Nautilus #4", Enamel, Copper, Sterling Silver, 2.5" x 2.5", 2018

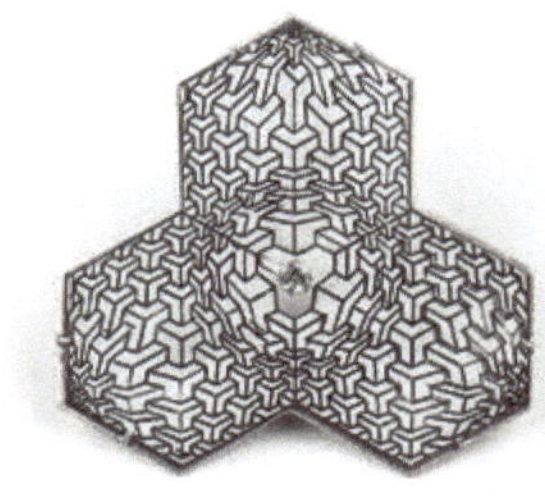

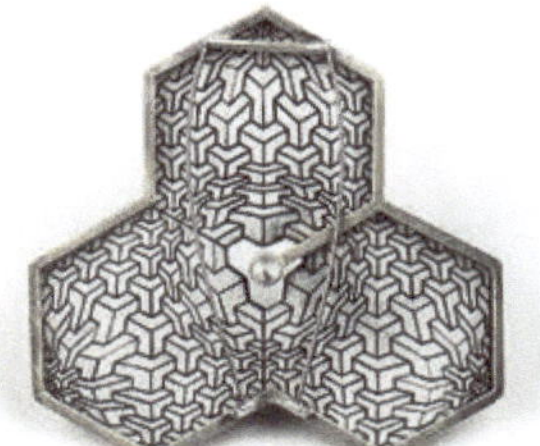

"White T-cube", Enamel, White Topaz, Sterling Silver, 3" x 3", 2018

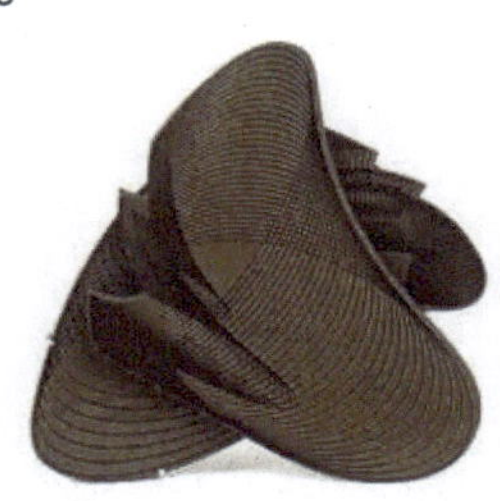

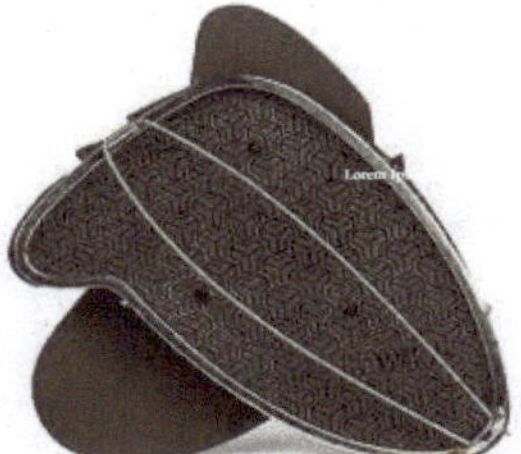

"Nautilus #3", Enamel, Copper, Sterling Silver, 2.5" x 2.5", 2018

WENDY HAILEY KIM

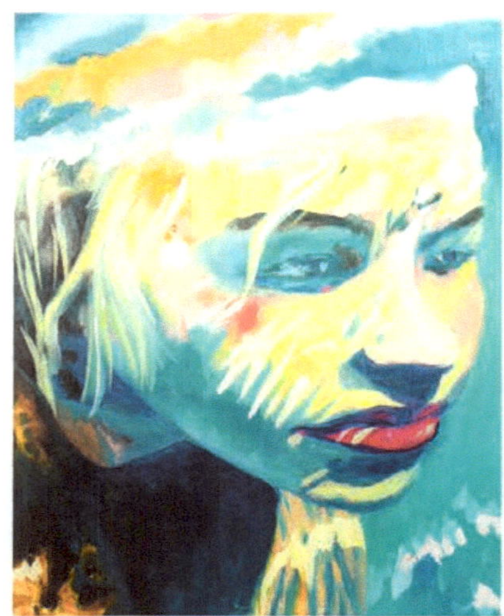

"Immersed" Water Soluble Oil on Canvas 22" x 30"

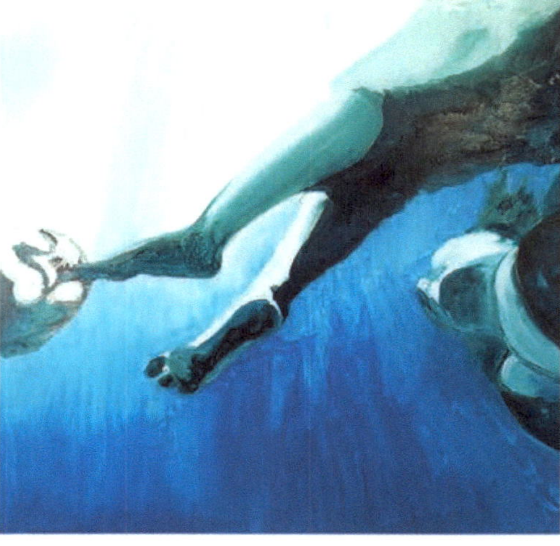

2 **"Family Pool"** Water Soluble Oil on Canvas 40" x 40"

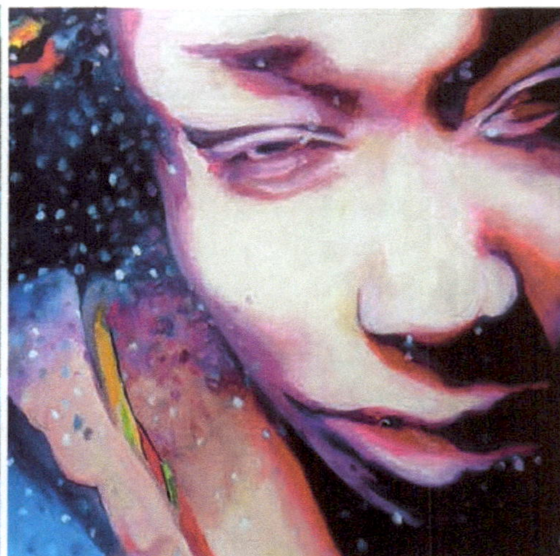

"Bobbie" Water Soluble Oil on Canvas 12" x 12"

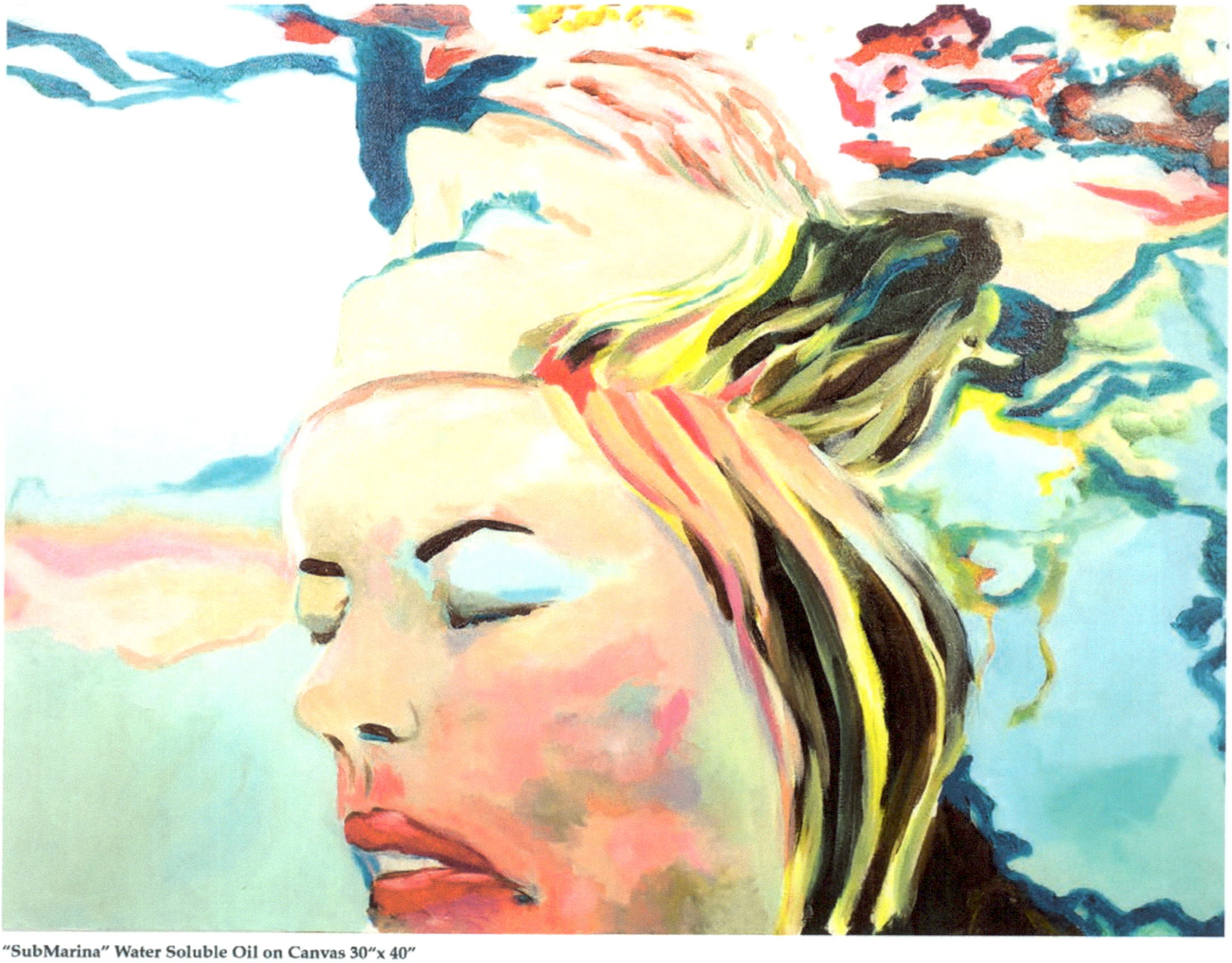

"SubMarina" Water Soluble Oil on Canvas 30"x 40"

KIMCHIPEACHSTUDIOS.COM

INSTAGRAM: lemonlushie

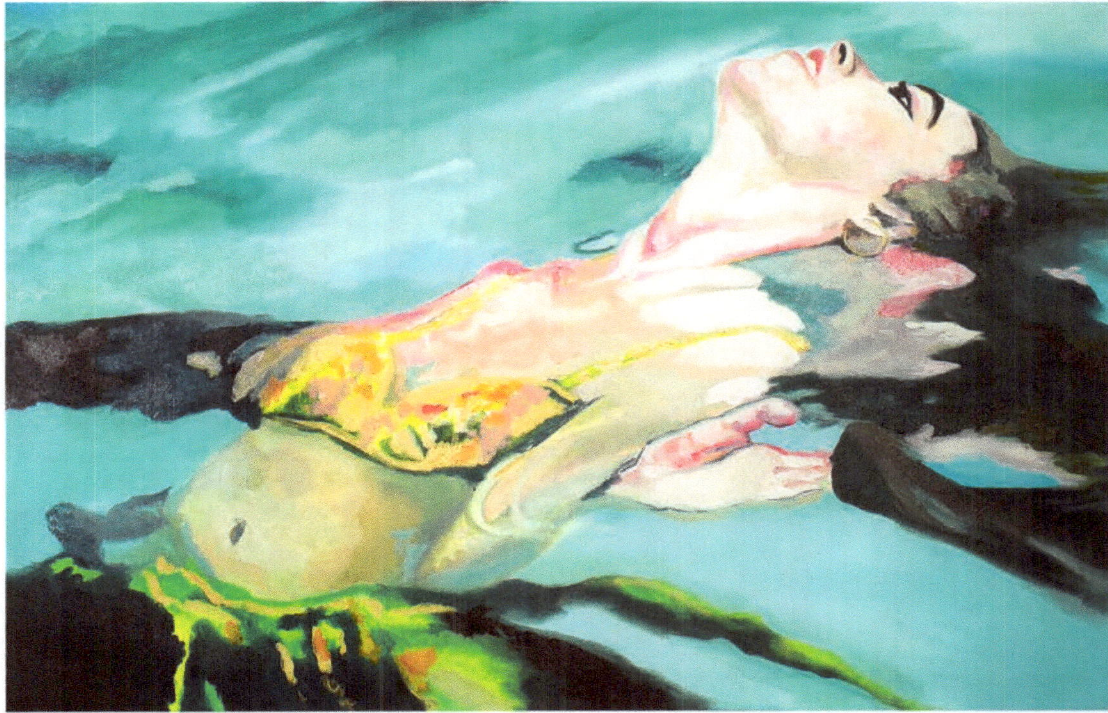

A "Dylan 2" Oil on Canvas 46" x 30"

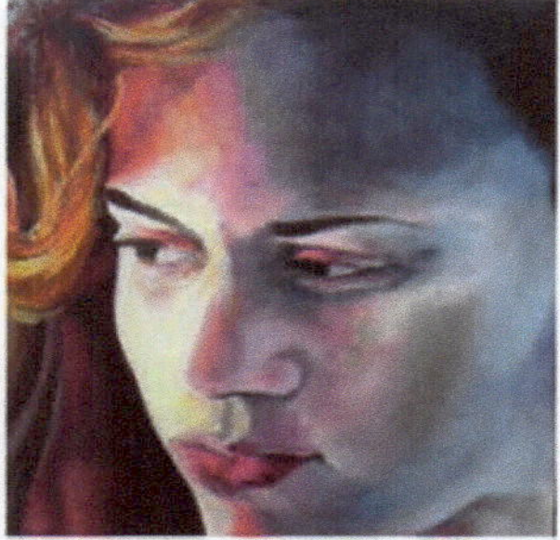

C "Chrissy" Oil on Canvas 12" x 12"

"I remember childhood summers at the pool, when swimming underwater felt like a new world I had discovered. Wendy's work is a vibrant reflection of the abstract way we see the world refracted through water. It evokes the brightness of summer and the nolstalgia of being submerged in another world."

~ Courtney Searcy

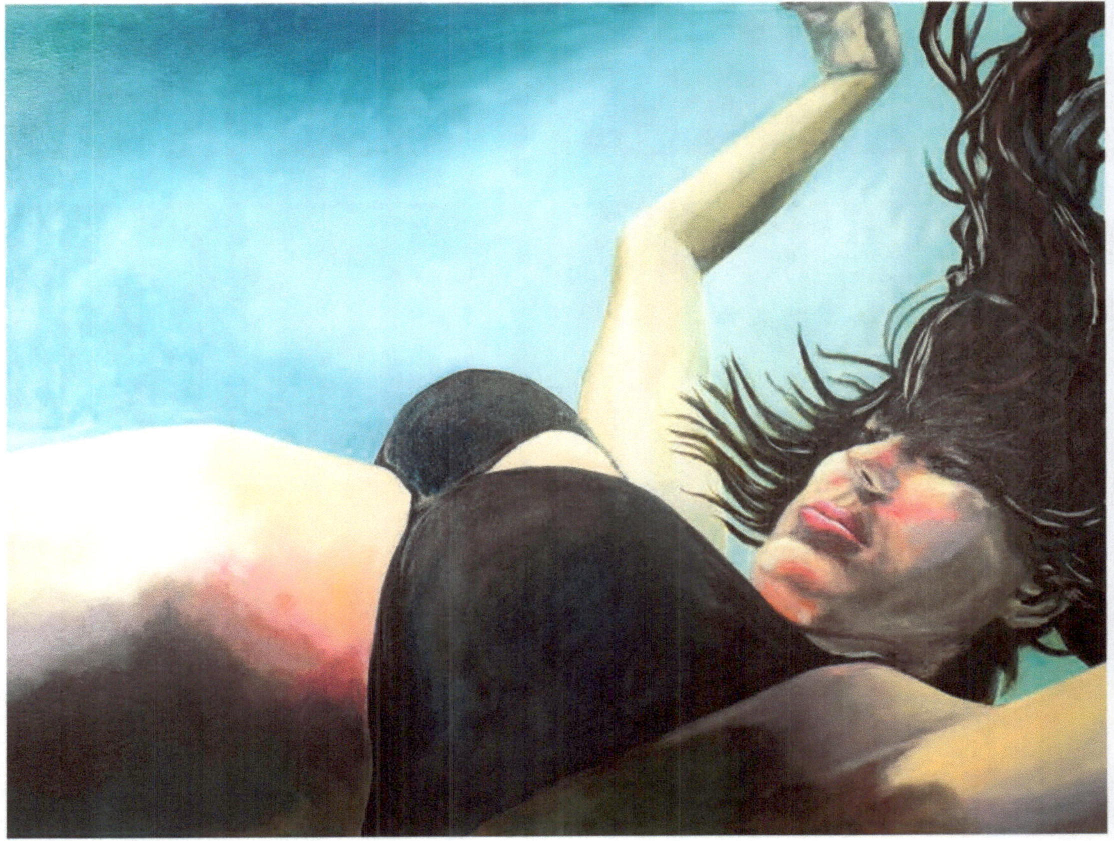

B. "Dylan 1" Oil on Canvas 40" x 30"

Corey Michael Smithson

I have dedicated my life to the service of art. My work explores various dimensions of queerness, identity, gender, eroticism, self-expression, biology, history, structure, myth, beauty, shock, fear, and love. I work in several media ... including painting, drawing, photography, film/video, animation, drag, and text ... but all of my creative output stems from the same drive: an ongoing search for beauty, connection, new experiences, and moments of grace.

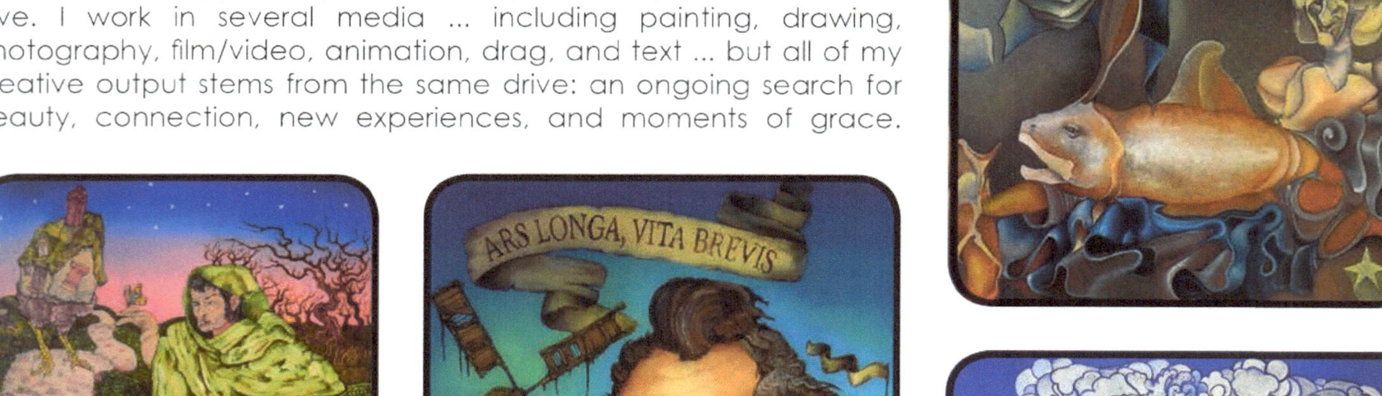

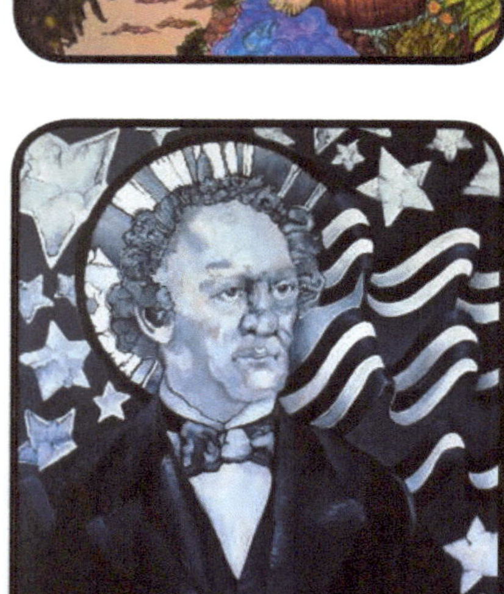

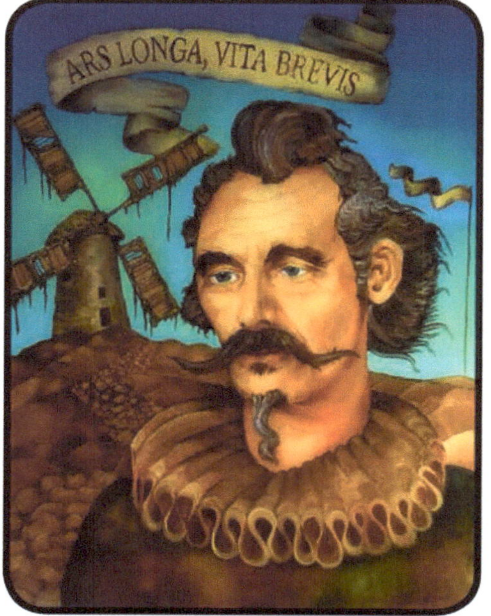

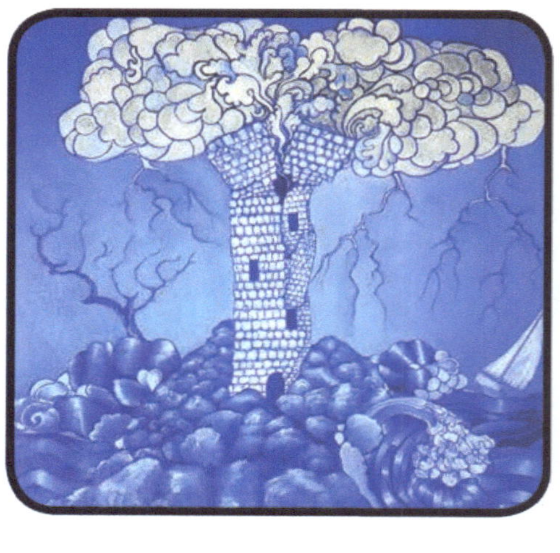

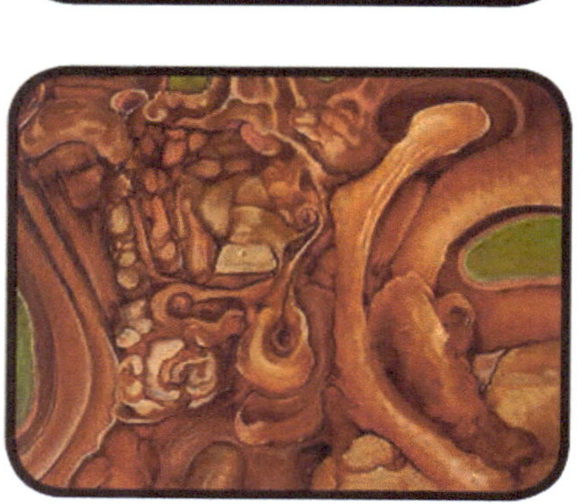

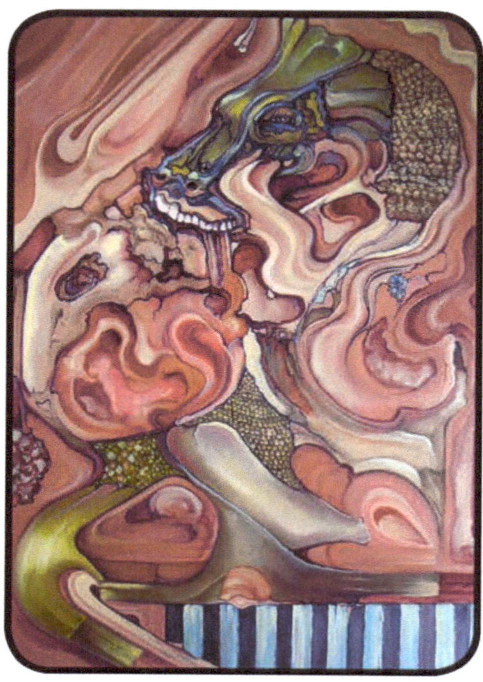

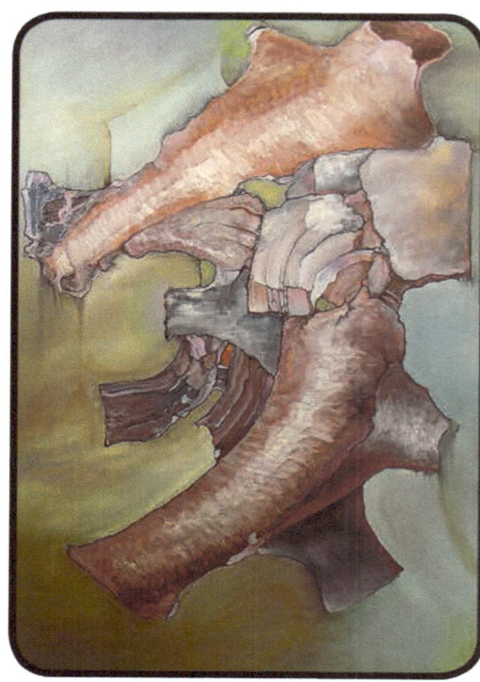

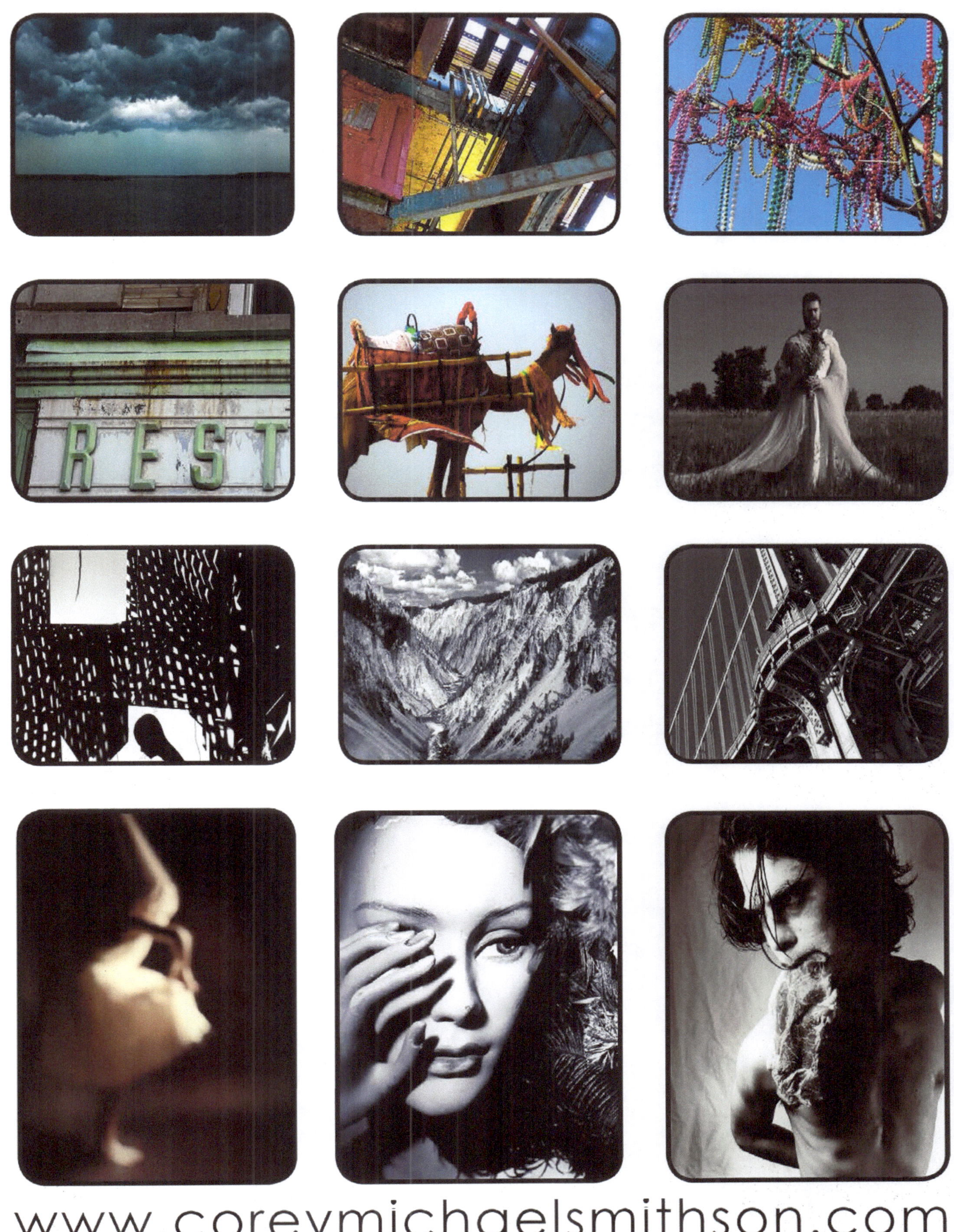

www.coreymichaelsmithson.com

BRONCO SLOAN CREATIONS

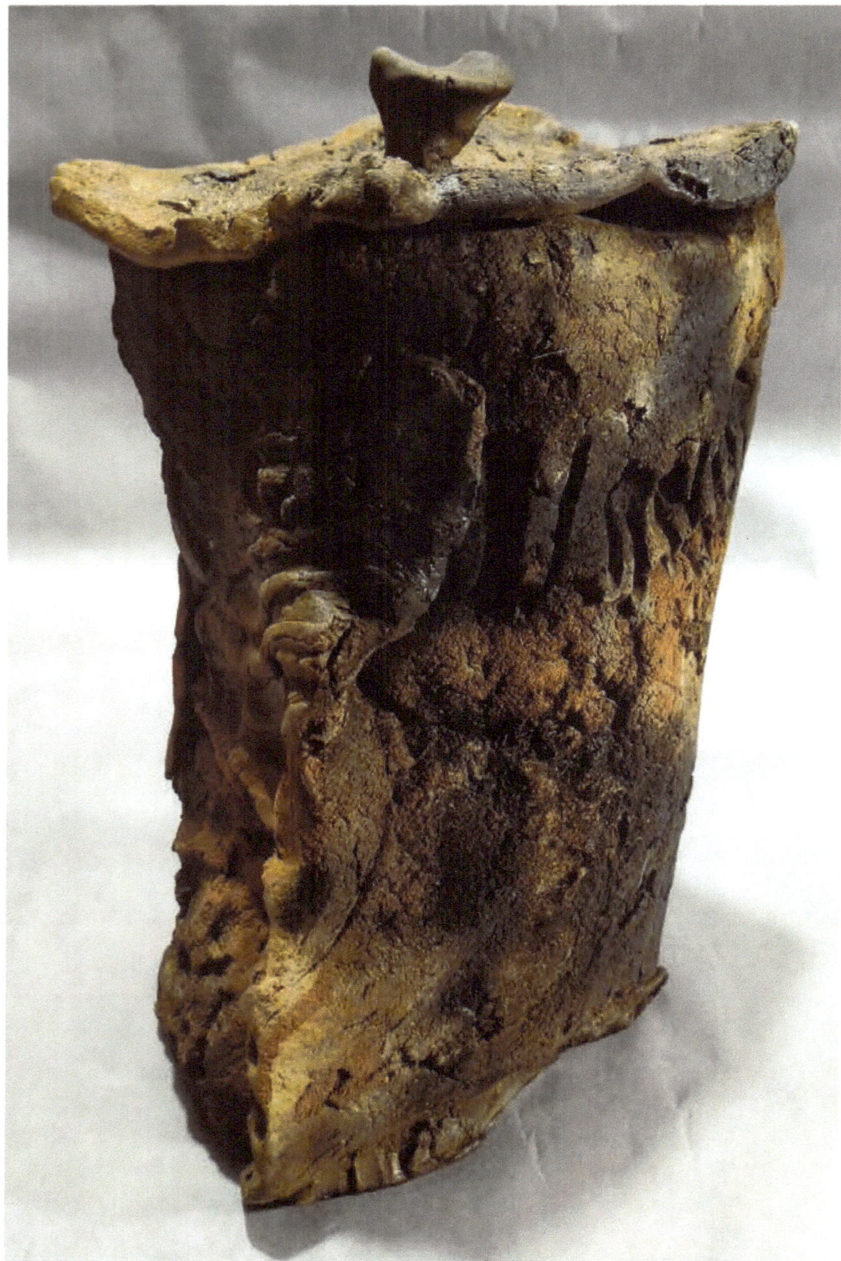

This series of boxes continues the discovery of my favorite voice, clay.
I love the alchemy involved in realizing these pieces.
I love the anticipation and labor of finding, digging, and processing the mud from the Earth.
I love the immediacy of the mark, and the texture brought to bear by tensions and torsions of my hands and tools.
I love every fluke of the flame and smoke, lapping at the surface to lend its own layers to each one.
There is a Taoist influence that allows the work to be a conversation between the materials and my self.
I seek to create a journey for the senses and a record of the generative instant.
A piece is most successful when my hands let the it become, rather than force it into being.

Pit-Fired Boxes with Wild Clay from Mobile, Alabama, 2020

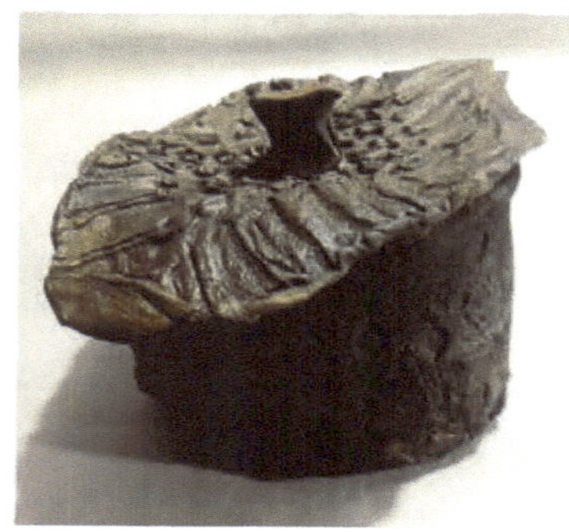

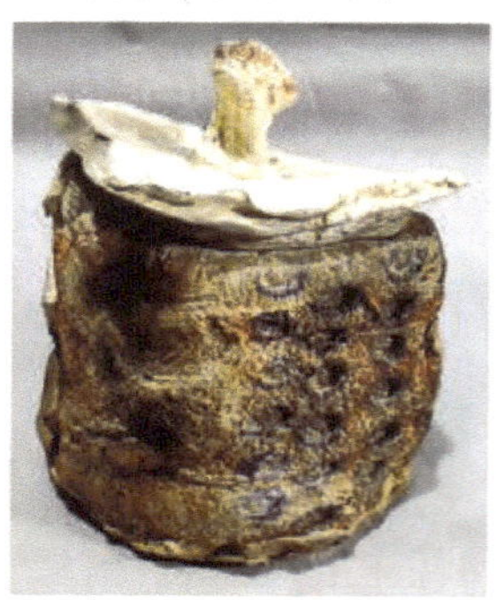

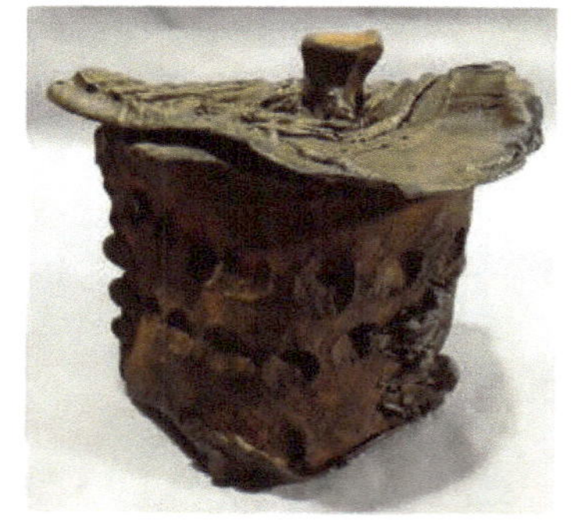

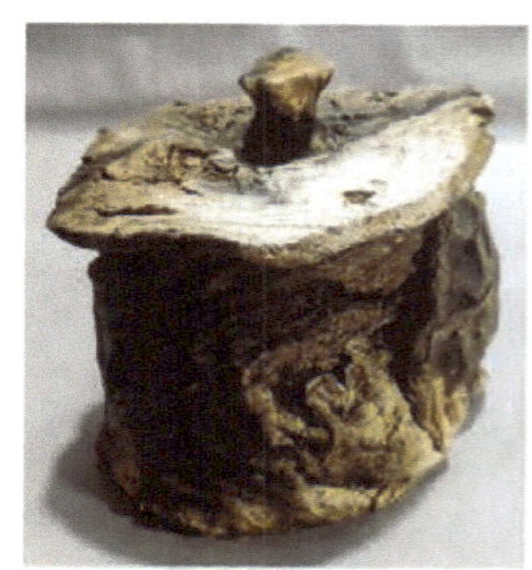

BRONCO SLOAN

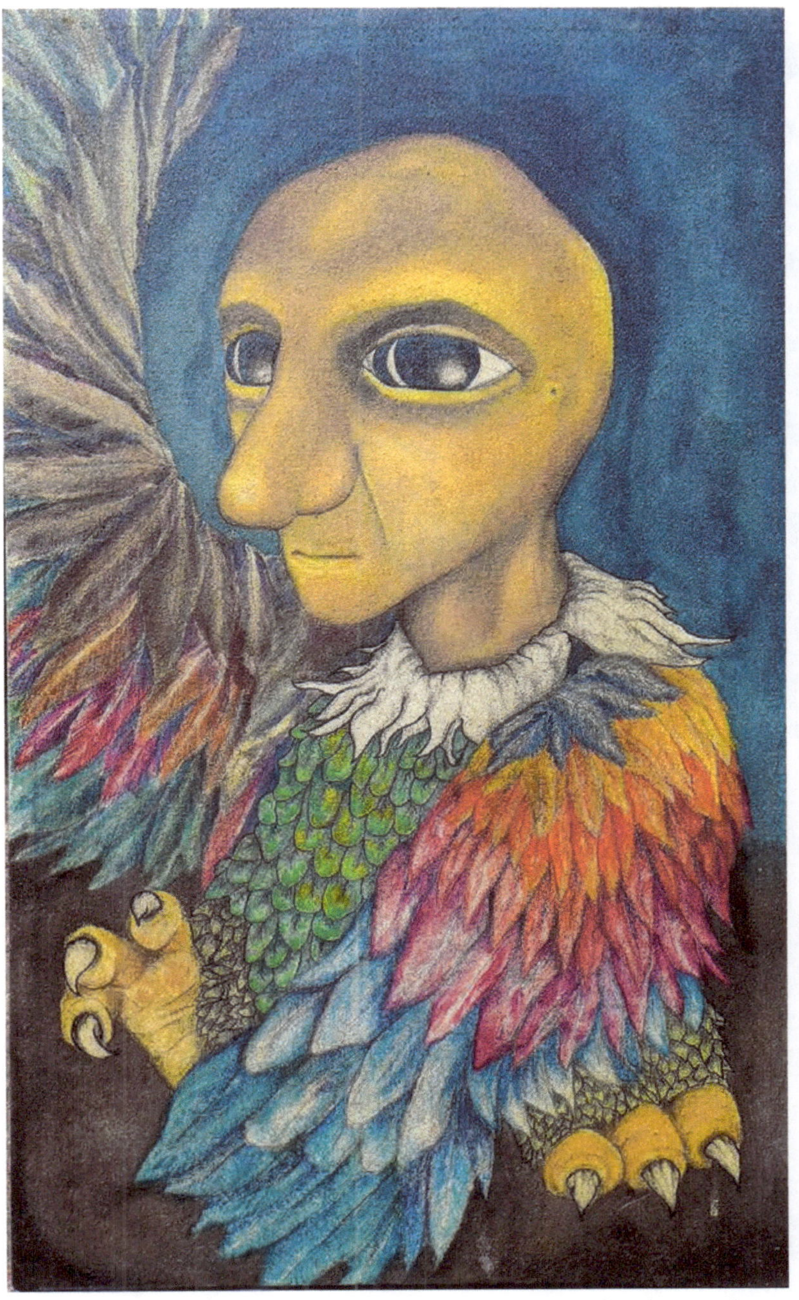

"A Bird with the Head of a Bird-Headed Boy Dancing the Dance of His People", 2015, oil and enamel on canvas, 30" x 18"

This fool has manifested in many media and many iterations over the past twenty years of my work. I always wonder what it is he's getting up to. For me, he brings mystery, humor, and a touch of the weird to focus while allowing me to play through material meditation. I think he is open to questions, but the answers might only serve to question the viewer's perspective.

Maritza Dávila-Irizarry

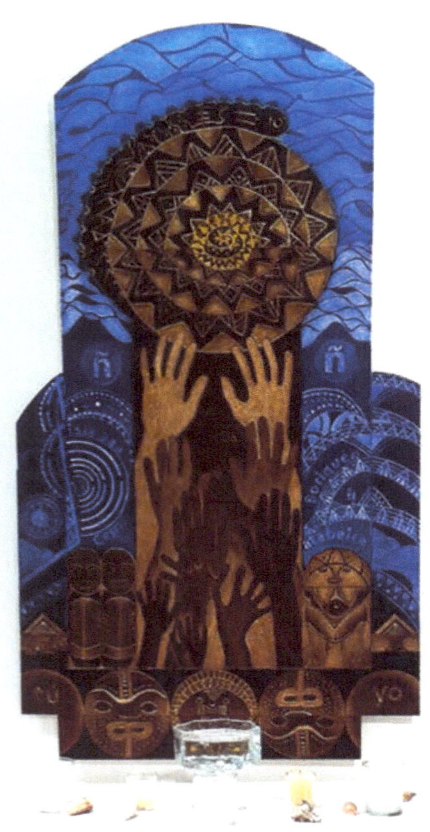

"Capilla Ancestral (Ancestral Chapel)"
Silk aquatint collagraph 43" x 28"

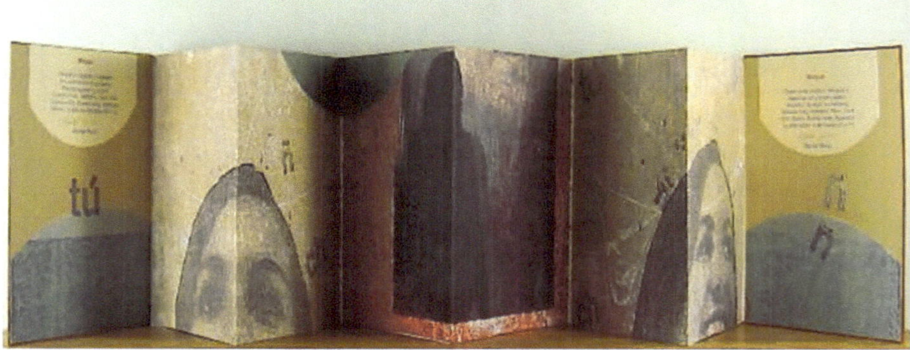

"BlilingueYagrumo (Bilingual)" Accordian binding structure 15" x 11"

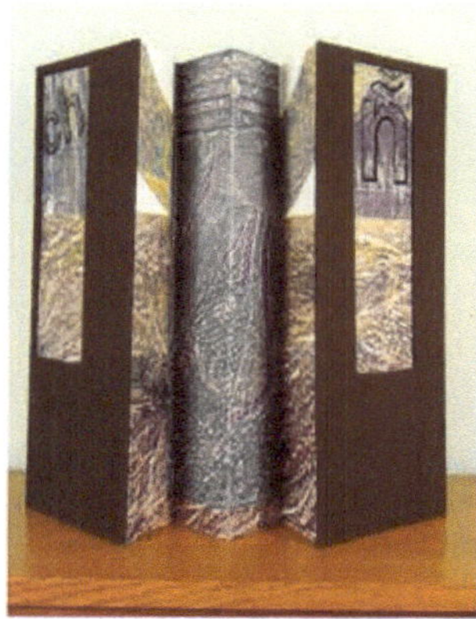

"manos en búsqueda de un idioma
(hands in search of something)"
Flag structure accordion book/
screen print 14" x 15"

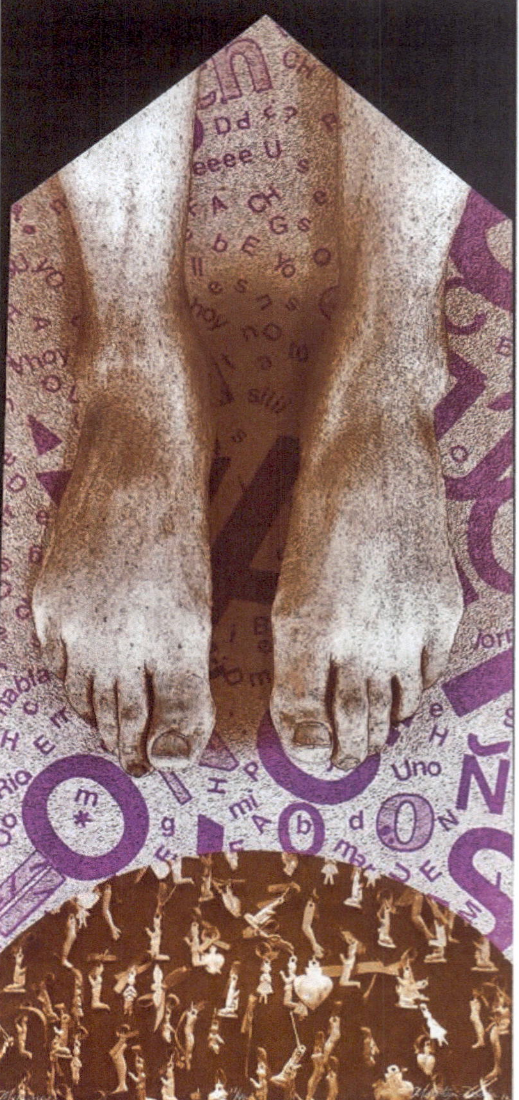

"Milagros (Miracles)" Lithograph 30" x 18"

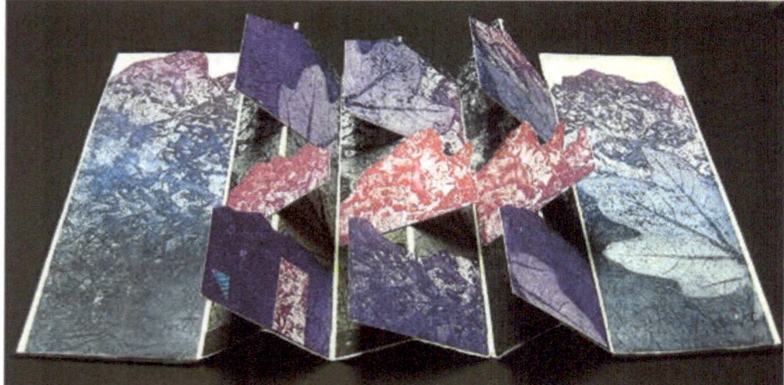

"Yagrumo" Flag structure accordion book/ Intaglio 11" x 5"

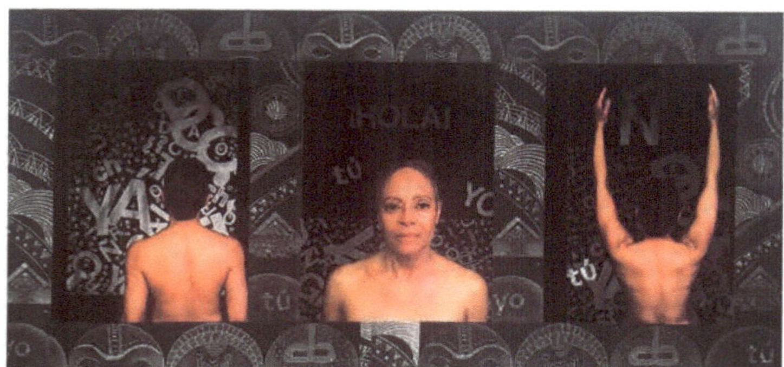

"Hola! (Hello!)" Digital prints with silk aquatint collagraph 68" x 32"

atabeira.com

Maritza Dávila-Irizarry is Professor Emeritus at the Memphis College of Art where she was professor of fine arts and the head of printmaking. She began teaching there in 1982 and received the prestigious Klyce Family Fund Benjamin Goodman Faculty Award in 2018 for her long service to MCA.

Professor Dávila-Irizarry has exhibited around the world and has works in collections in the United States, Europe, the Caribbean and Asia. She has received awards in the United States, Puerto Rico and France. Her work is included in collections at the National Library in Madrid, Spain; the National Library of Paris France; Taller ACE of Buenos Aires, Argentina; Museum of Art and History at the University of Puerto Rico; and the National Library of Congress in Washington, D.C., among others.

She is owner of the Atabeira Press studio and has collaborated with poet Kay Lindsey and visual artist Indrani Nayar Gall from India on various art projects. She was also a visiting artist at University of Bilbao, Spain in 2011 and the School of Fine Arts of the Institute of Culture of Puerto Rico among others. Residencies include Taller ACE in Buenos Aires, Argentina in 2011 and Illinois State University's Normal Editions in 2016.

As part of her research, exhibitions and in the making of her work, Professor Dávila-Irizarry has also travelled to Spain, France, Poland, England and Japan.

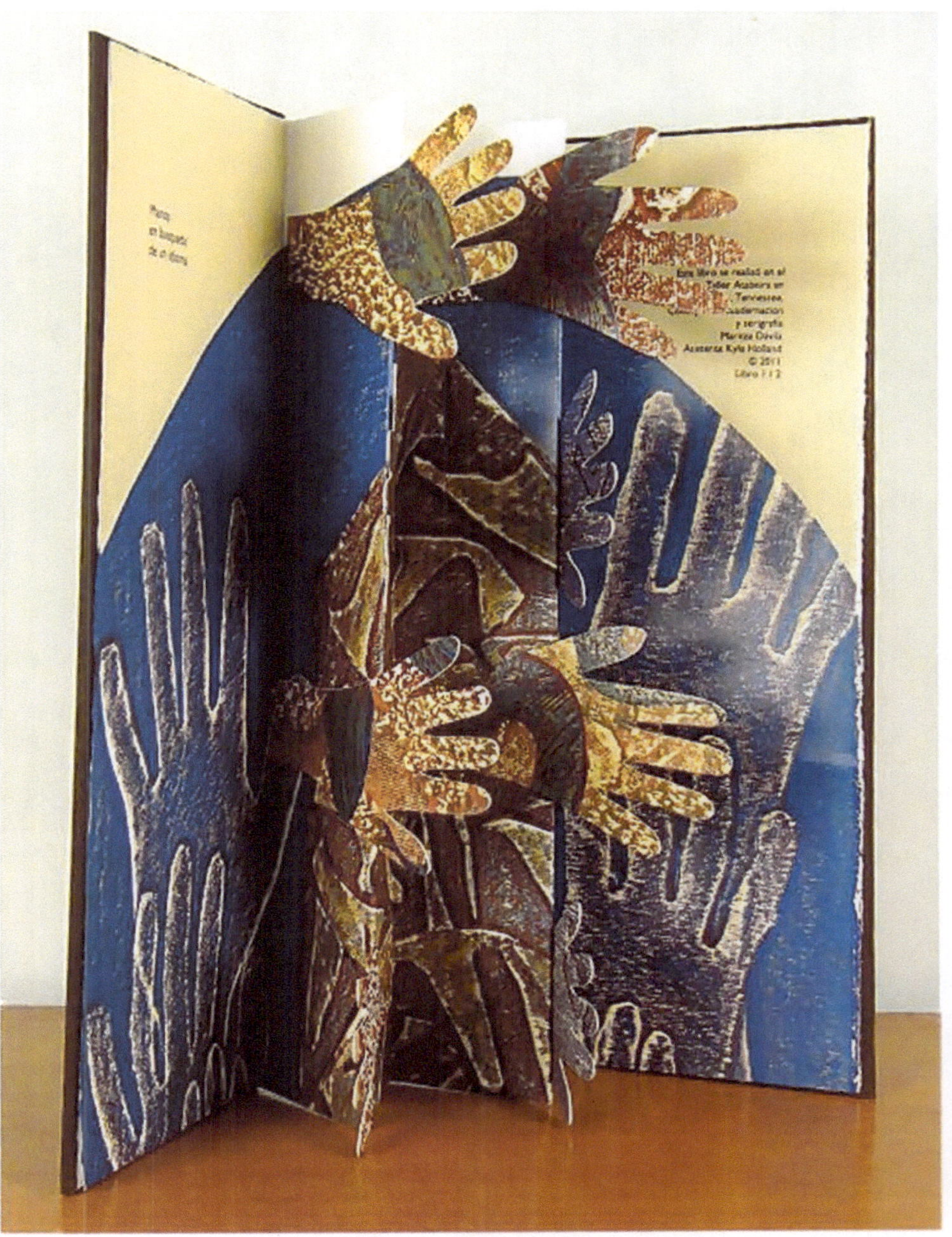

"Manos (Hands)" Flag structure acordian book/screen

"And while we may not be able to consent to the qualities of the past that have shaped us, we do exercise choice in how we regard our essential selves."

~Maritza Dávila-Irizarry

TOMMY MAVRA

"I am interested in how we negotiate our place in nature."

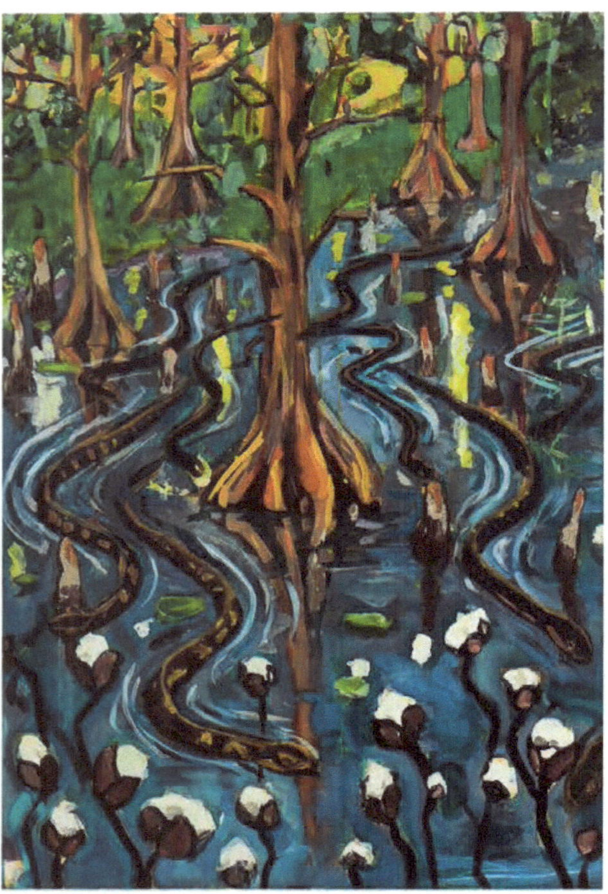

"Riches and Infamy", 2018, acrylic 35"x24"

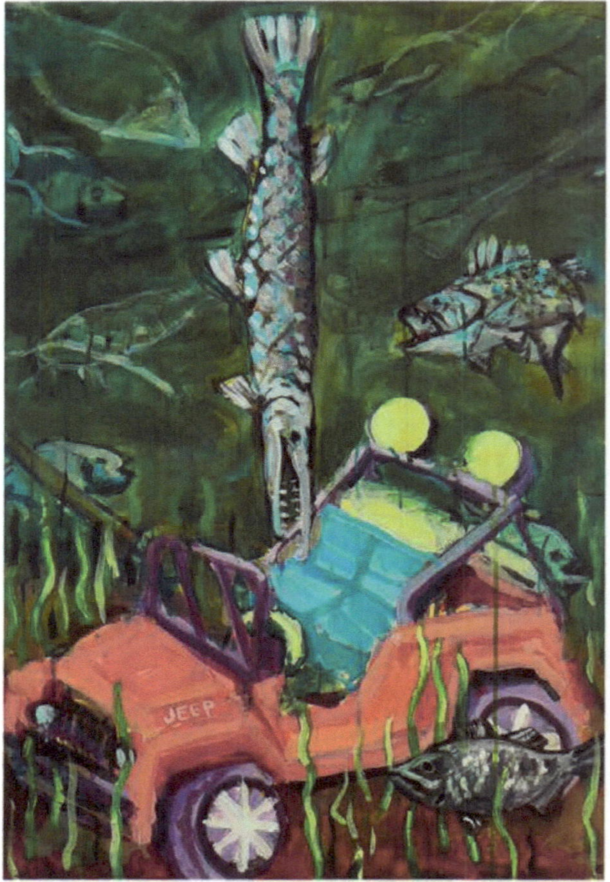

"Sunken Jeep", 2018, acrylic 35"x24"

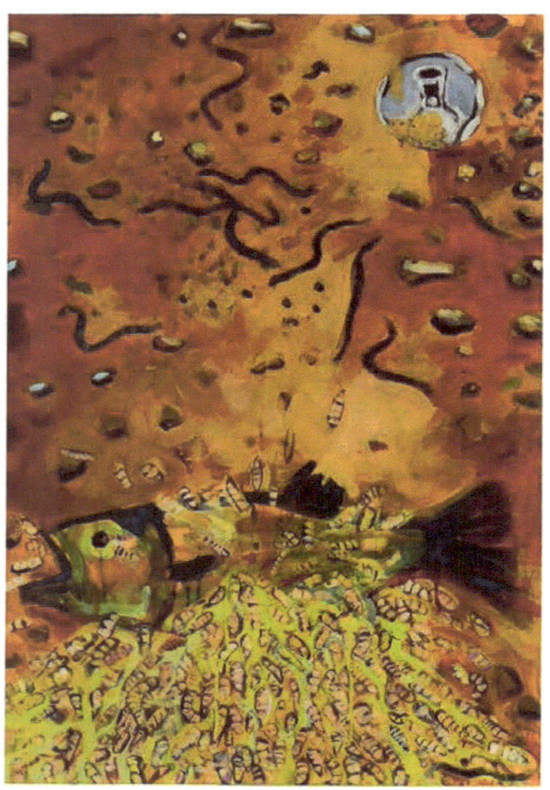

"the way things go", 2018, acrylic 35"x 24"

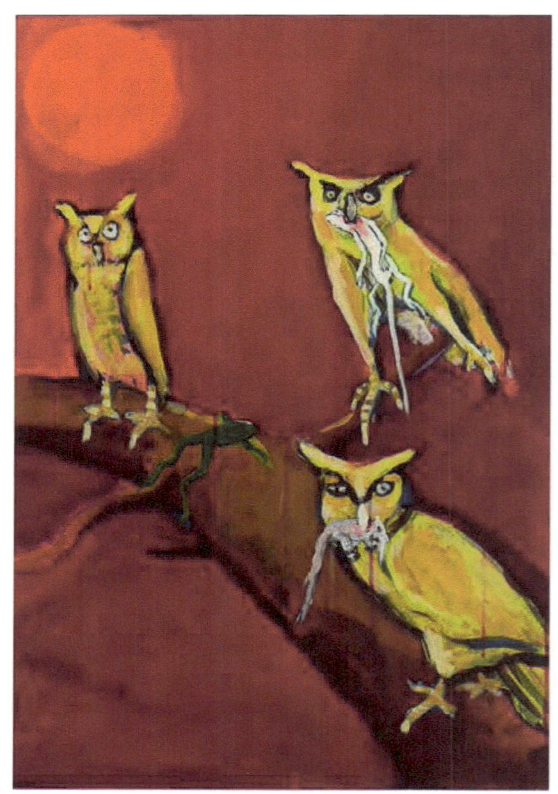

"Night Shift", 2018, acrylic 35"x 24"

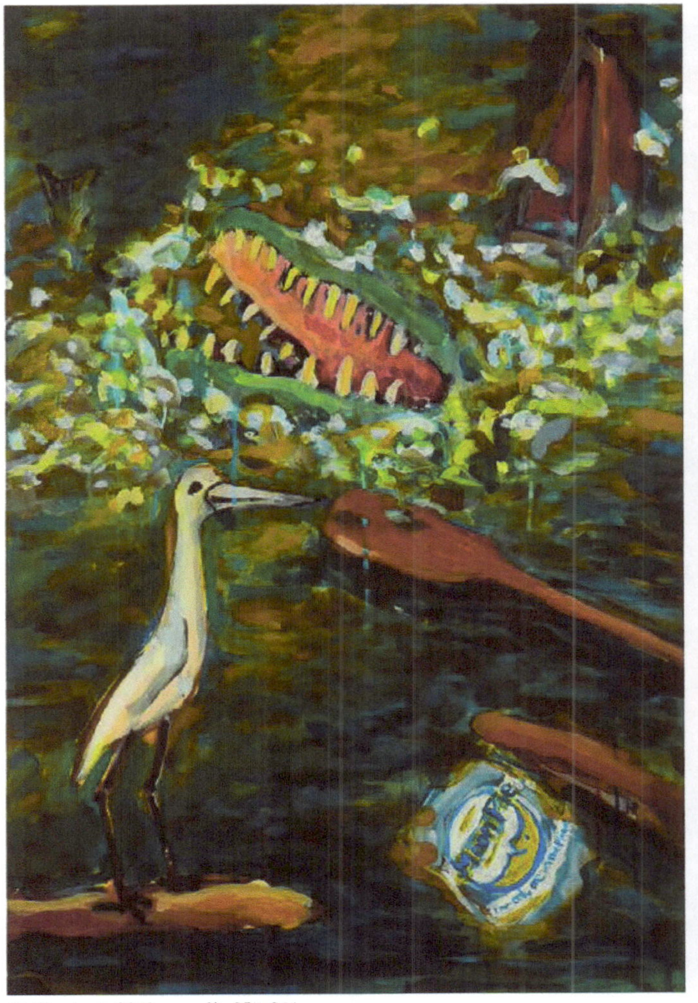

"Alligator", 2018, a crylic 35"x24"

"Pineapple Farms", 2017, acrylic 35"x24"

Tommy Mavra

www.tmavra.com

tmavra@gmail.com

instagram.com/tommymavra

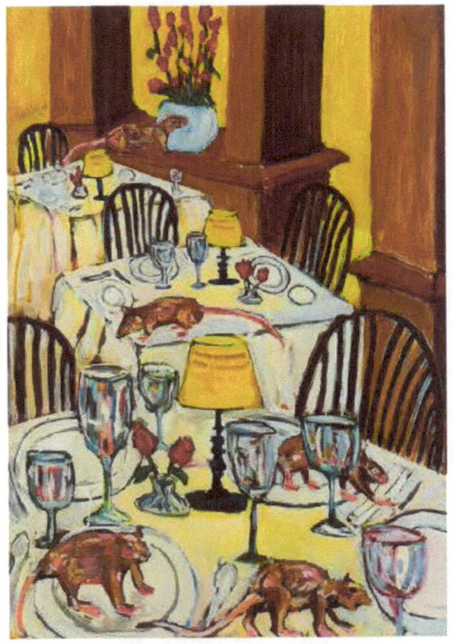

"Dining Rats", 2017, acrylic 35"x24"

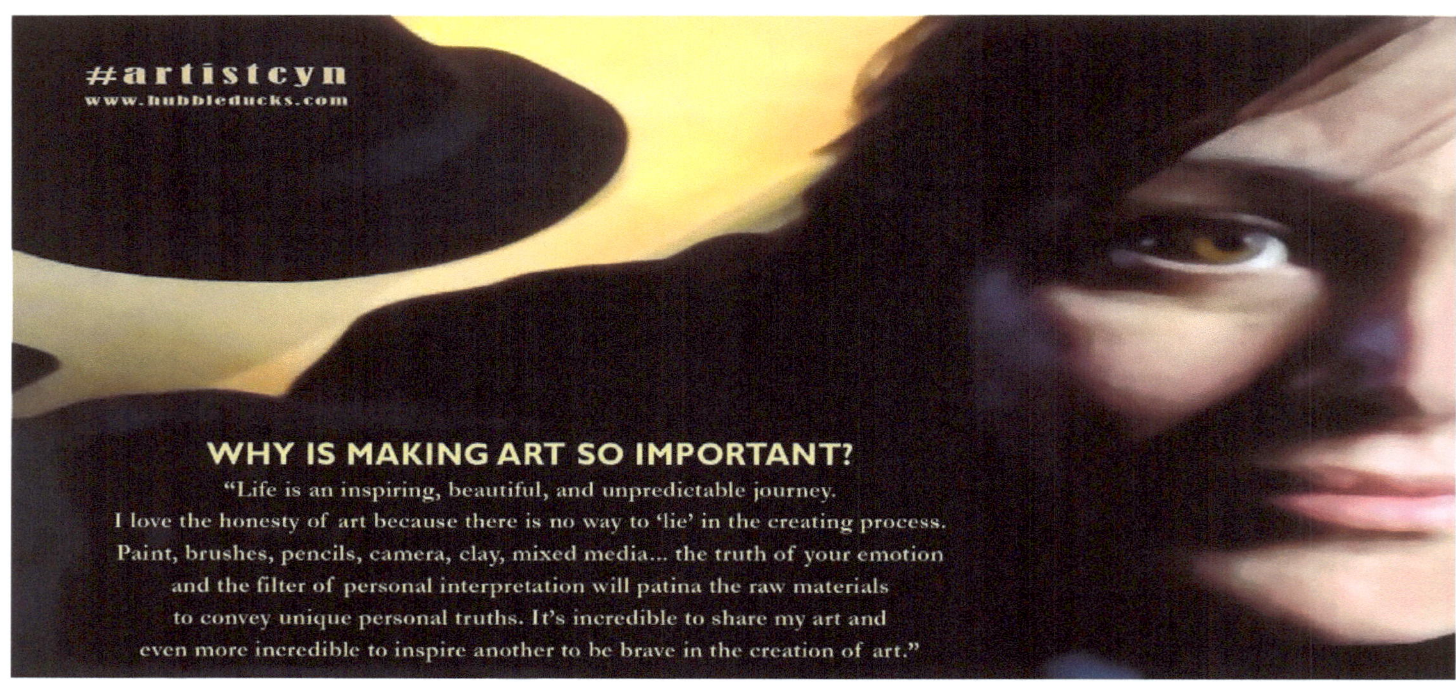

WHY IS MAKING ART SO IMPORTANT?

"Life is an inspiring, beautiful, and unpredictable journey. I love the honesty of art because there is no way to 'lie' in the creating process. Paint, brushes, pencils, camera, clay, mixed media... the truth of your emotion and the filter of personal interpretation will patina the raw materials to convey unique personal truths. It's incredible to share my art and even more incredible to inspire another to be brave in the creation of art."

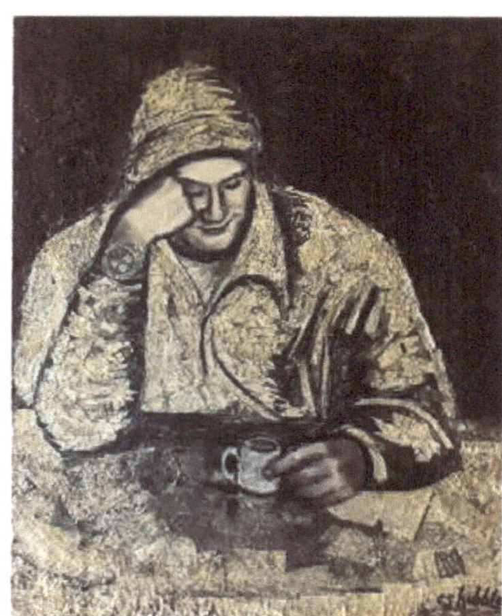

"Solo", 2003, 28.5" x 35.5", Coffee Grounds and Newspaper

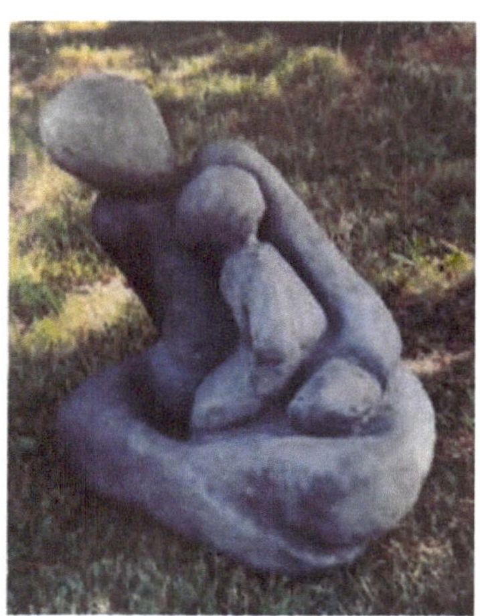

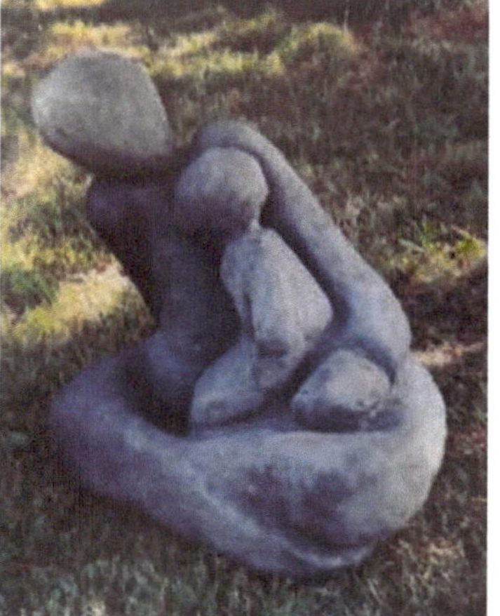

"Mother & Child", 2002, 36" x 24" x 30", Concrete

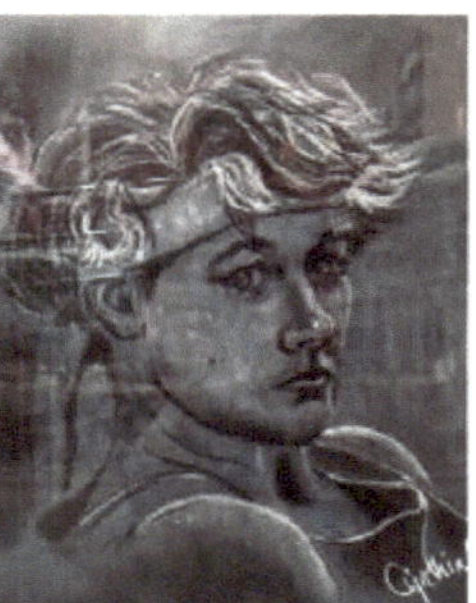

"Melancholy", 1989, 16" x 20", Conte'

"Portrait" 2018, 6" x 5", Graphite

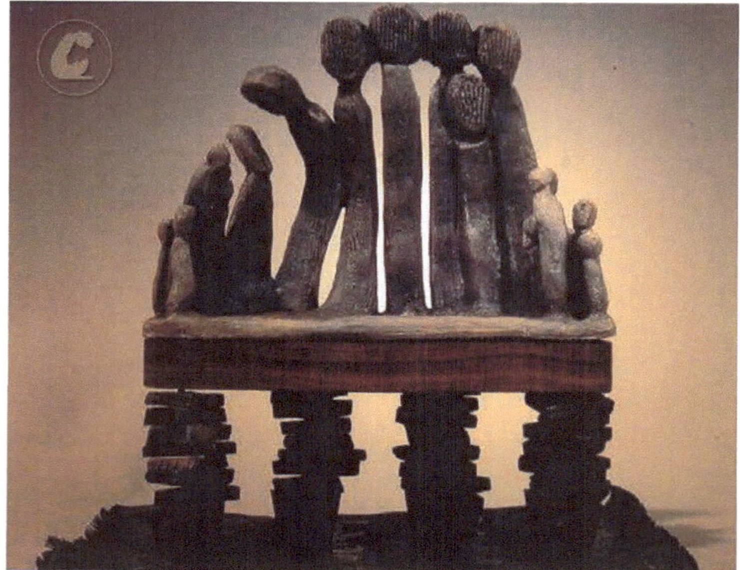

"Ancestors", 2002, private collection, 12" x 8" x 6", Stoneware and Copper

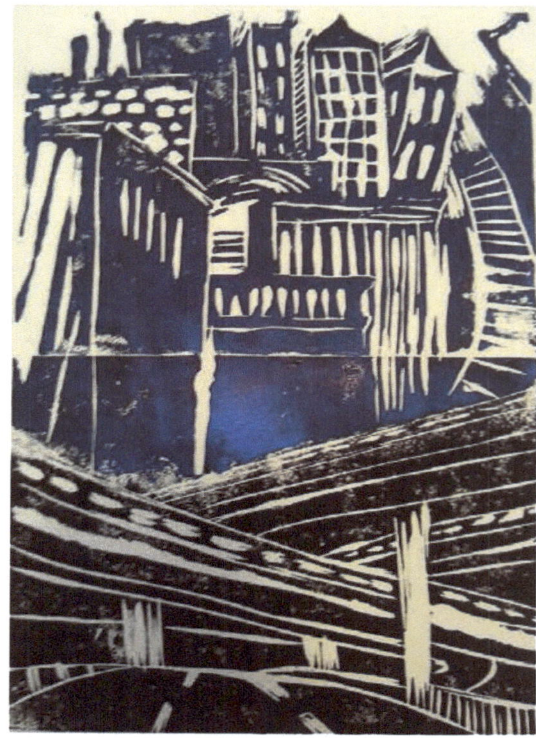

"City Impressions", 2020, 10" x 7", Linocut Print

C.S. HUBBLE

WWW.HUBBLEDUCKS.COM INSTAGRAM: @ARTISTCYN

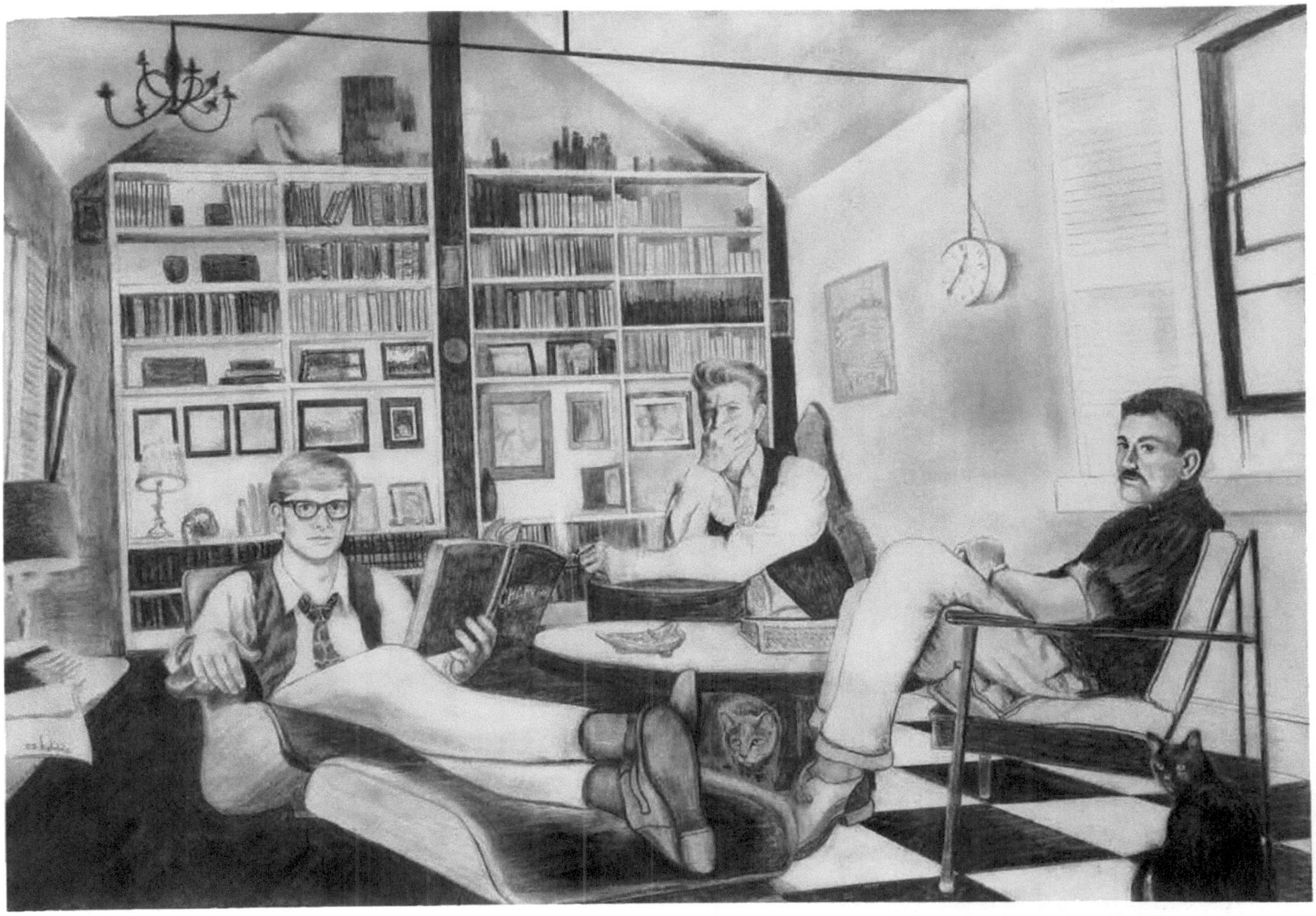

"before the moment became legendary, it was just another day in the studio", 2018, 30" x 20" graphite, private collection

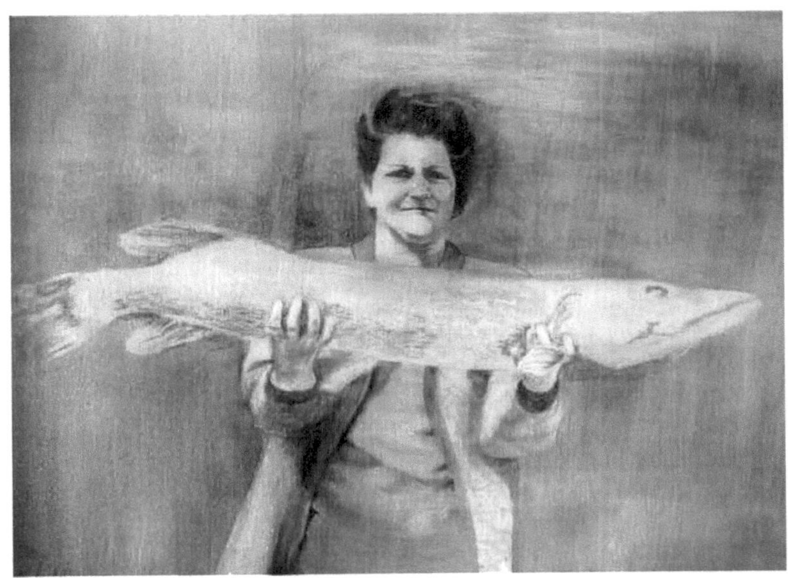

"Grandma Vivian", 2018, 18" x 24", Acrylic

"before the moment became legendary, it was just another day in the studio" was created to honor Doug Wells, who passed away in 2017 after a brave battle with Lewy Body Dementia. His son commissioned the piece to honor his father's memory. A younger Doug reclines with his copy of "Breakfast of Champions" as Kurt Vonnegut, his favorite author, and David Bowie, his son's favorite musician, are gathered inside Mr. Vonnegut's writing studio. Within the drawing, the words "Make me young" are hidden three times in tribute to the final sentence of the book in Doug's hand: "Here was what Kilgore Trout cried out to me in my father's voice: 'Make me young, make me young, make me young!'"

Mueller LOW LIFE .COM

ART AND DESIGN BY DAVID C. MUELLER

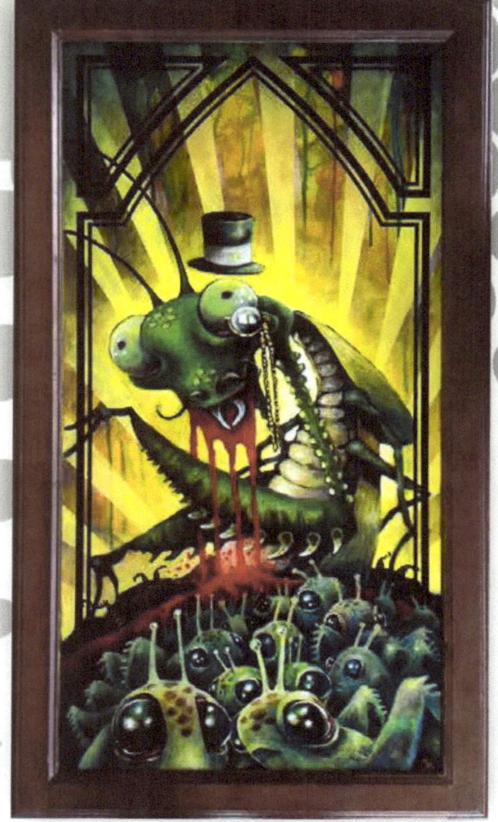

"Trickle Down" - Acrylic on Wood

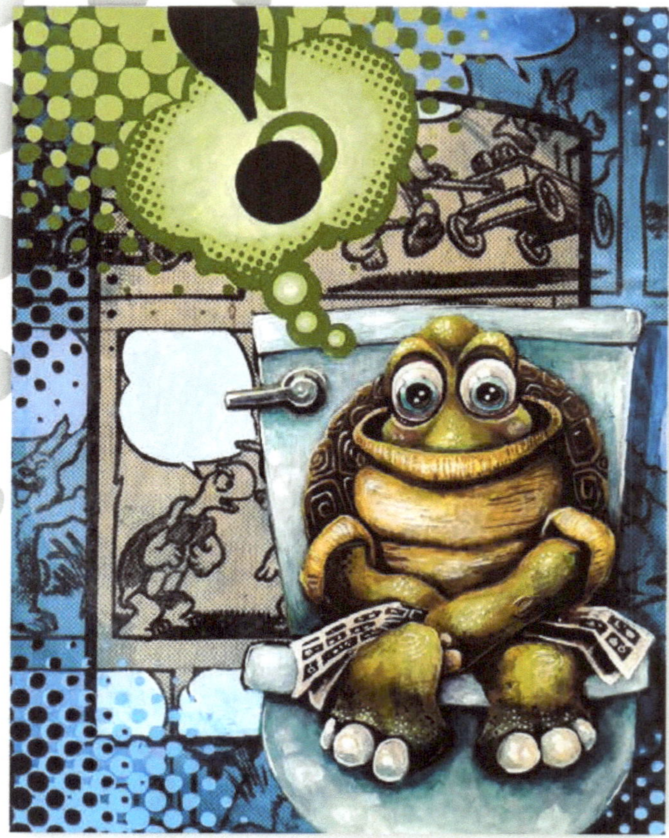

"Turtlehead" - Acrylic on Wood

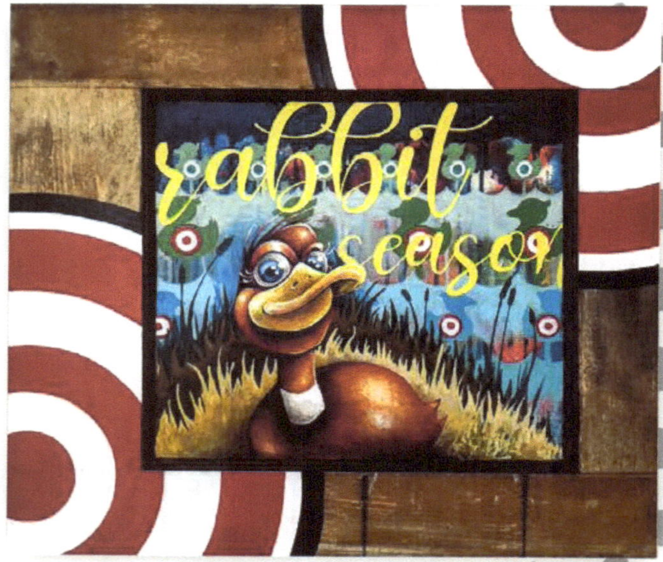

"Rabbit Season" - Acrylic on Wood

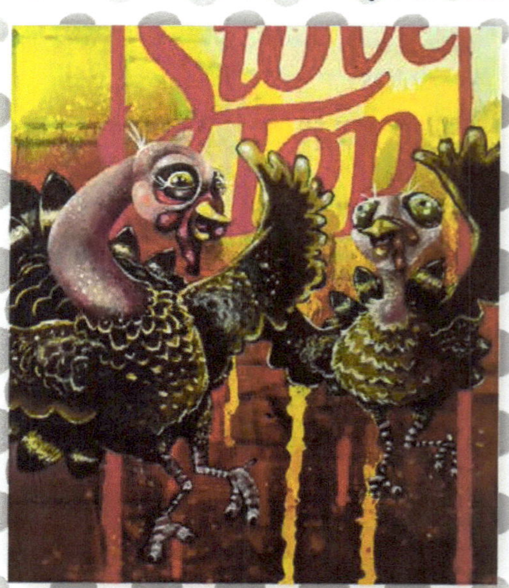

"The Mashed Potato" - Acrylic on Wood

@MUELLERLOWLIFE ★ MUELLERLOWLIFE.COM

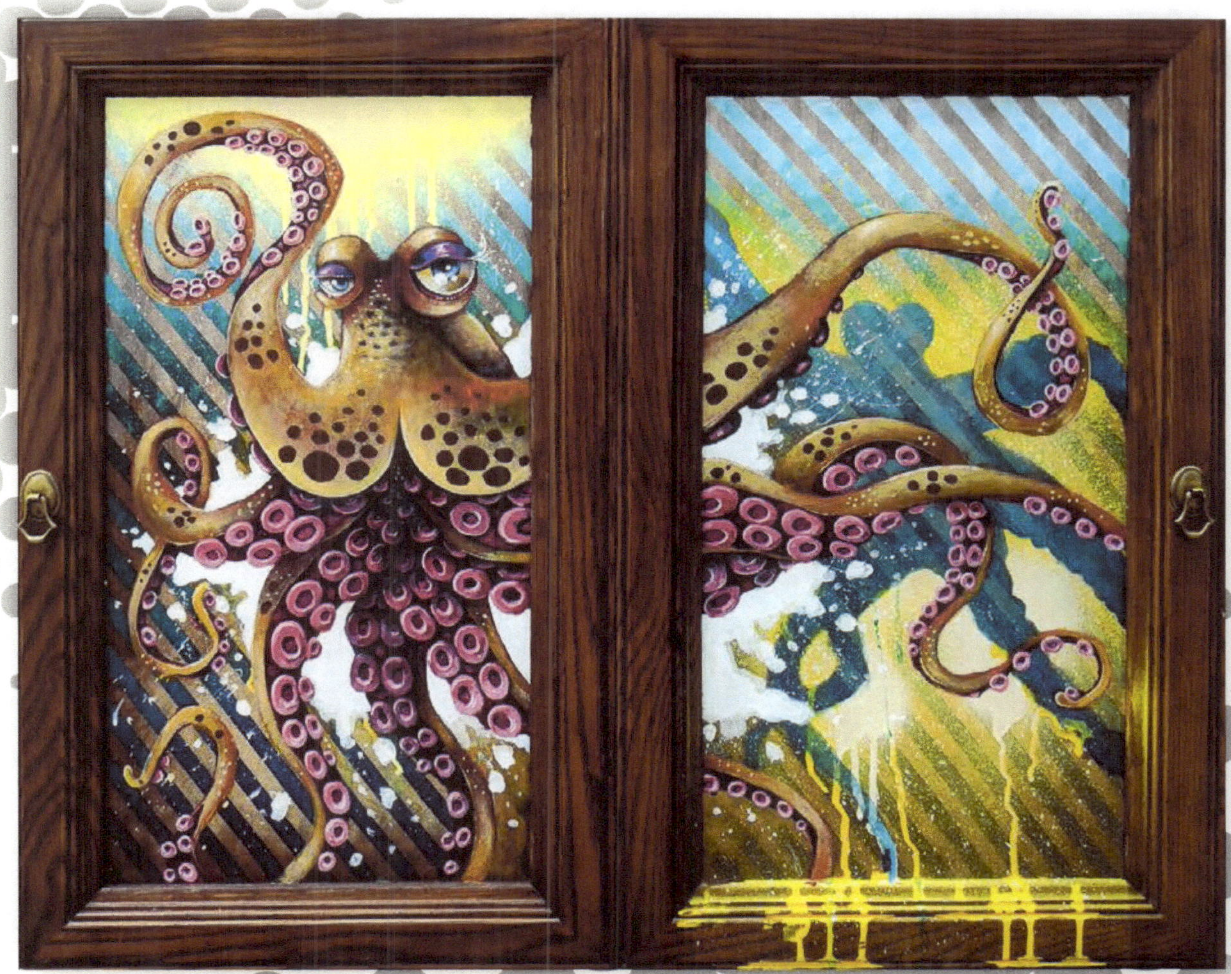

"Leave a Mark" - Acrylic on Wood

I'm a cheese-eating, beer-drinking, working class artist, based in Milwaukee, Wisconsin. My paintings reflect an individual raised on Saturday Morning Cartoons, inspired by the day to day and grounded in traditional painting and printmaking techniques. I primarily work on salvaged wood due to it's affordability and the fact that it prevents a few things from being put into a landfill. As an artist, I focus on narrative and the accessibility of art to broader audiences.

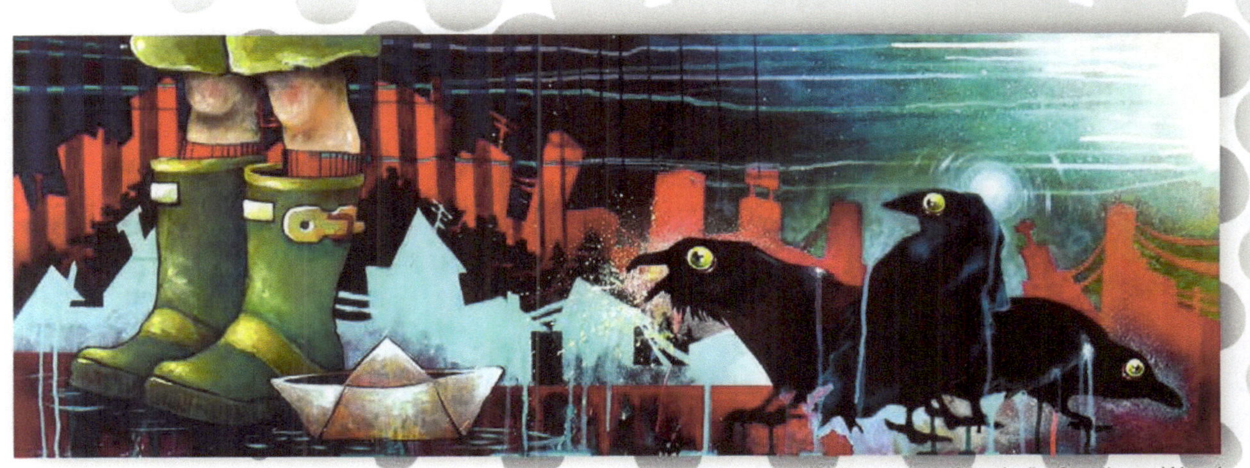

"Witness to a Murder" - Acrylic on Wood

@MUELLERLOWLIFE ★ MUELLERLOWLIFE.COM

JUSTIN TOLENTINO

Instagram: @studiotolentino

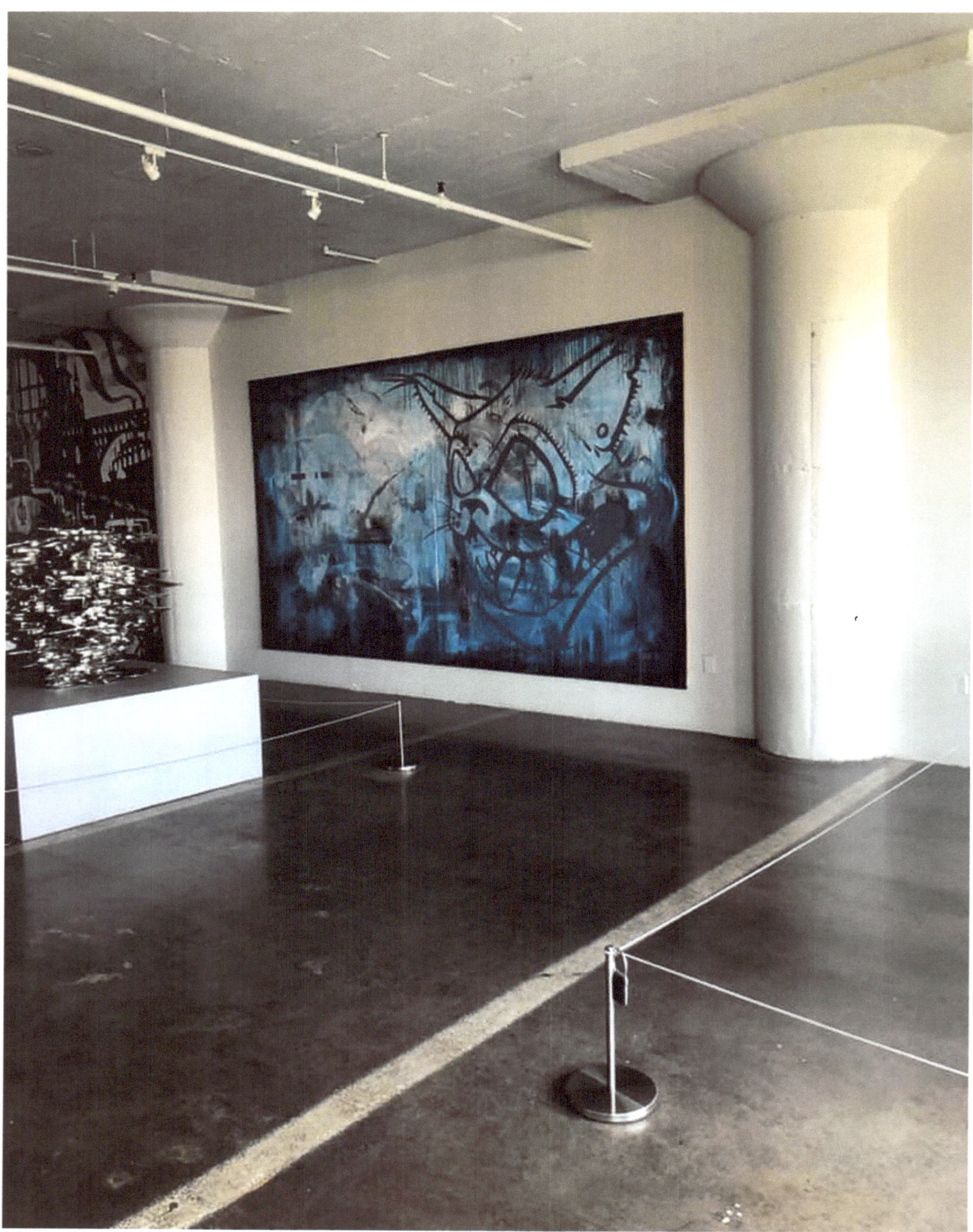

"Gato Silvestre" 2017 Acrylic and Graphite on Panel 168" x 96"
Permanent Collection of "City Museum" St. Louis, Missouri

STUDIOTOLENTINO.COM

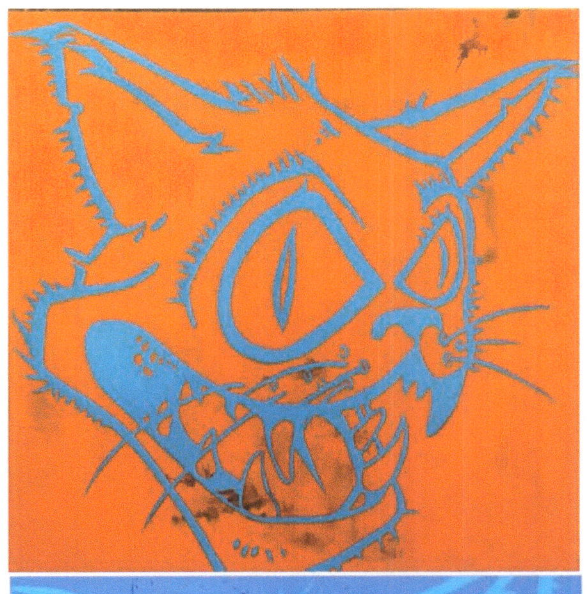

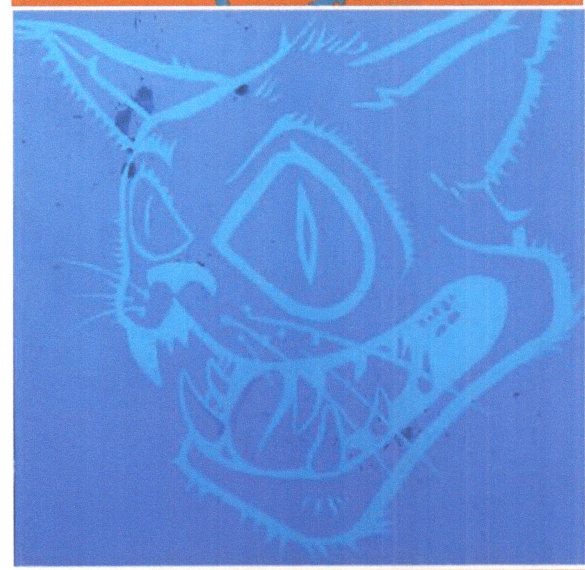

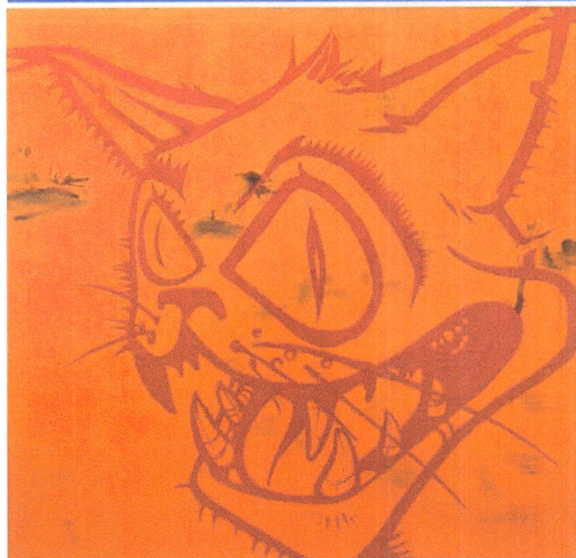

"Gato colorido" 2018 Acrylic on Canvas 24" x 24" Private Collection

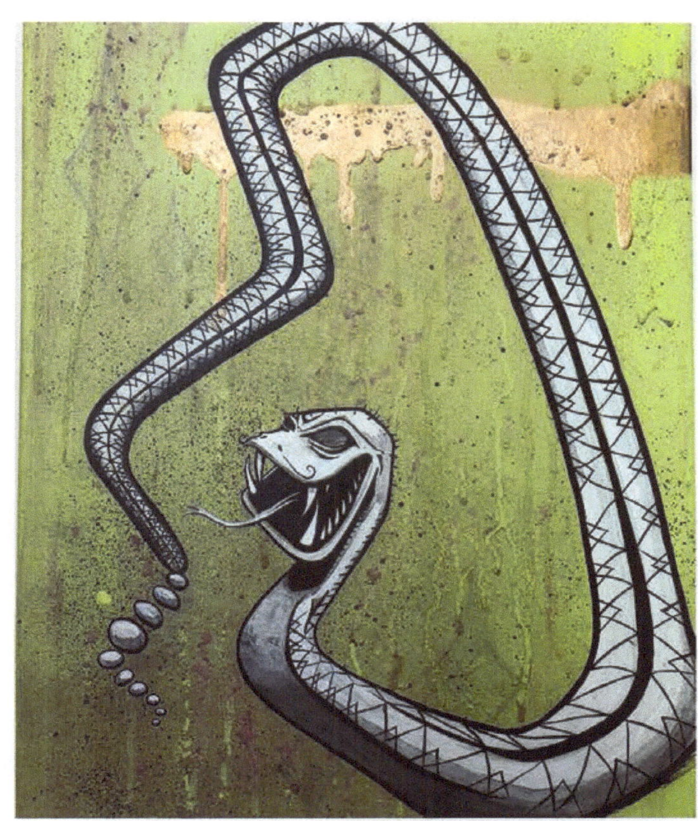

"Serpentine" 2018 Acrylic on Canvas 16" x 20" Private Collection

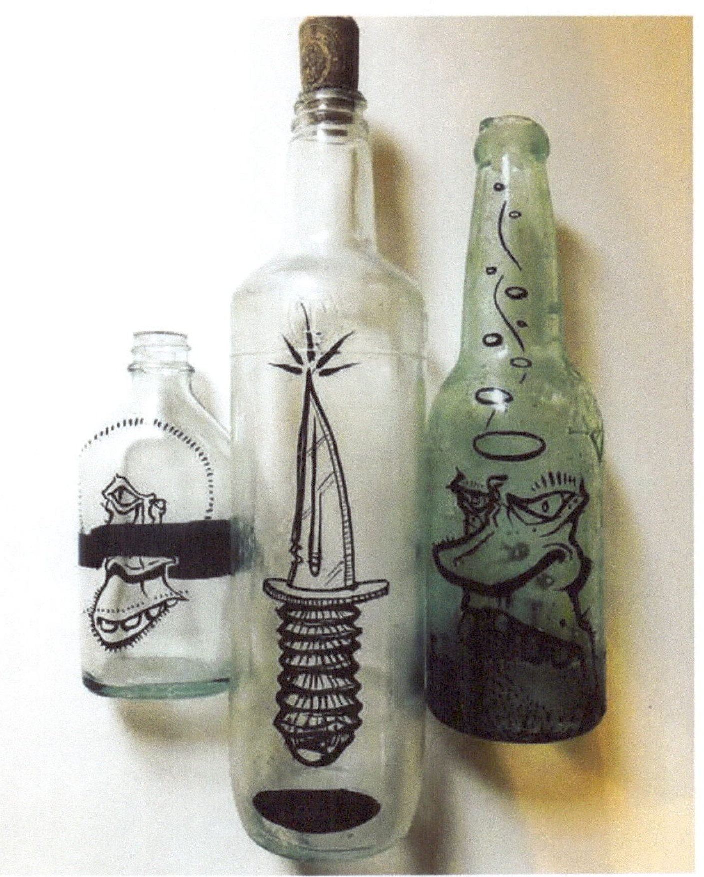

"Untitled" 2018 Acrylic and Enamel on found antique bottles various sizes. Private Collection

HEIMING CHAN

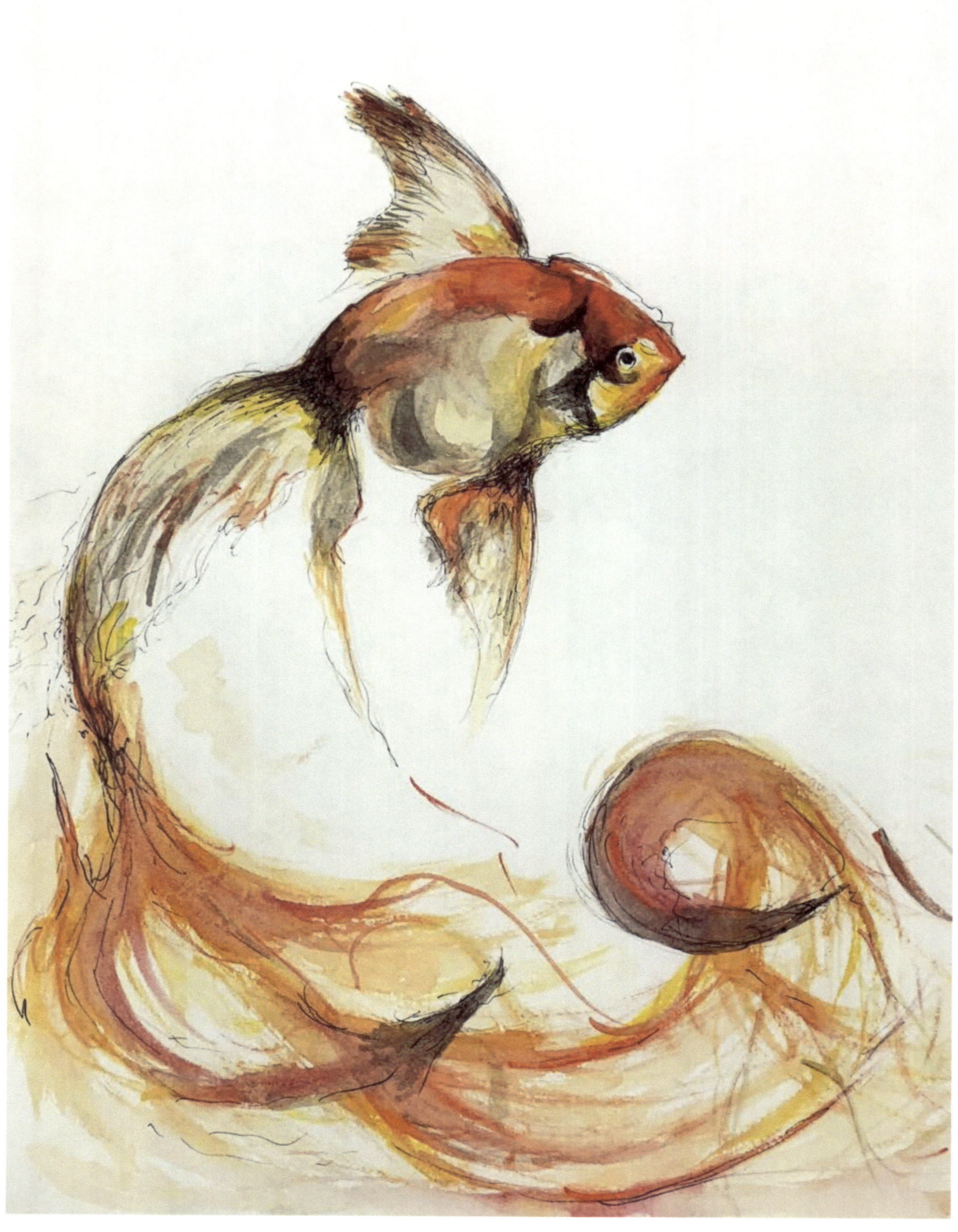

Goldfish on fire
Watercolour and pen illustration on paper
380 x 284 mm

heiming
heiming@gmail.com

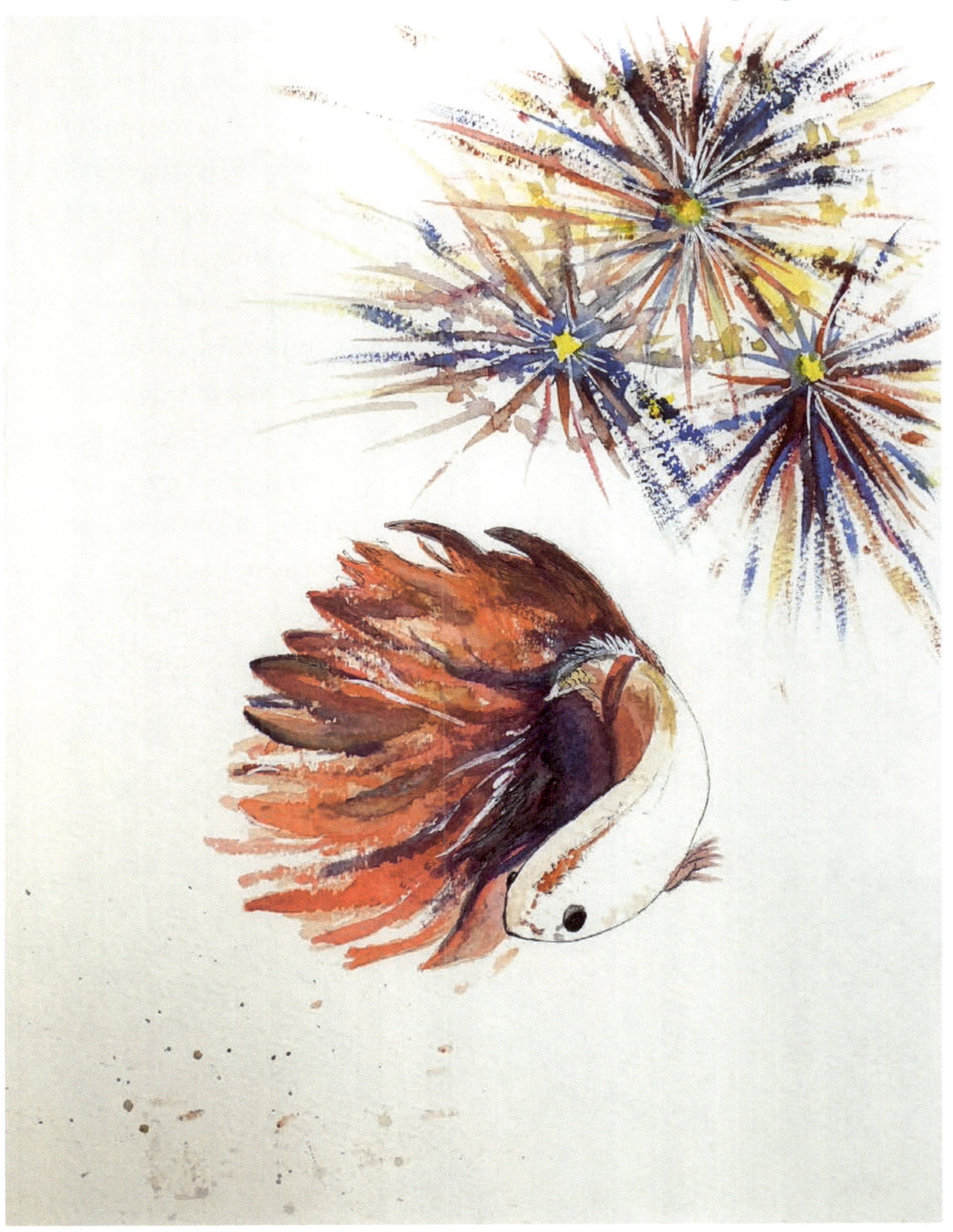

Goldfish under firework
Watercolour and pen illustration on paper
380 x 284 mm

AMBER PALECEK

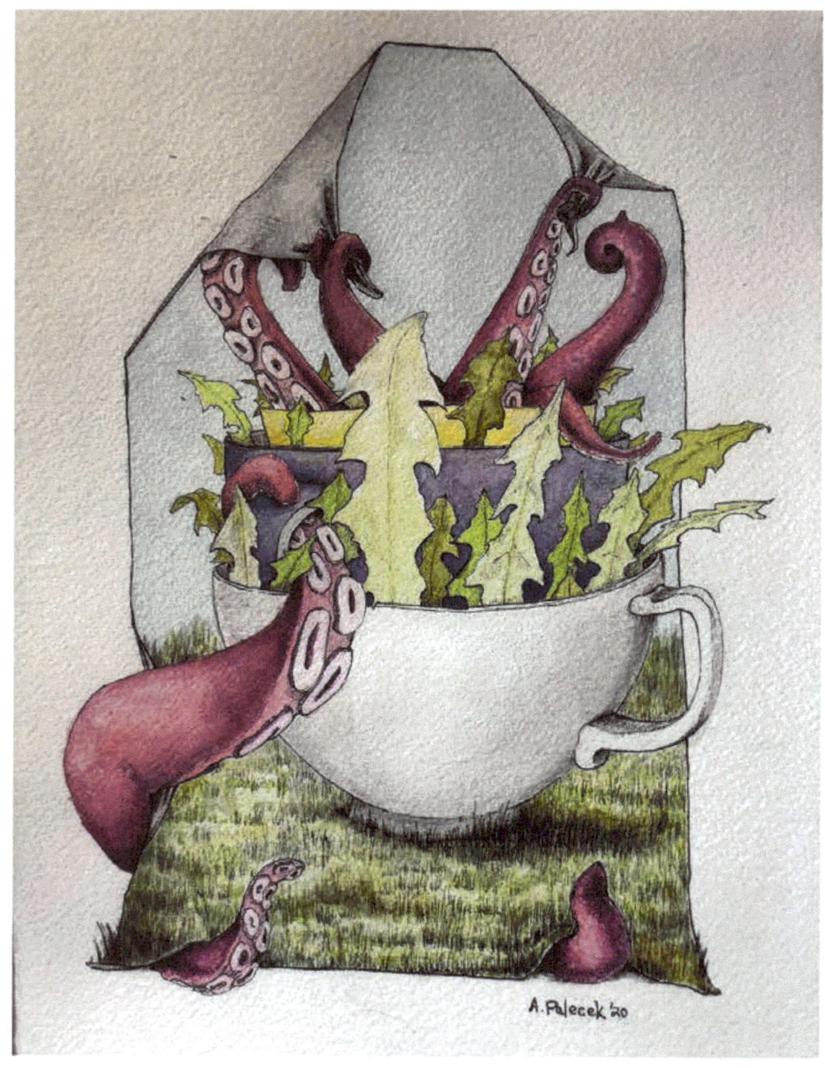

"untitled" 2020 7"x 5" Watercolor and Pen on Paper

I work with mix media on paper, acrylics and sometimes digital photography. Though I hate to be creatively limited to any particular material, working on paper is my favorite creative outlet. I have always found that there is a higher level of honesty achieved and creative intimacy experienced when creating on paper compared to working in other materials. I think it's because paper was my first drawing material and that intrinsic connection to paper allows me to explore themes such as Love, anxiety, fears, memory, nature and travels.

Memphis College of Art 2003
BFA in Printmaking with a minor in Art History
School of Visual Arts 2007
MA in Art Education
Instagram - @Palechickstudios

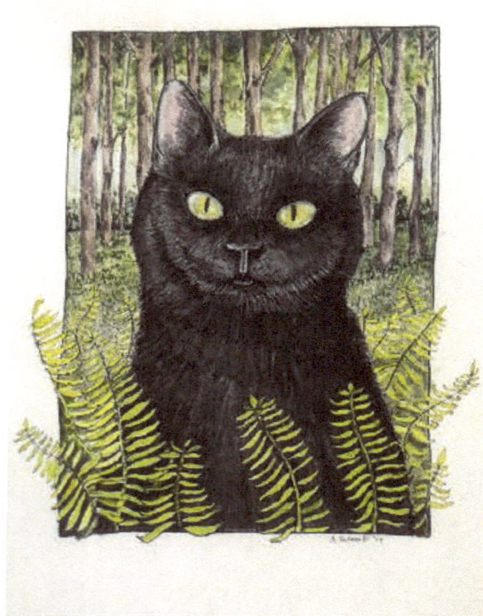

"Gheera in the ferns" 2018 7"x 5" Watercolor & Pen on Paper

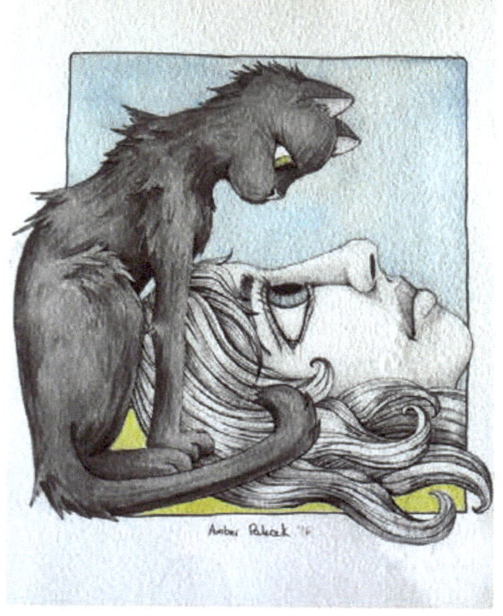

"Mine" 2016 5"x 3.5" Watercolor & Pen on Paper

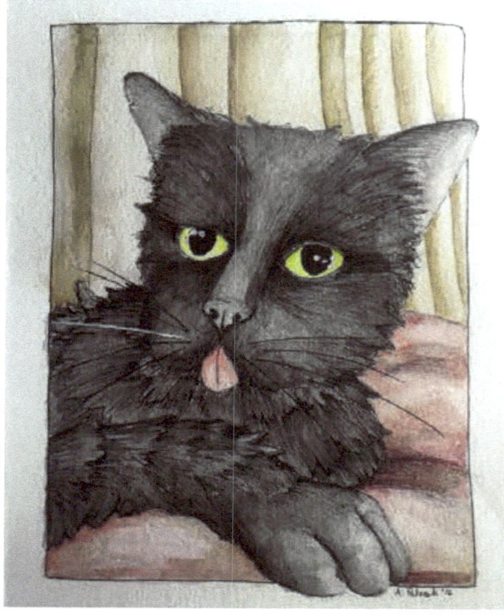

"Tamlin" 2016 7"x 5" Watercolor & Pen on Paper

PALECHICKSTUDIOS.com

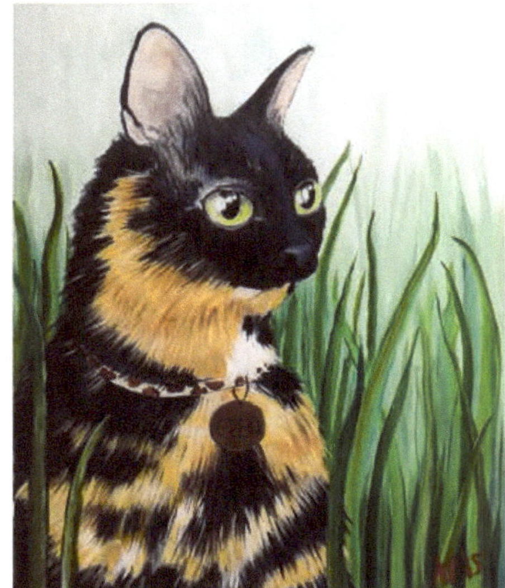

"Cleo" 2015, 16" x 20" Acrylic on Canvas

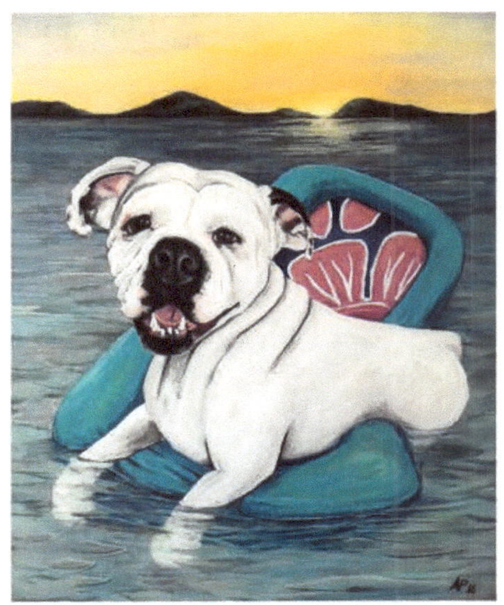

"Gia" 2018, 18" x 24" Acrylic on Canvas

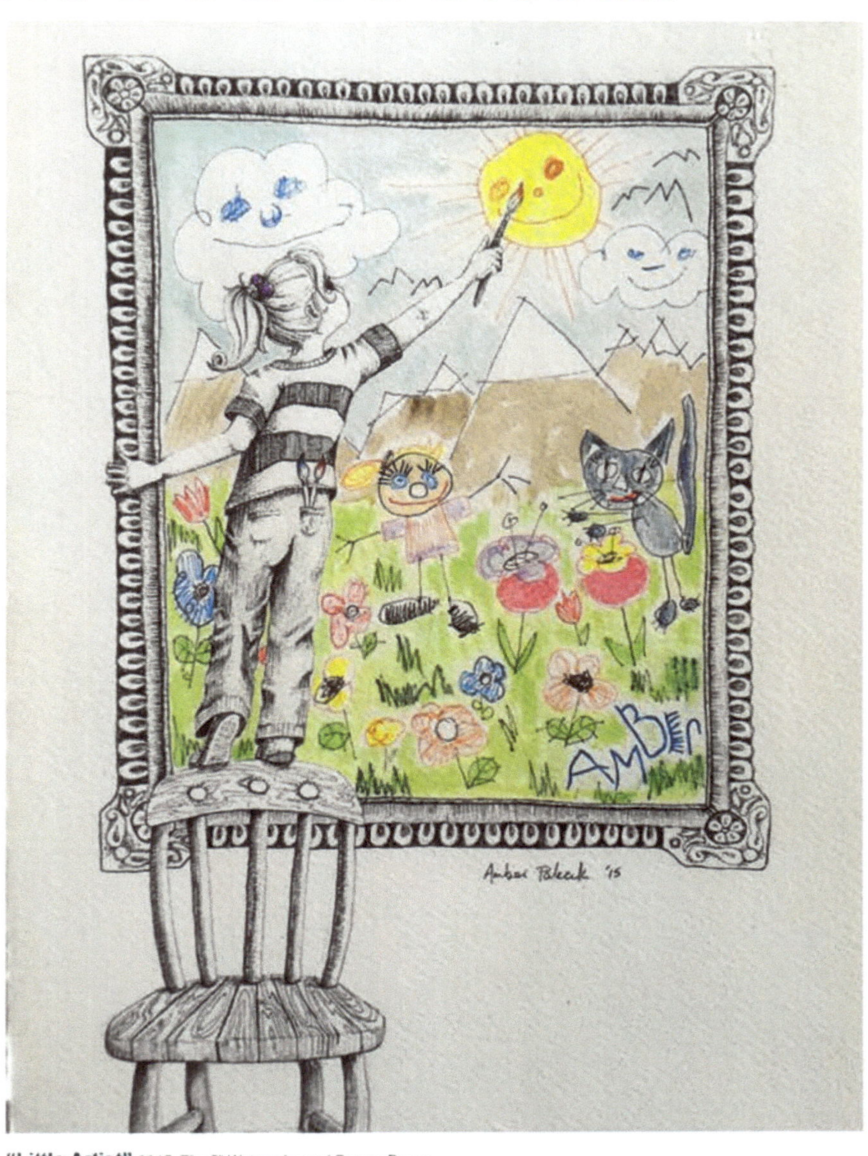

"Little Artist" 2015, 7" x 5" Watercolor and Pen on Paper

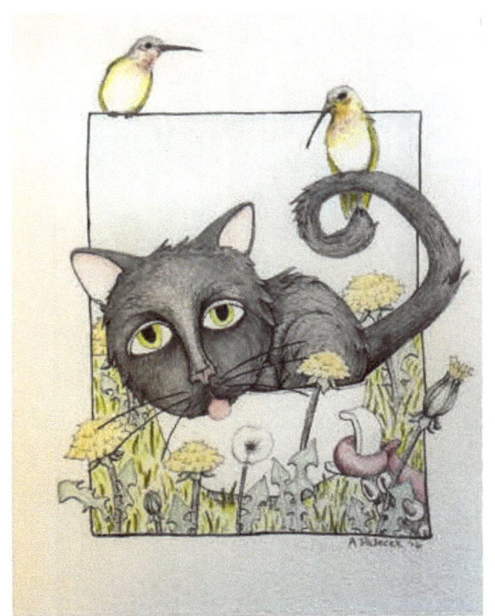

"Tamlin in a teacup" 2016, 7" x 5" Watercolor on paper

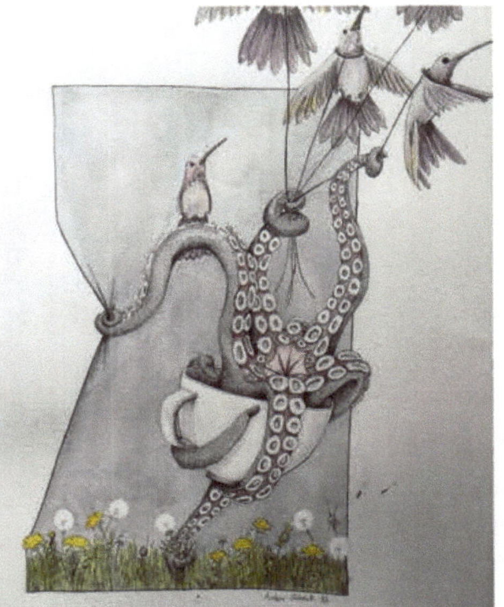

"Extroverted Introvert" 2016, 12" x 8" Watercolor on paper

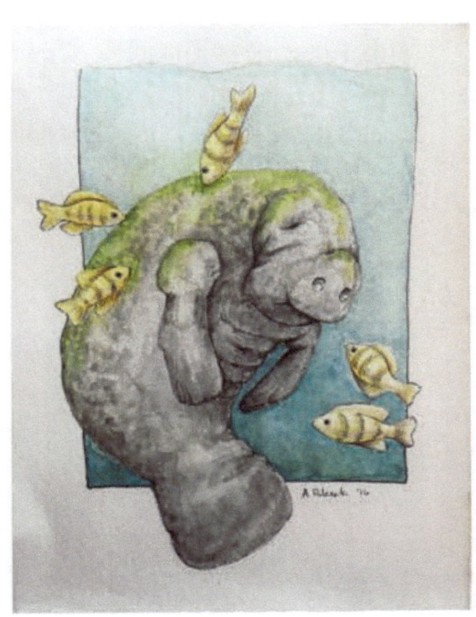

"Manatee" 2016, 7" x 5" Watercolor on paper

Nona Bolin

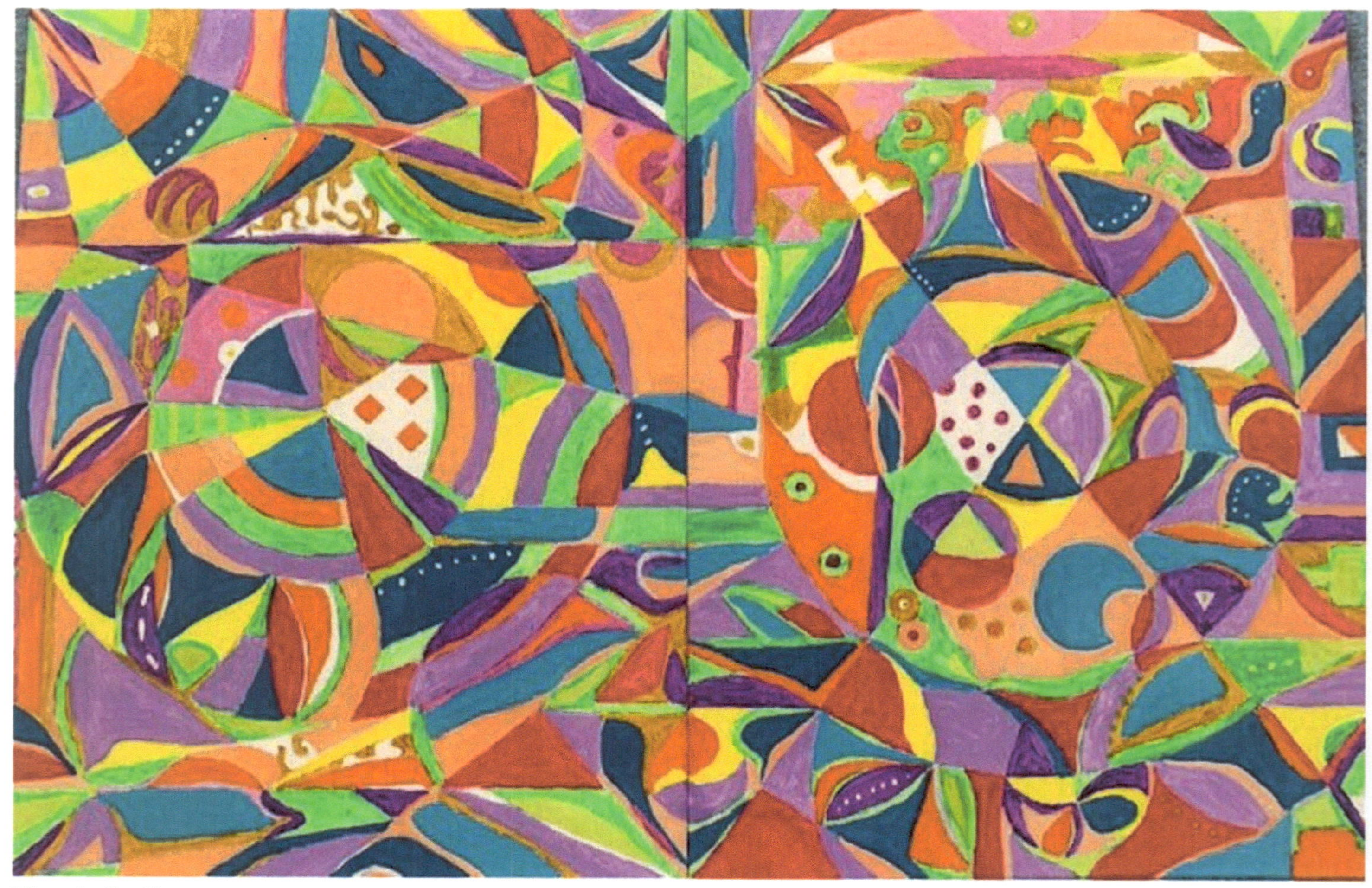

"Mazurka Op. 2" 2019 18"x 24" Acrylic

Mazurka Op. 2

A mazurka is a lively musical composition accentuating irregular rhythms often accompanied by a dance of couples in a flow of semi-circles to a syncopated downbeat. The most famous composer of mazurkas was Chopin, a favorite of my mother's, whose music *enlivened my childhood.*

Nona Bolin

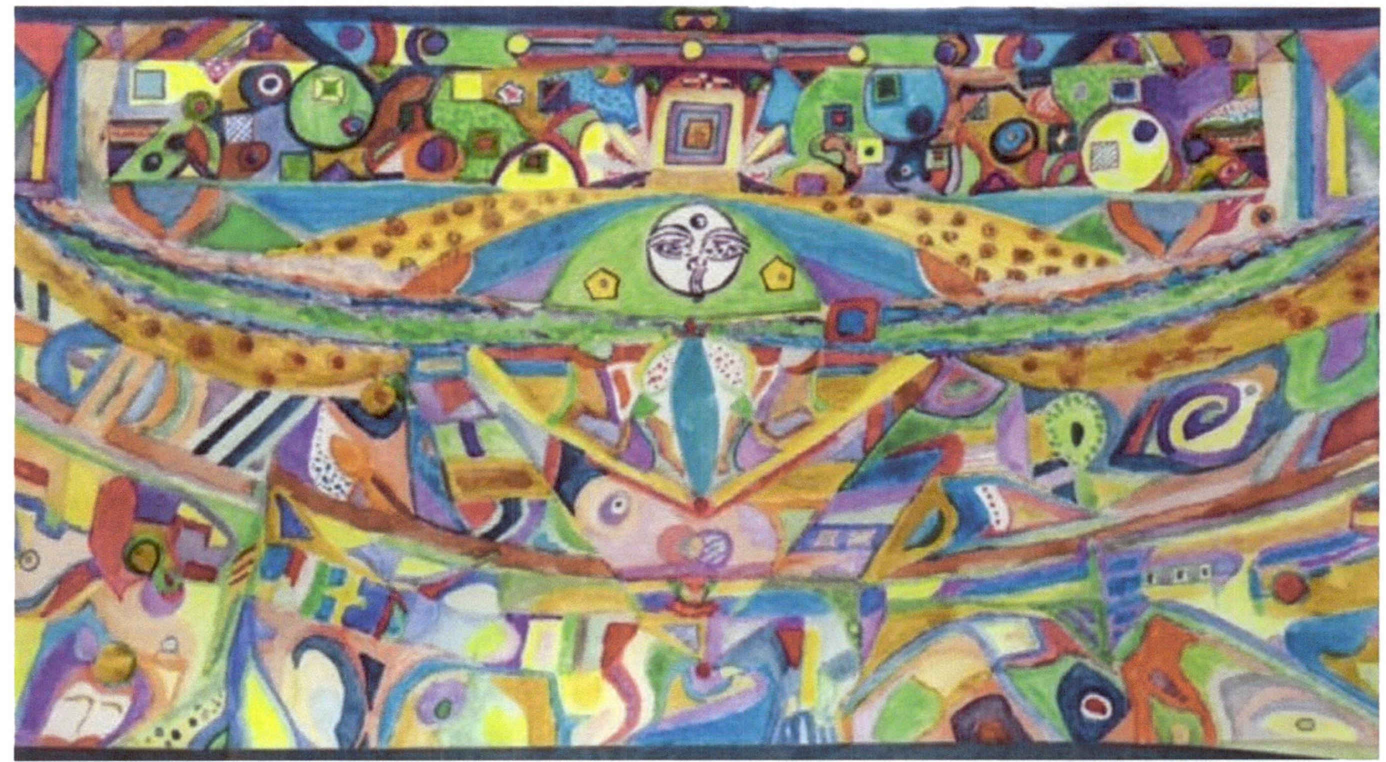

"Buddist Drive-In" 2019 8"x 15" Watercolor

Buddhist Drive-in

A myriad of beings trapped in samsara is comforted by a compassionate teacher who speaks in enigmatic parables meant to lead the devotee to embrace The Middle Way. The sites of these sermons were often venues free from enclosure such as a park. Updating this scene, I have chosen the outdoor theater as a place wherein a congregation might assemble to hear the words of enlightenment.

Killean Evans

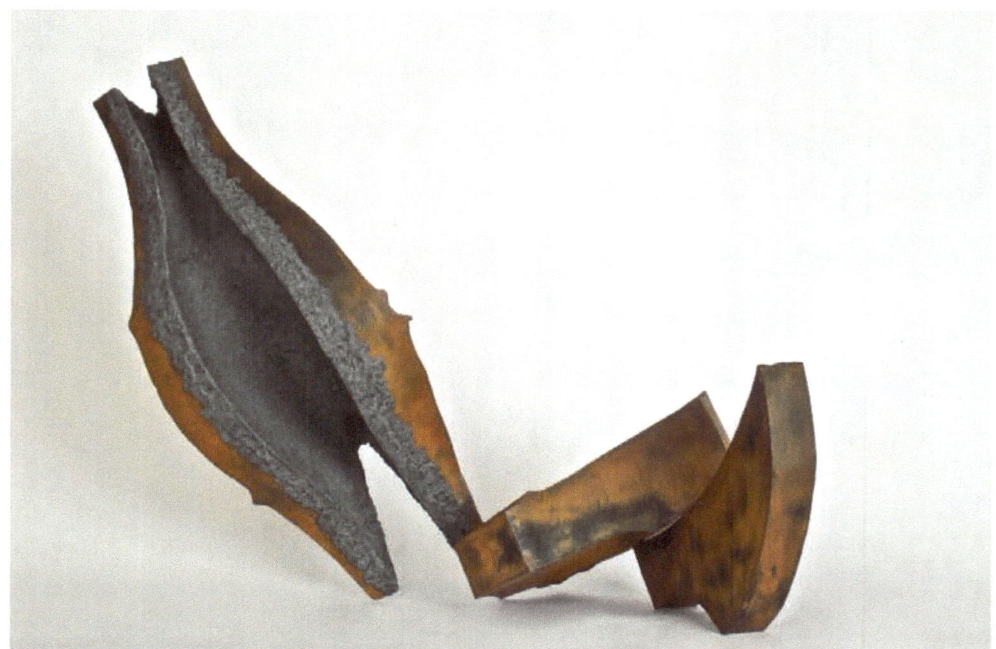

Almost 2010 4'x 2'x3' Steel and Paper

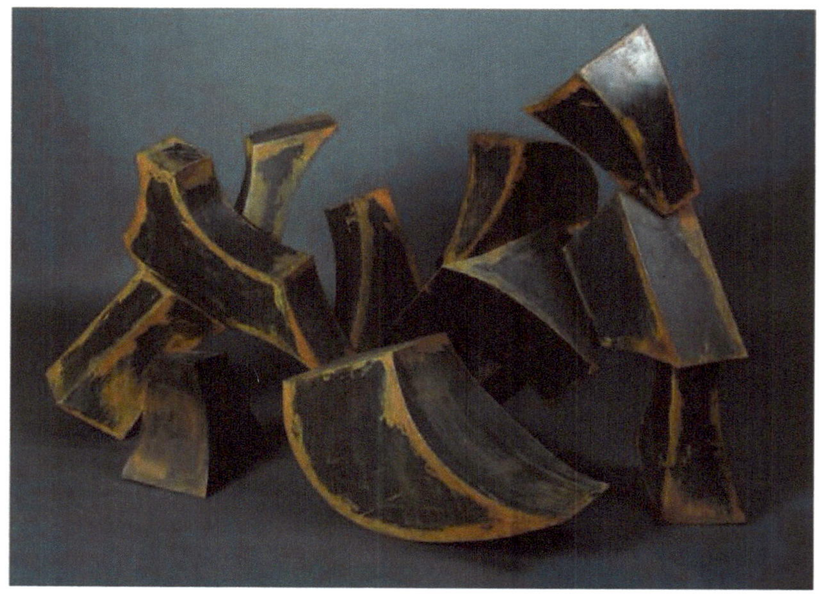

Untitled 2009 5'x4'x3' Steel

Killeanevans.com

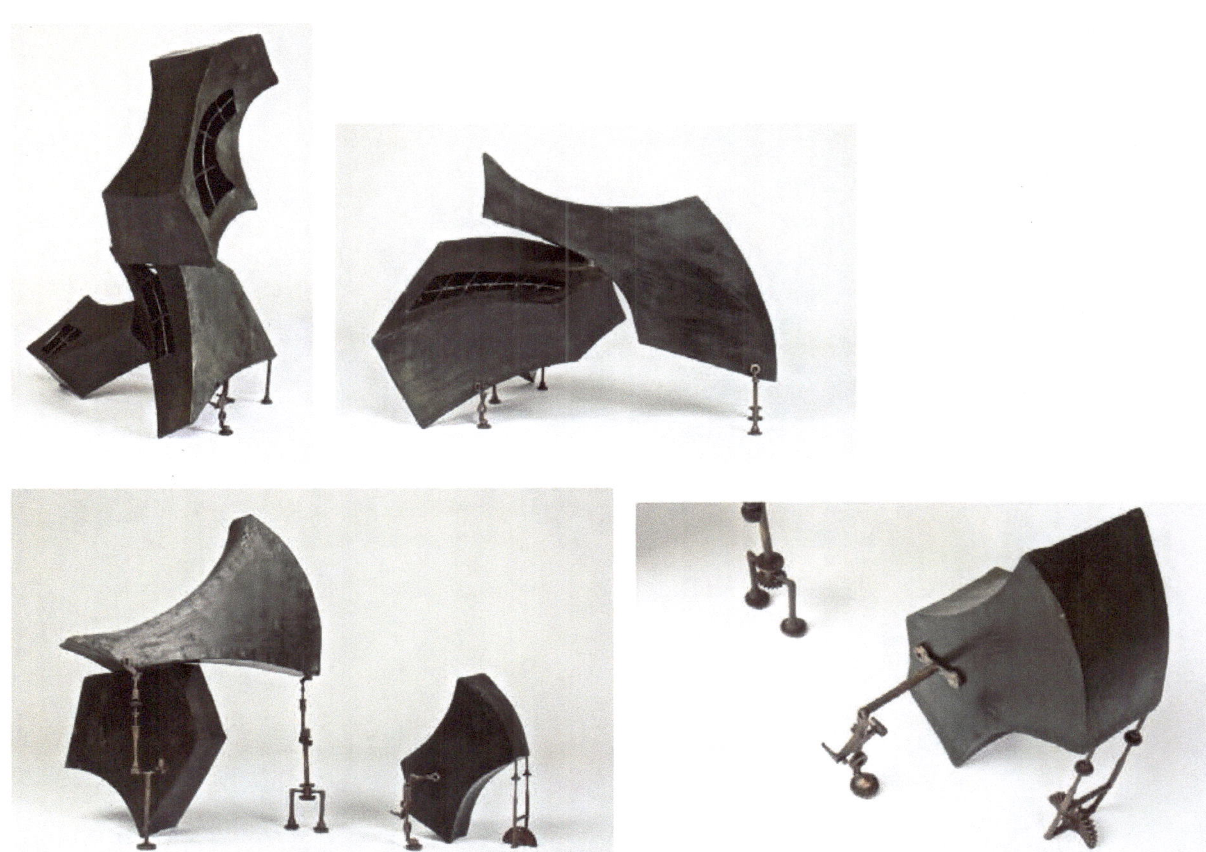

Built Upon 1, Built Upon 2, Built Upon 3 and Detail 2010 Steel and Bronze

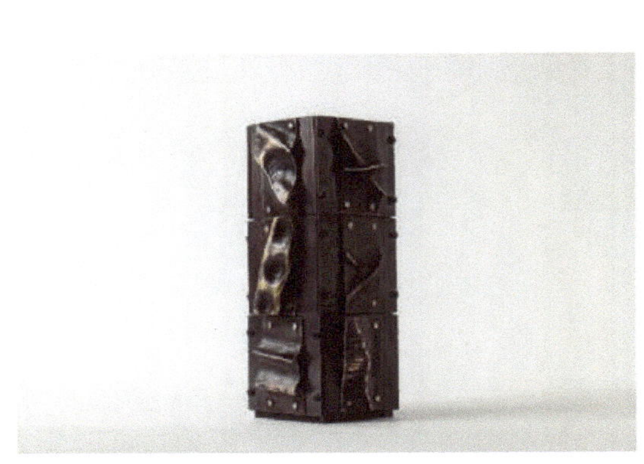

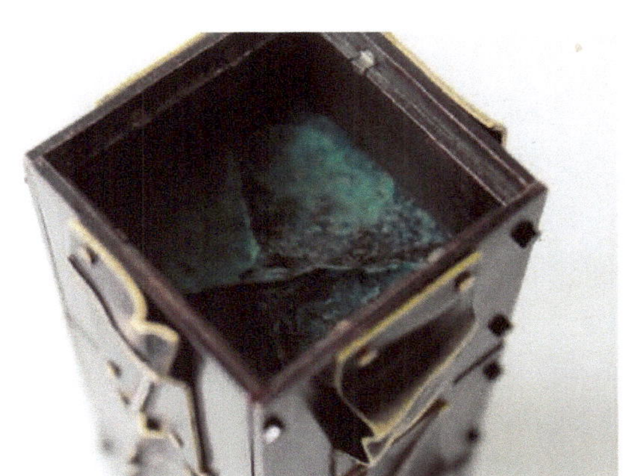

Contained, Detail 2018 3"x3"x6"

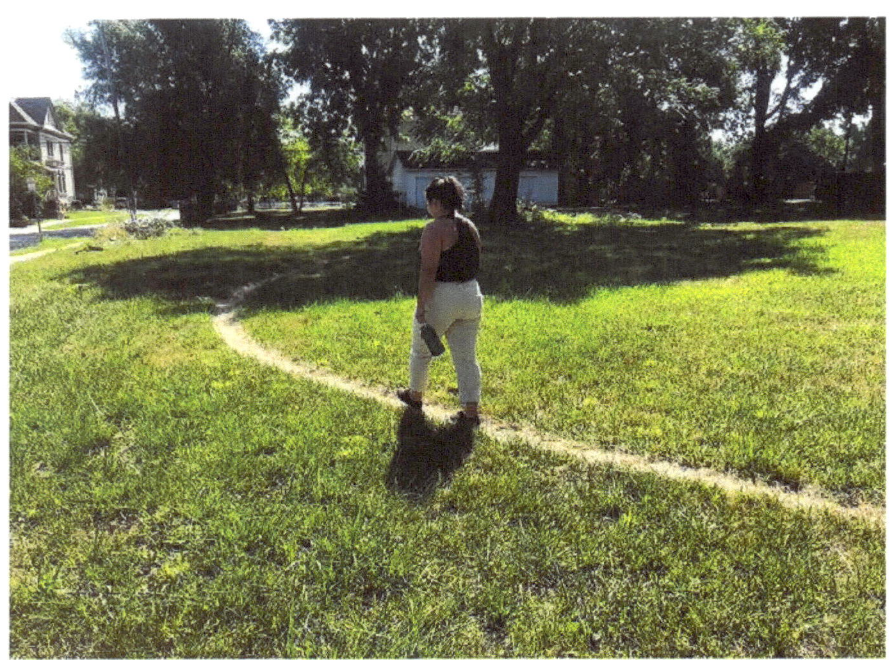

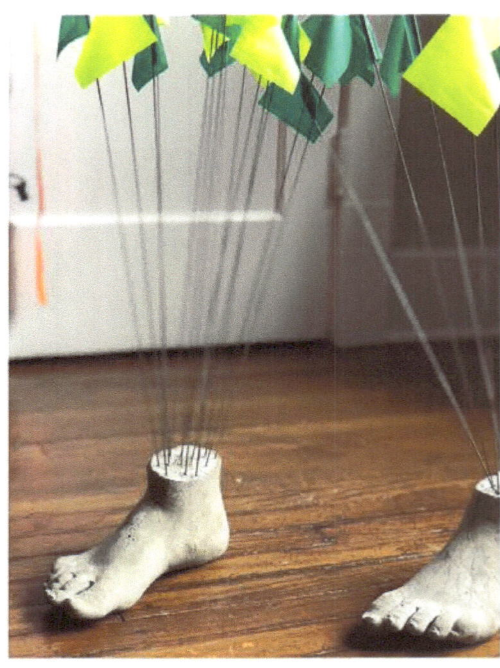

KELLI BLACK

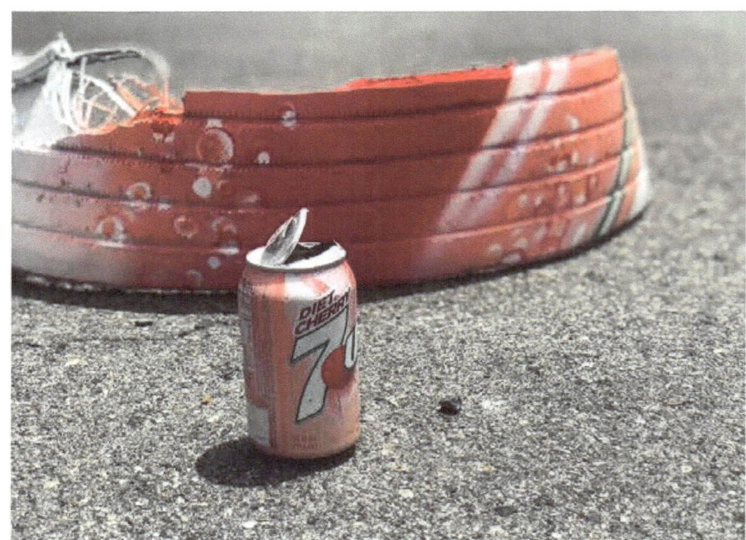

Kelli Black is an interdisciplinary artist whose work explores the in-between, the transient, and what it means to navigate conditioned, binary social structures. Kelli earned her BFA from Memphis College of Art in 2014 and her MFA from The School of The Art Institue of Chicago in 2016.

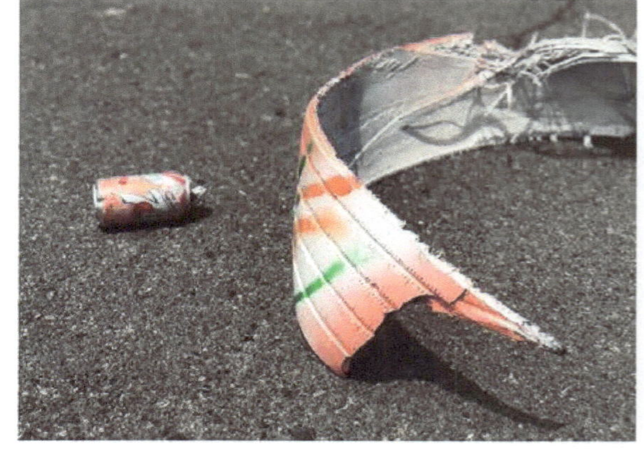

Kelli Black

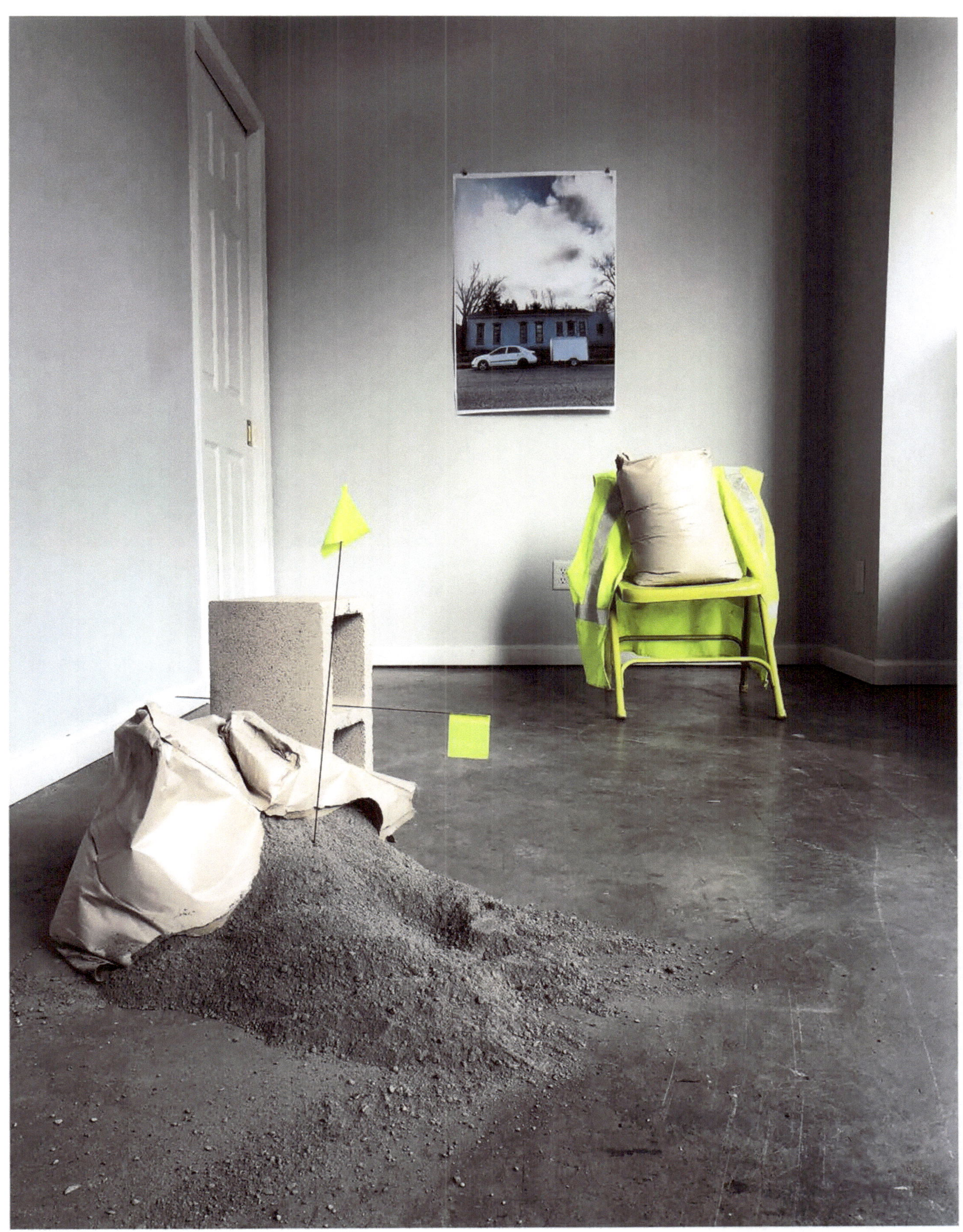

ANNA TILLETT ILLUSTRATION

ANNATILLETT.COM

@ANNATROBOT

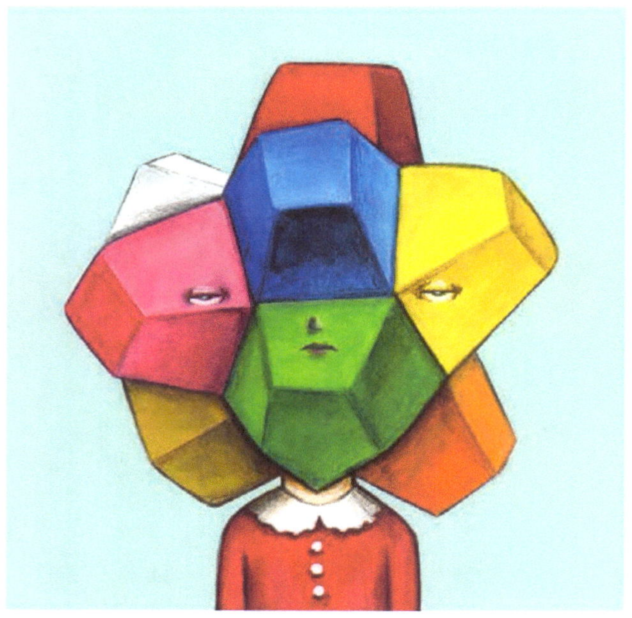

Can't Stop Won't Stop

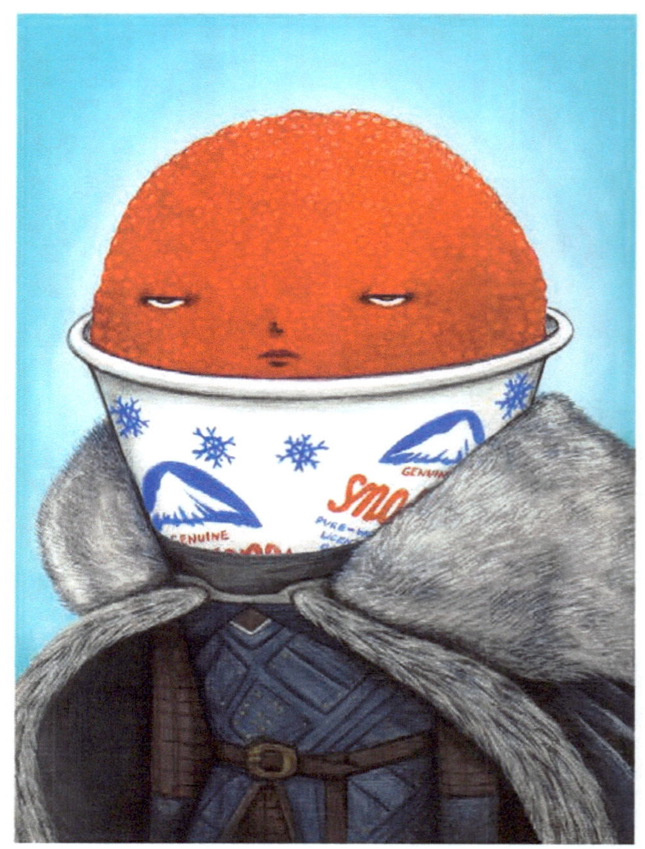

Jon Snow Cone

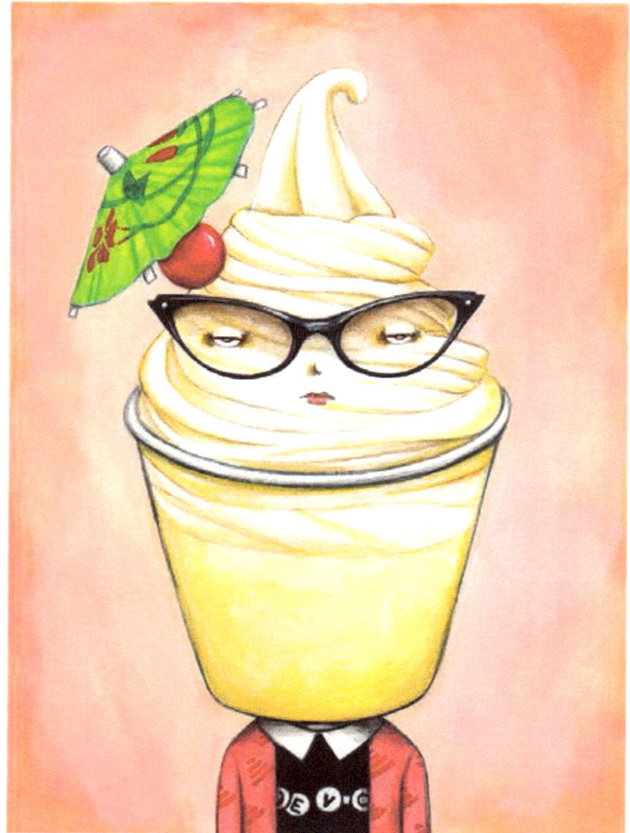

Dole Whip It Good

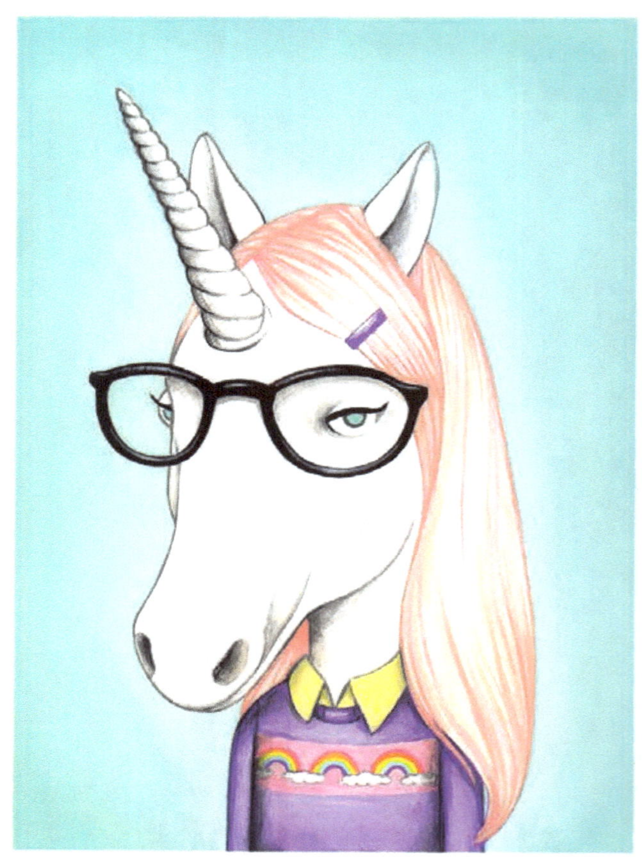

Nerdicorn

ANNA TILLETT ILLUSTRATION

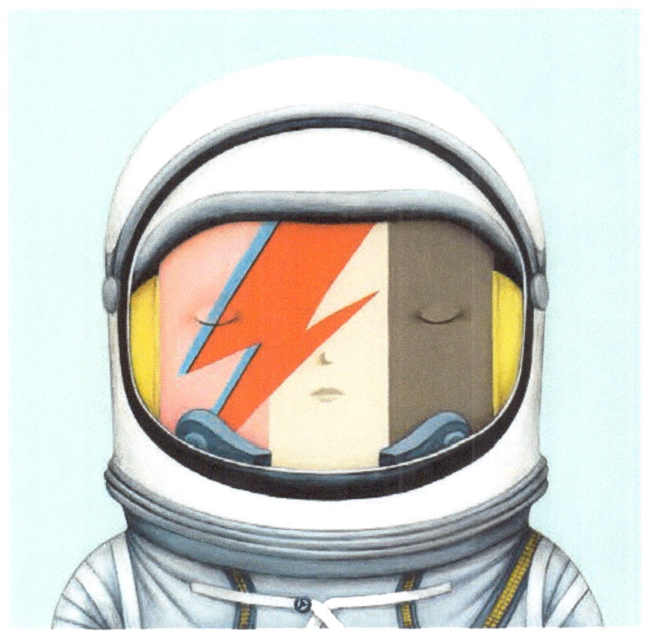

Astronaut Ice Cream - Major Tom

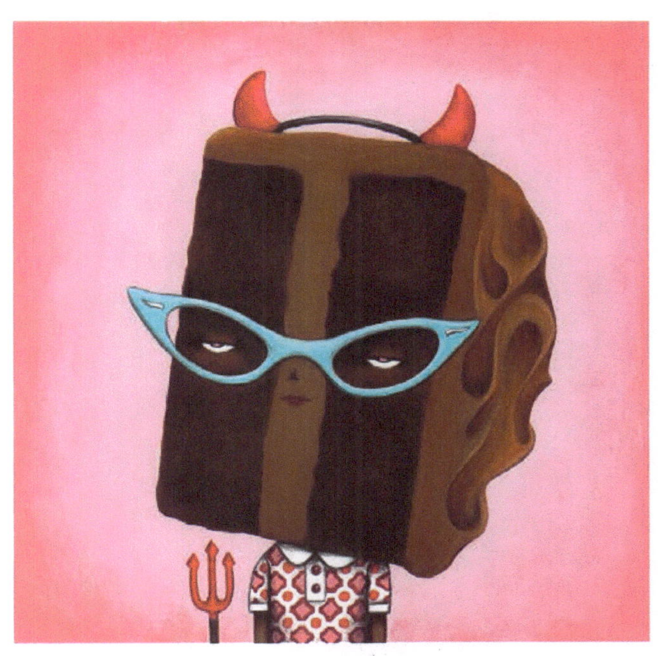

Devil's Food Cake

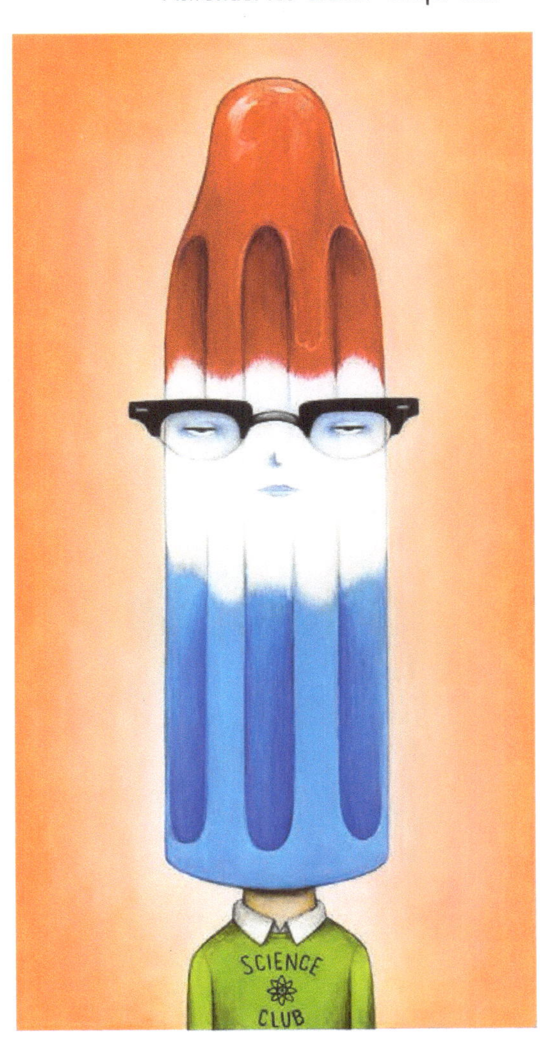

Ill Humored Ice Cream - Rocket Science

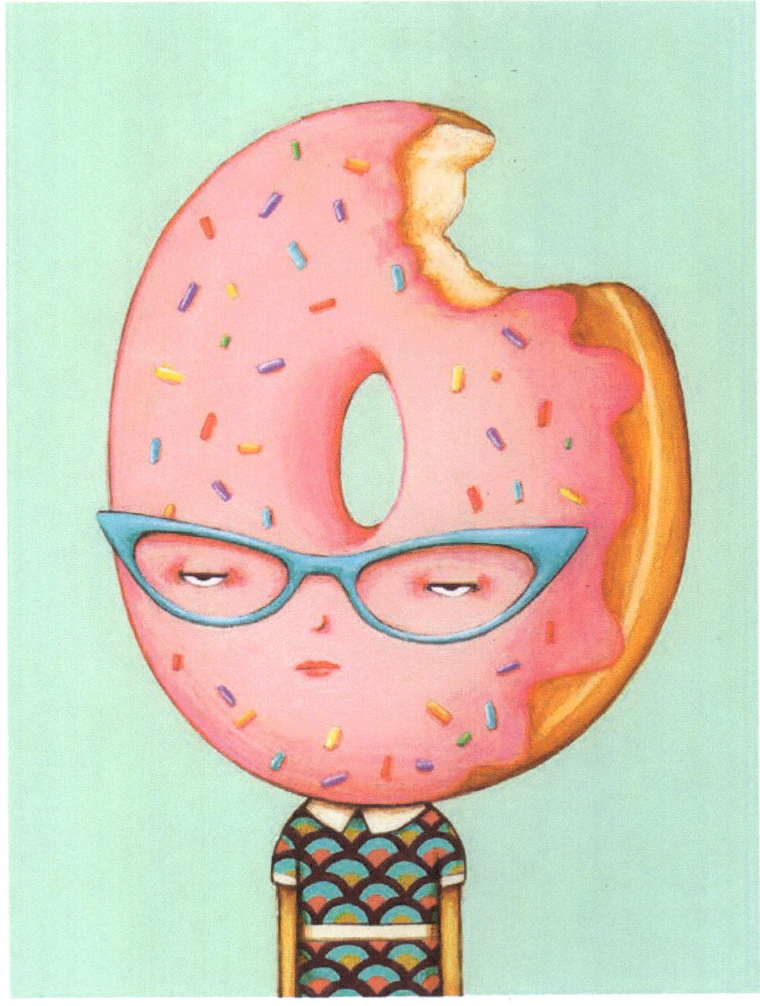

Glazed and Confused with Sprinkles

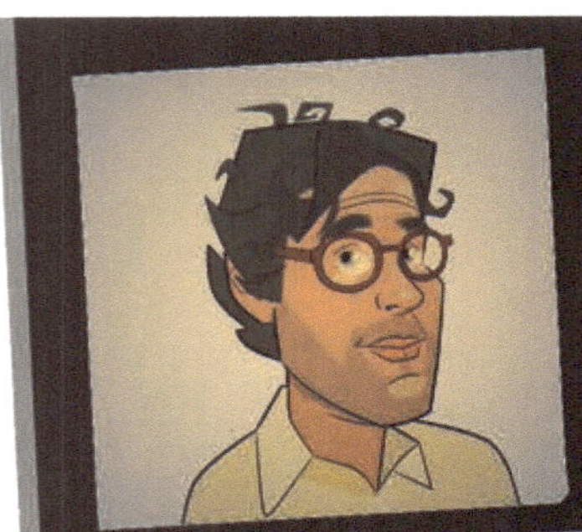

MATTHEW MOSS

MCA ALUMNI 2000-2003

ILLUSTRATION BFA

matthew@touchtouchstudio.com

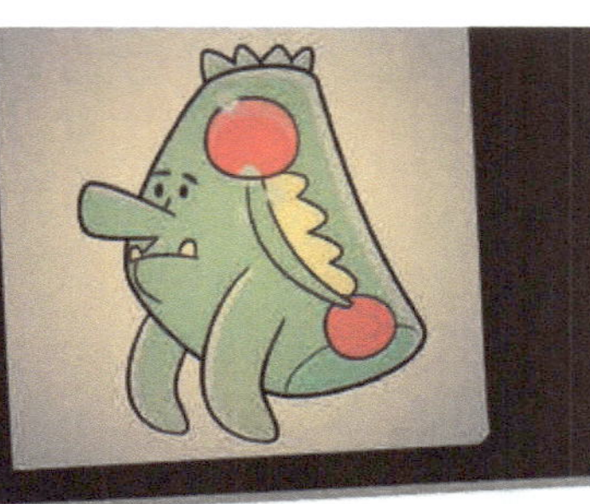

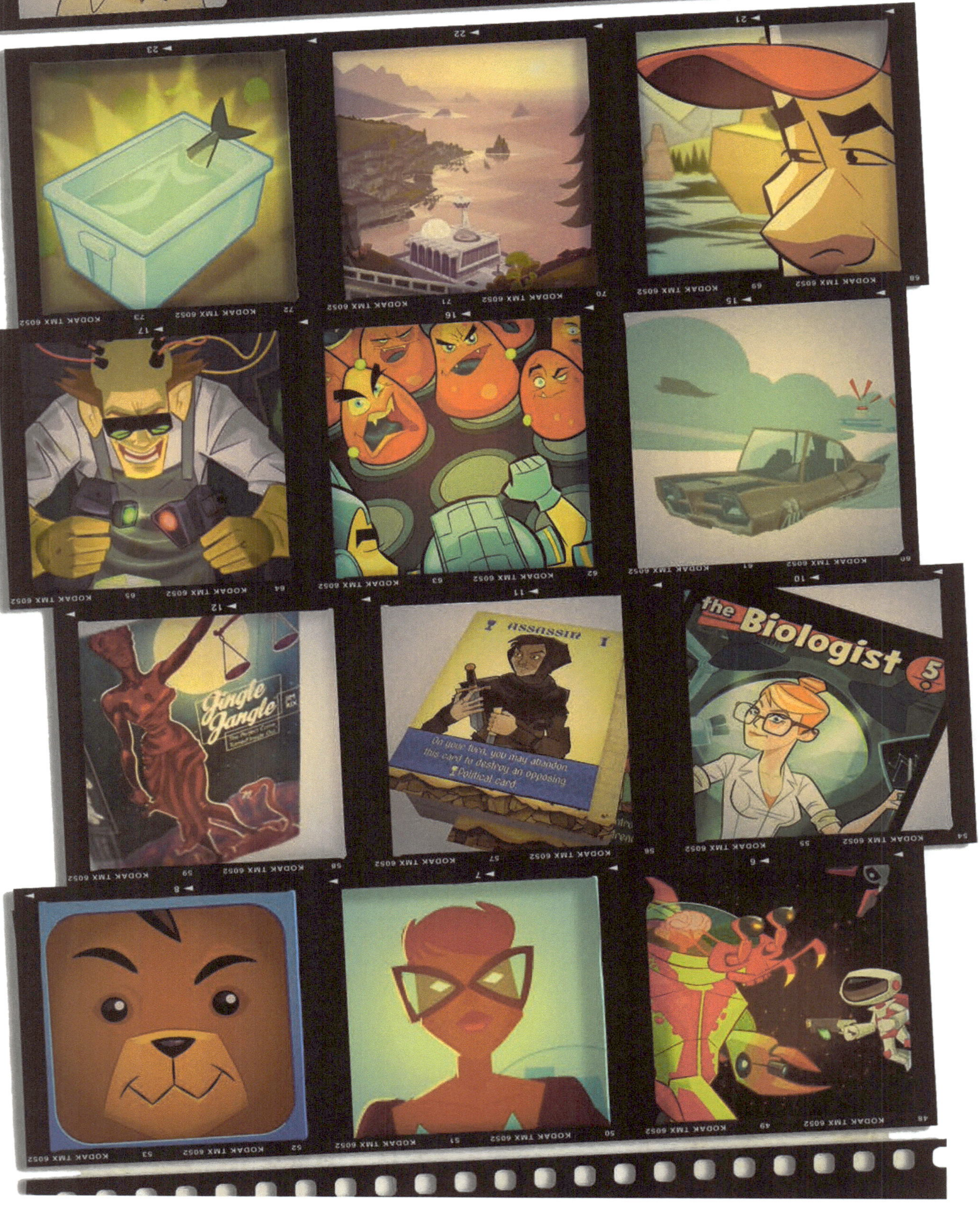

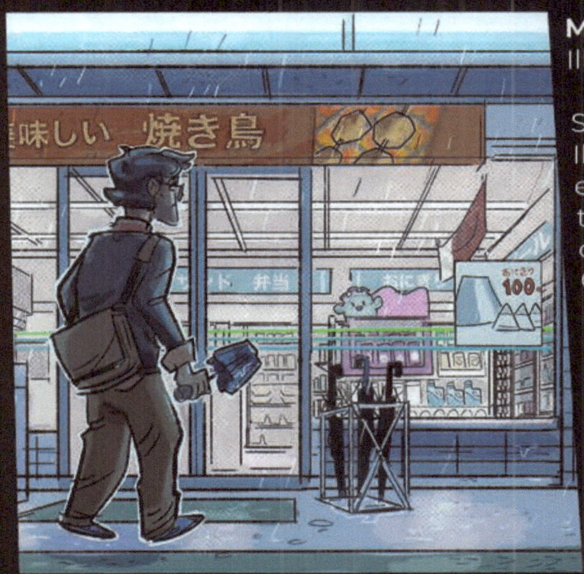

Matthew Moss, Creative Director and Illustrator.

Since Graduating from MCA with a BFA in Illustration in 2003, I've been an award winning editorial cartoonist, an in-house art director in the game industry working on projects for clients including Disney, Lego, National Geographic and an independent creative professional operating my own studio.

Currently based in Tokyo, Japan, my business Touch Touch Studio creates art and design that ranges from game development to comics, print, application development, branding, character design and design consultation.

Along with ceramicist Akiko Geirin, we formed Team Ping-Pong, 2018 in Tokyo, an art collaboration unit creating gallery exhibitions and performance art with focus on cross-disciplinary fine art that incorporates a healthy dose of humor.

Since the start of the Corona Virus pandemic, I've been co-creating the slice of life webcomic, 66 Days, with Argentinian cartoonist Luis Santamarina. In it we examine the perils of life in the Corona, using comedy and magic-realism to shine a light on the absurd situation created by the global upheaval.

The years since my time at MCA have passed incredibly quickly. However, there's never a day I don't communicate, reflect on, or feel the profound impact that my time at the Memphis College of Art has on my life and career. A heartfelt thank you to my educators, classmates and friends-- I love you all dearly and hope you continue to be creative and successful long into the future.

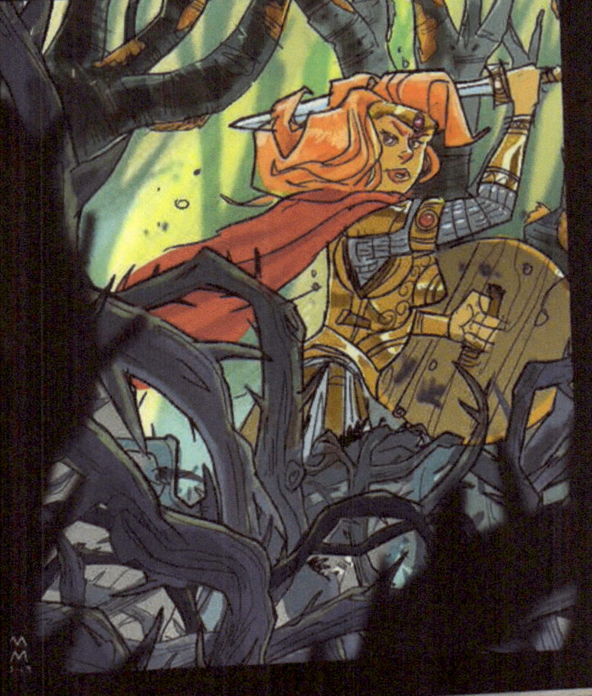

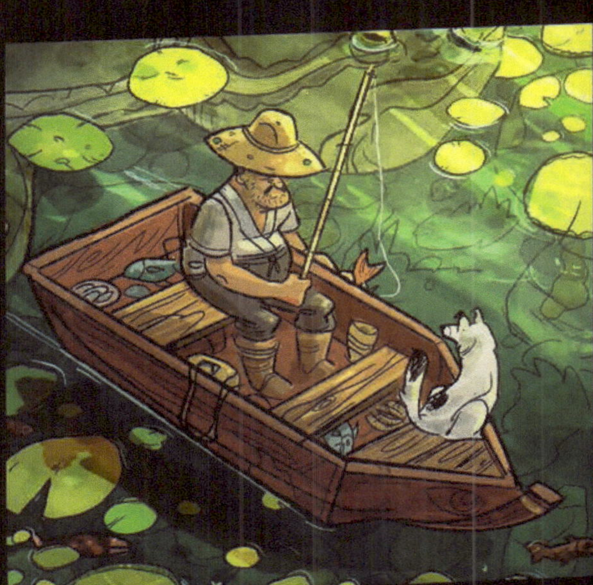

AMANDA MICHAEL HARRIS

Instagram: @ _a_m_harris

I've worked through many forms over the last twenty years, scattering my ideas through painting, drawing, bookmaking and sculpture. Over the course of my practice my work has morphed from folky, dream-like mythological worlds to pure observational drawing and painting. Currently, my artwork gravitates towards anthropomorphized shapes and forms that embody concepts of sex and interpersonal boundaries. Through playful compositions and colorful palettes, I toy with the squishes, cockles and constraints of the caricatured human body.

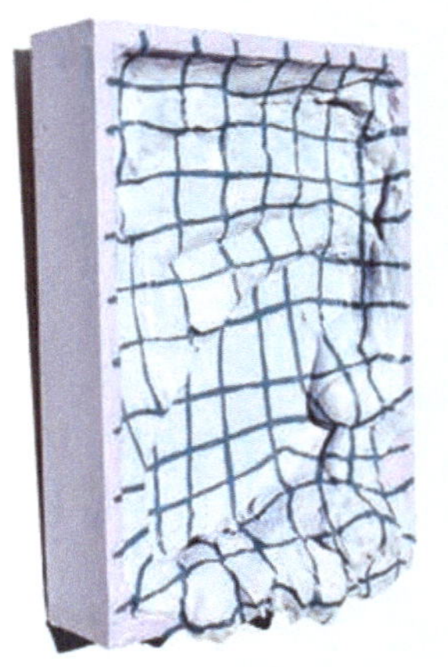
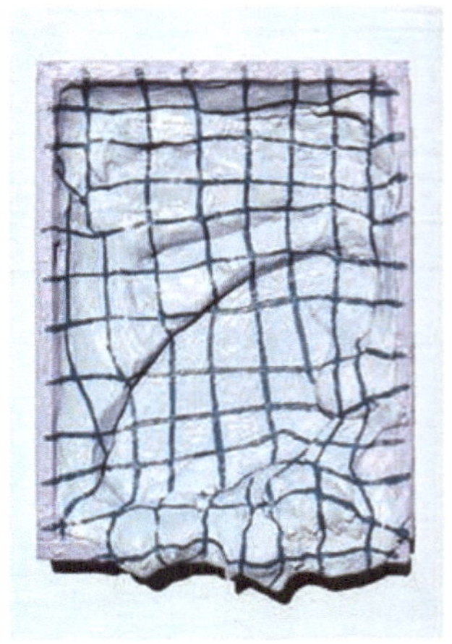

"Bajulate" 2017, 6" x 8" acrylic, joint compound on wood

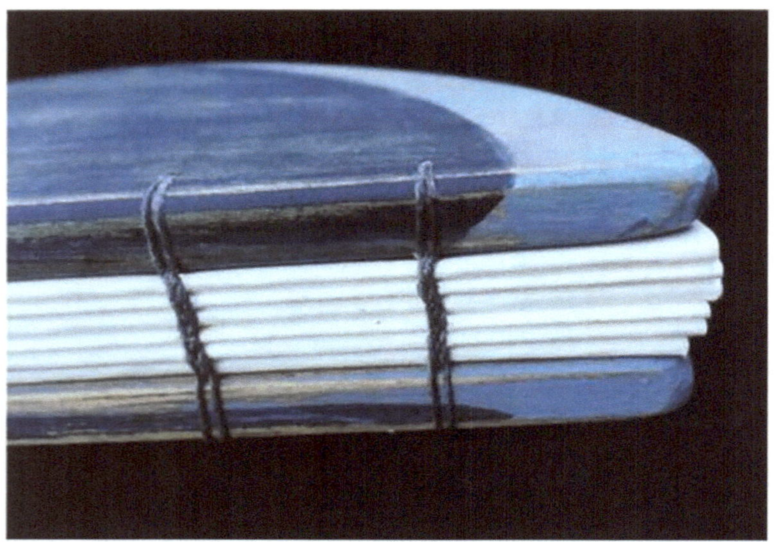

Moon Journals, 2015-17, various sizes, wood, paper, thread and acrylic

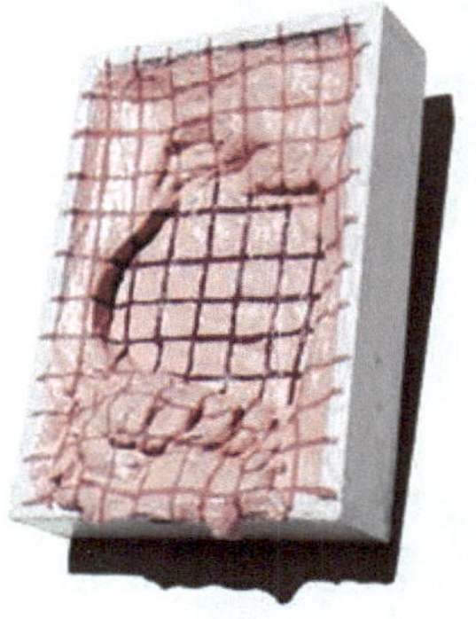
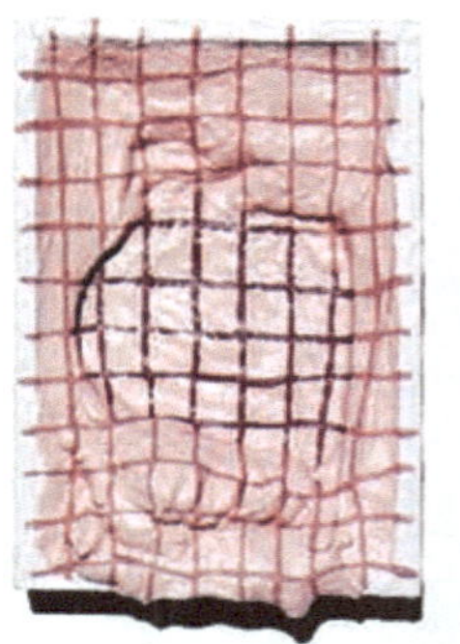

"Commendaces" 2017, 6" x 8" acrylic, joint compound on wood

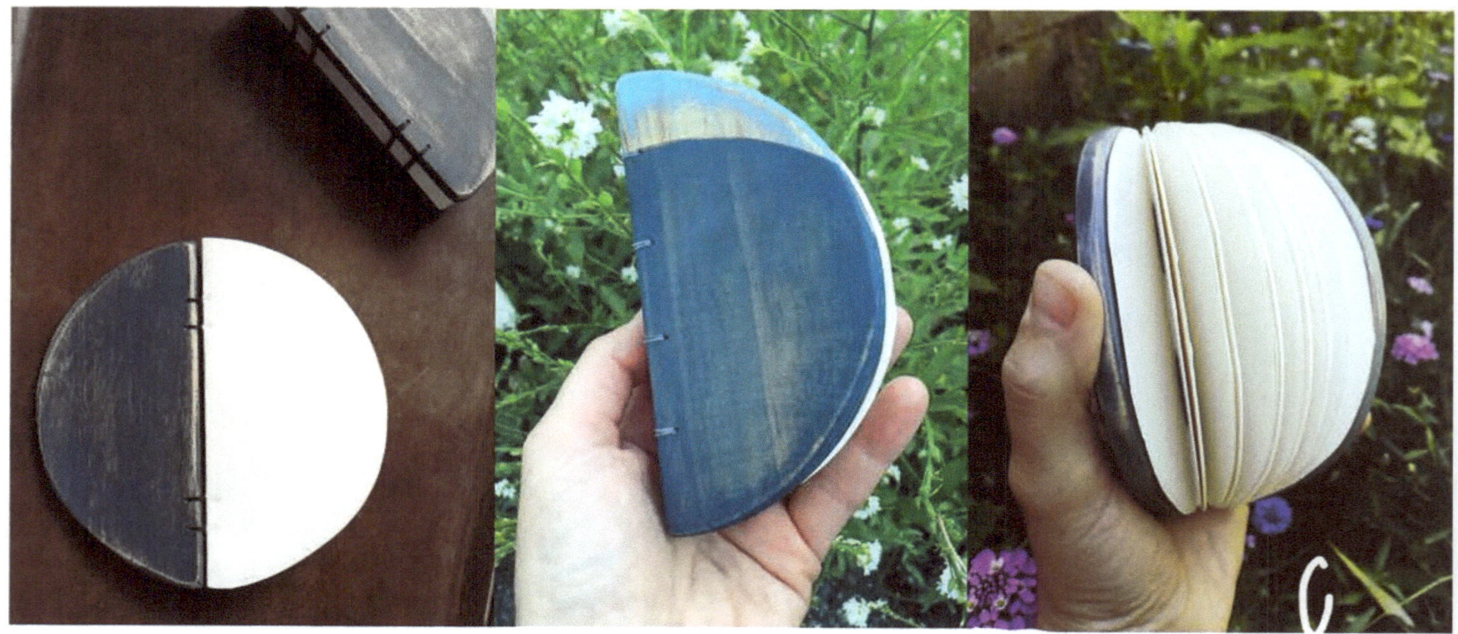

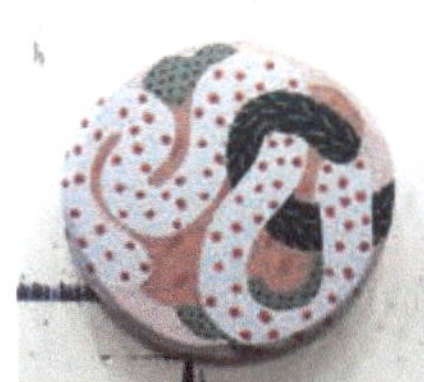

"Moosh Bokhoradet" 2018
10", acrylic on foam

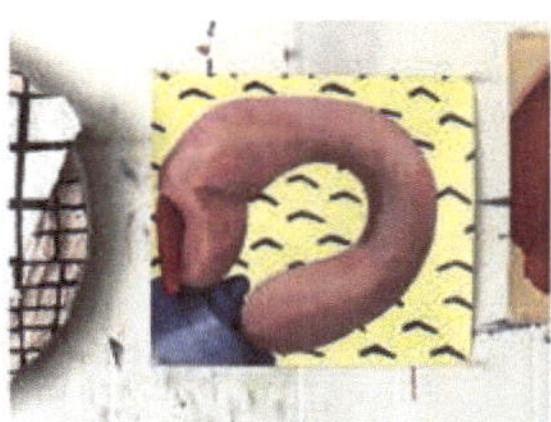

"Pang" 2019
11" x 15", acrylic on canvas

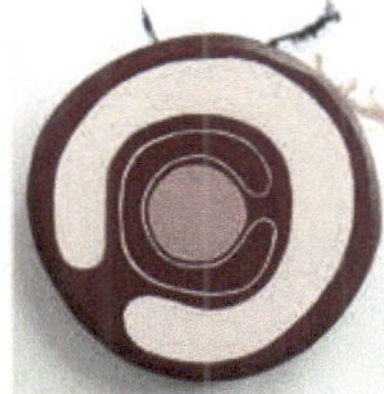

"Tosh" 2018
10", acrylic on foam

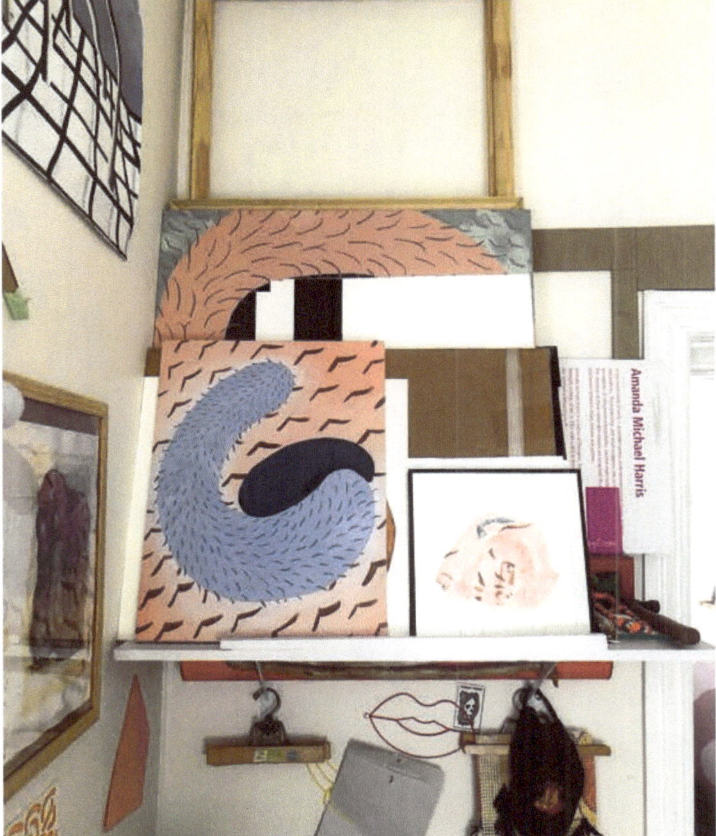

Studio Image

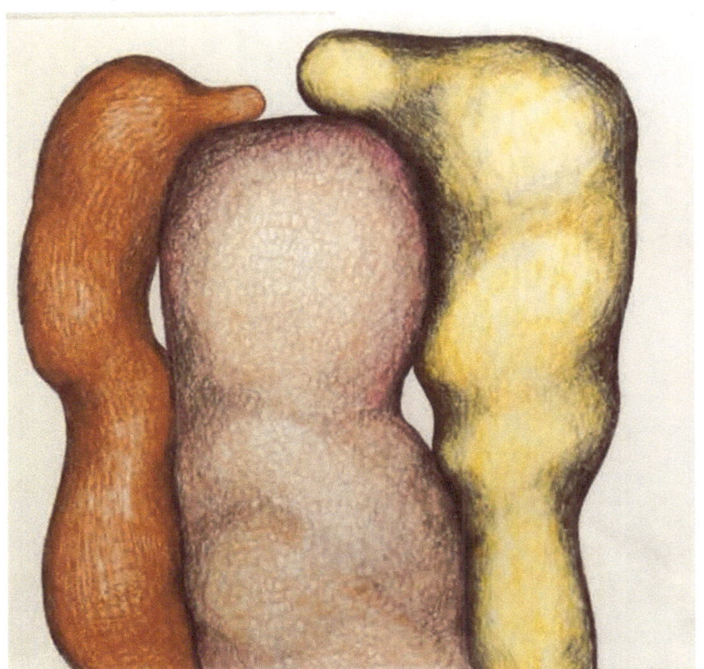

"My Little Round Thing" 2018, 36" x 42", acrylic on canvas

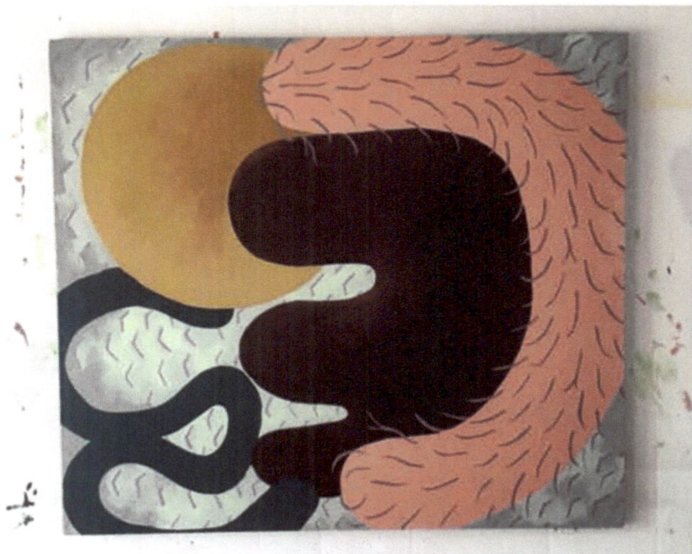

"Wring" 2019, 11" x 15", acrylic on canvas

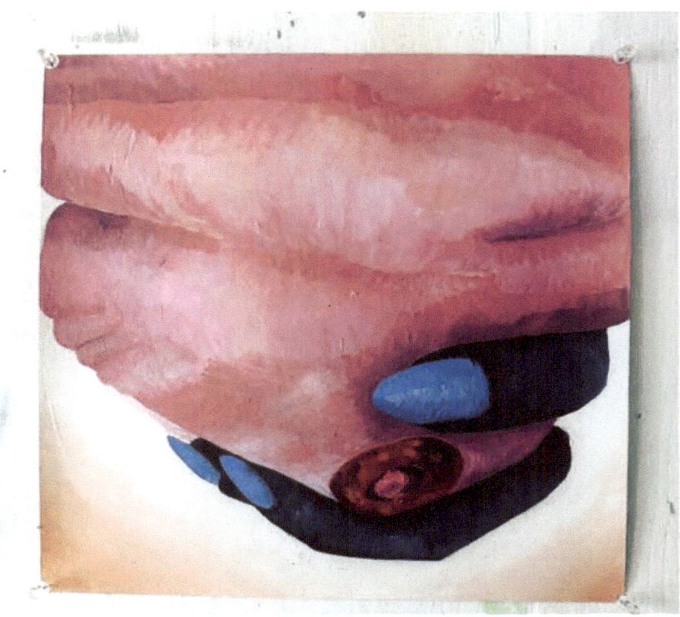

"Trois (orange)" 2019, 11.5" x 10", acrylic on canvas

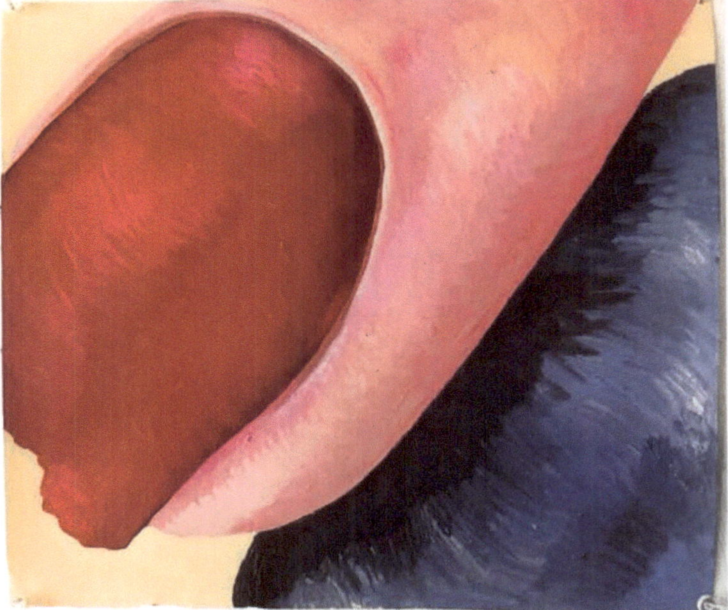

"Goad" 2019, 11" x 15", acrylic on canvas

Kohei Kato

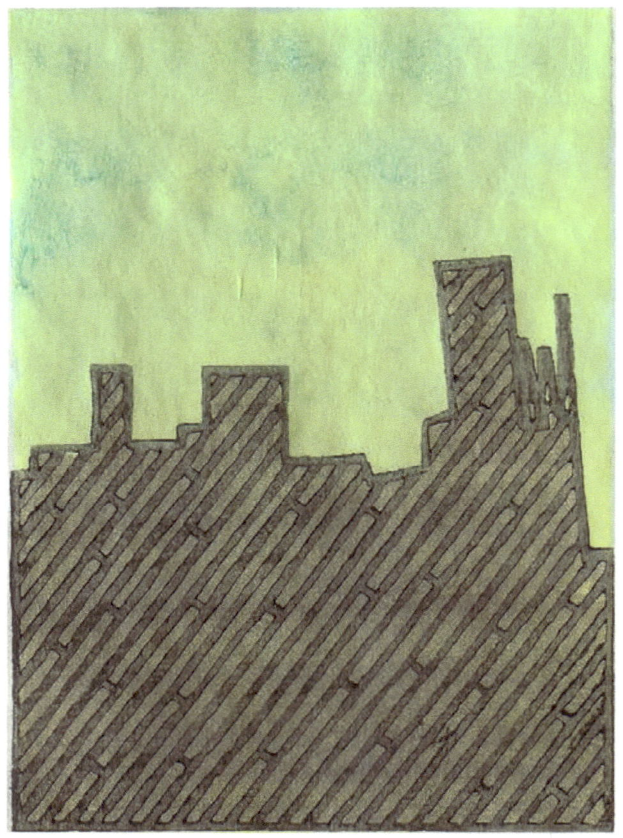

"Out side" 2016 wood cut 9"x6"

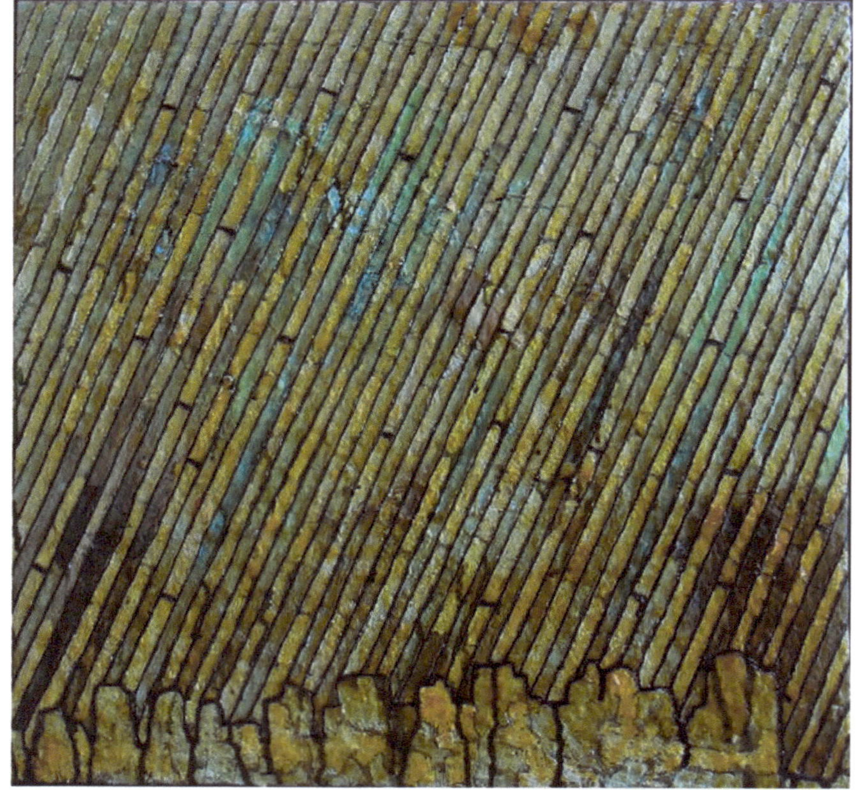

"Shower" 2010 oil 18"x18"

Kohei Kato

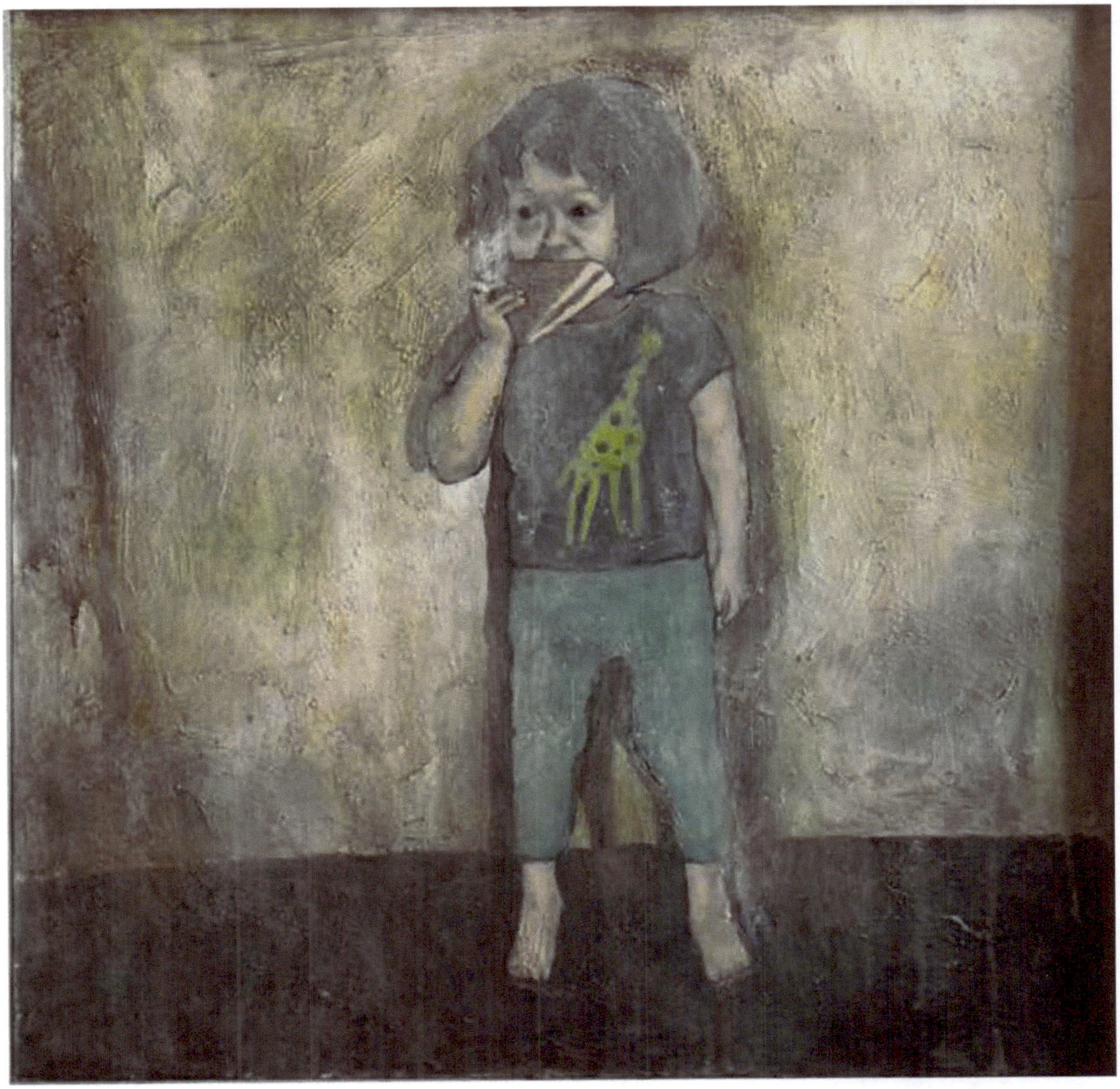

"Daughter" 2018 acryic 20"x20"

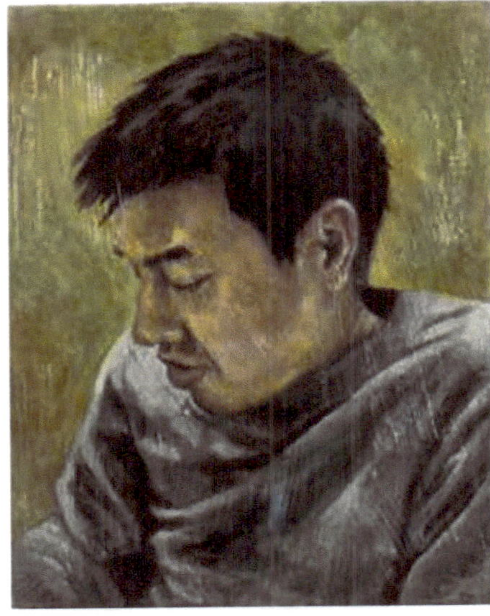

"Takao" 2020 acryic 7"x5"

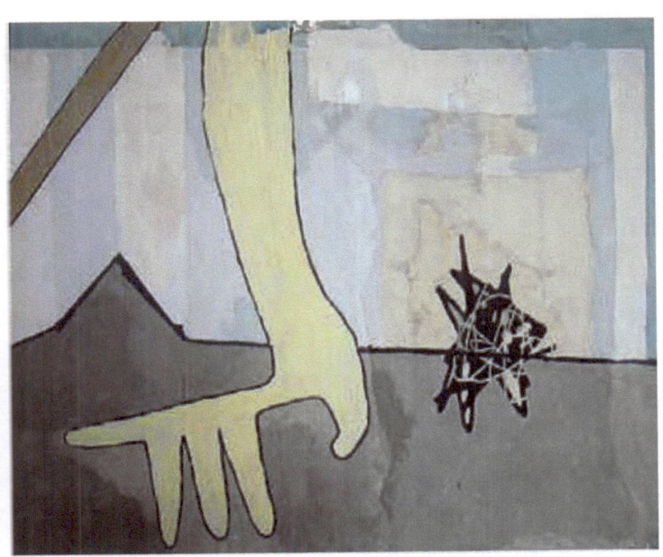

"unknown" 2002 mixed media 7"x5"

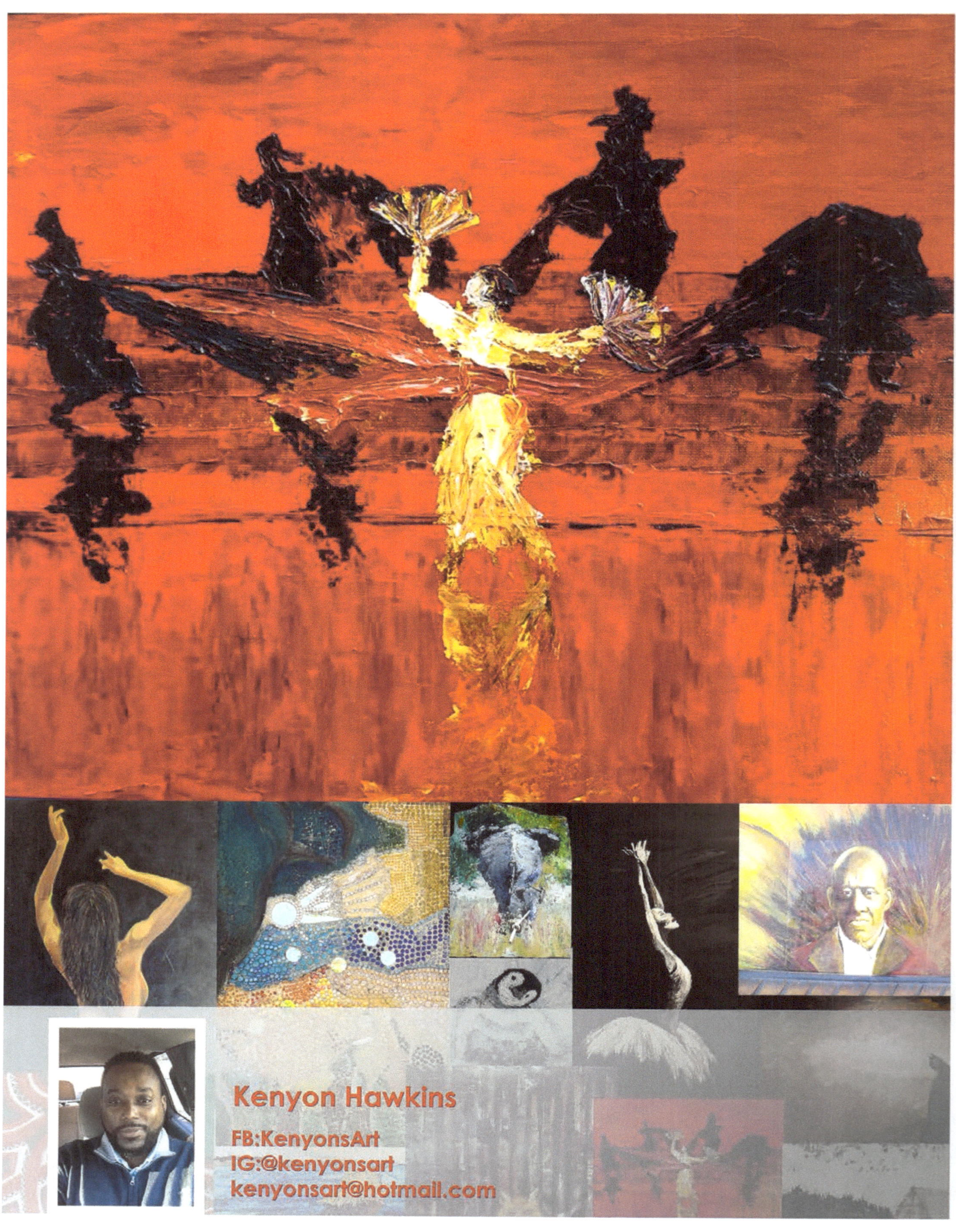

Kenyon Hawkins

FB:KenyonsArt
IG:@kenyonsart
kenyonsart@hotmail.com

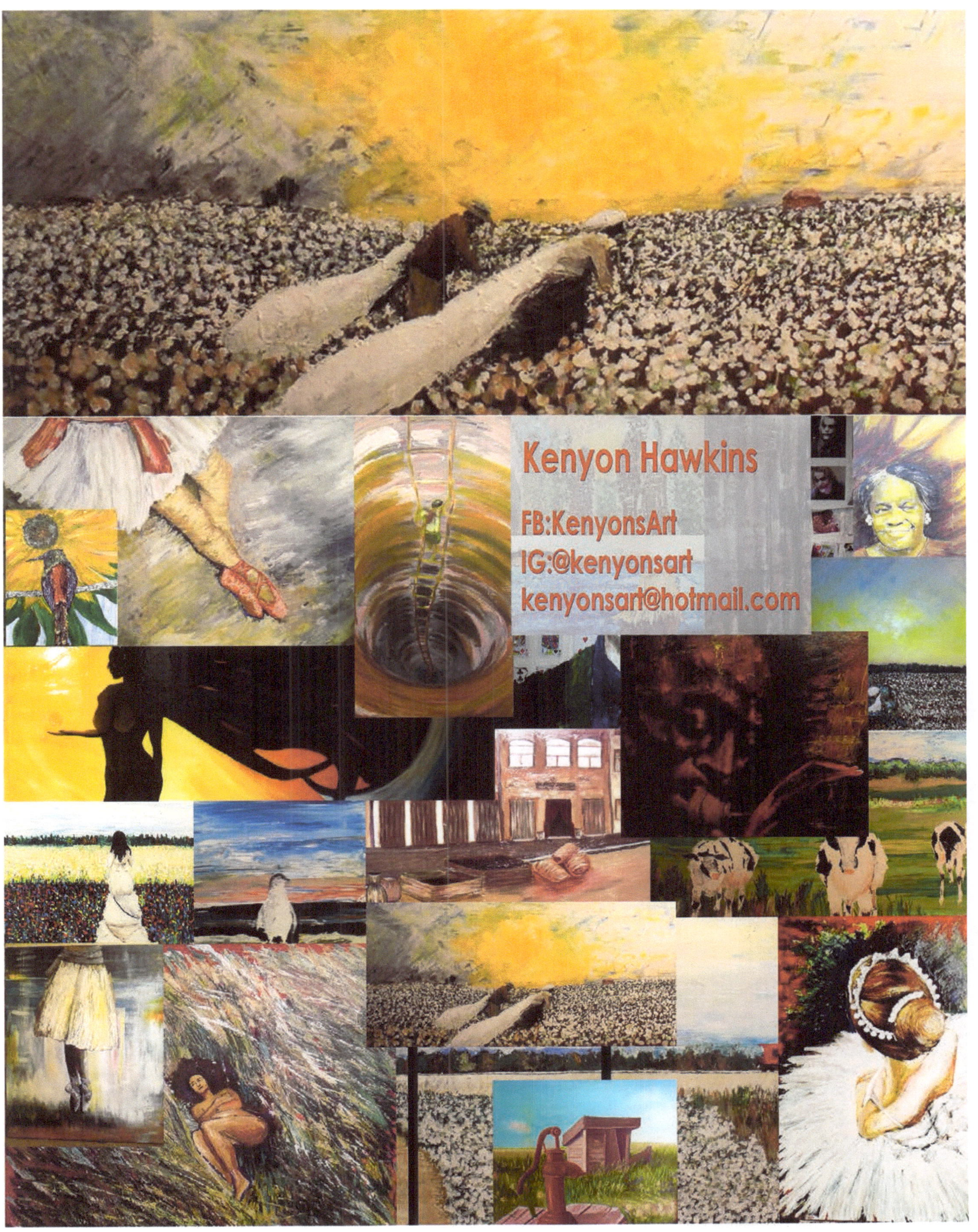
Kenyon Hawkins
FB:KenyonsArt
IG:@kenyonsart
kenyonsart@hotmail.com

MICHAEL COPPAGE

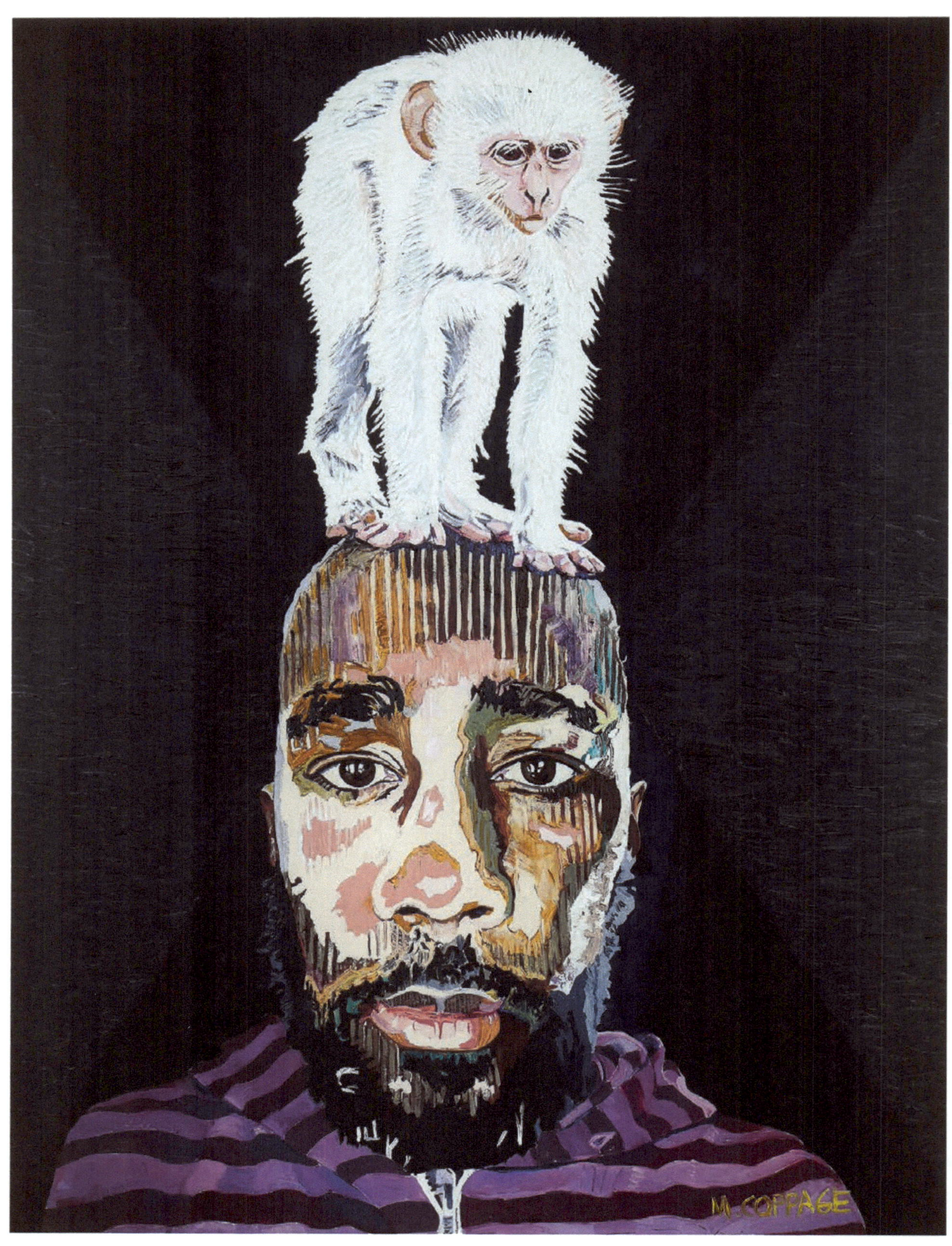

THE APPROPRIATION, 2018, oil on canvas, 36" x 48"

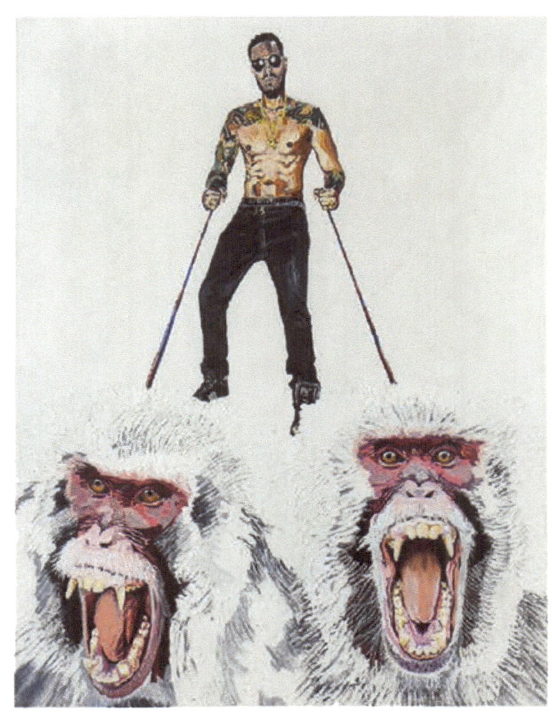

Three/Fifths, 2018, 36" x 48", oil on canvas

MichaelCoppage.com

Originally, from Chicago, Michael Coppage has lived and worked in Cincinnati since 2007. Coppage earned a B.F.A in Sculpture from Memphis College of Art and an M.F.A in Studio Art from The Pennsylvania Academy of the Fine Arts. Primarily a mixed media artist, Coppage has spent a number of years making work centered around stigmatized and marginalized individuals. He has recently been featured in print and online for a controversial and provocative series entitled "American +" where he addresses the appropriation of black culture and the simultaneous demonization of black men as well as depicts white Americans as monkeys. In addition to his more personal works, He co-created a therapeutic art program called PIECES at the Cincinnati Children's Hospital where he works with adolescent psychiatric patients and teams from other disciplines to create large-scale portraits. To date, over 300 images have been completed and exhibited around the Cincinnati area. He uses his artwork to address social justice issues in contemporary America through exhibitions and lectures and uses his business (PIECES) to combat the community issues highlighted in his artwork.

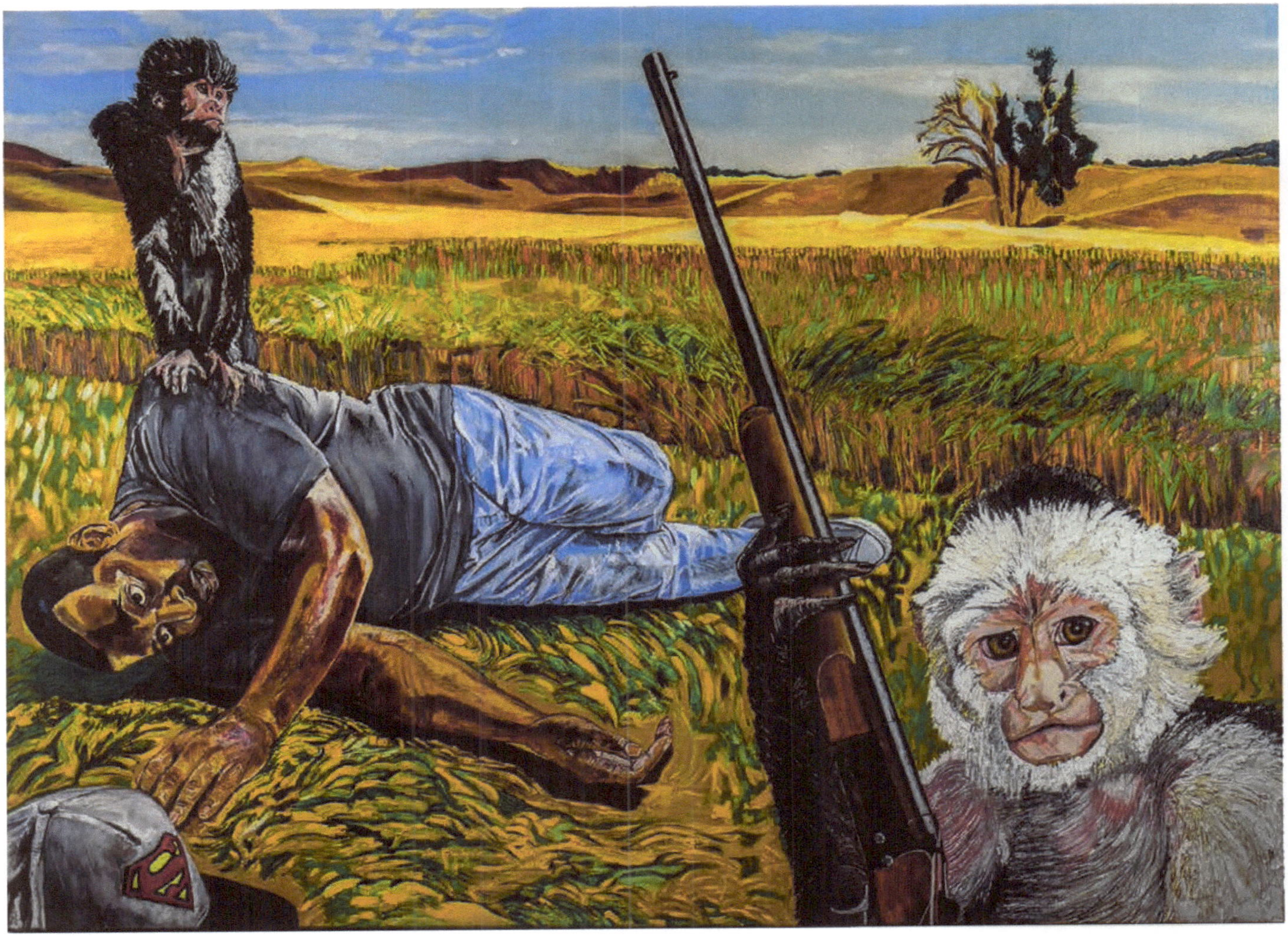

AMERICAN ELEPHANT, 2018, 36" x 48",oil on canvas

SUSAN MAAKESTAD.com

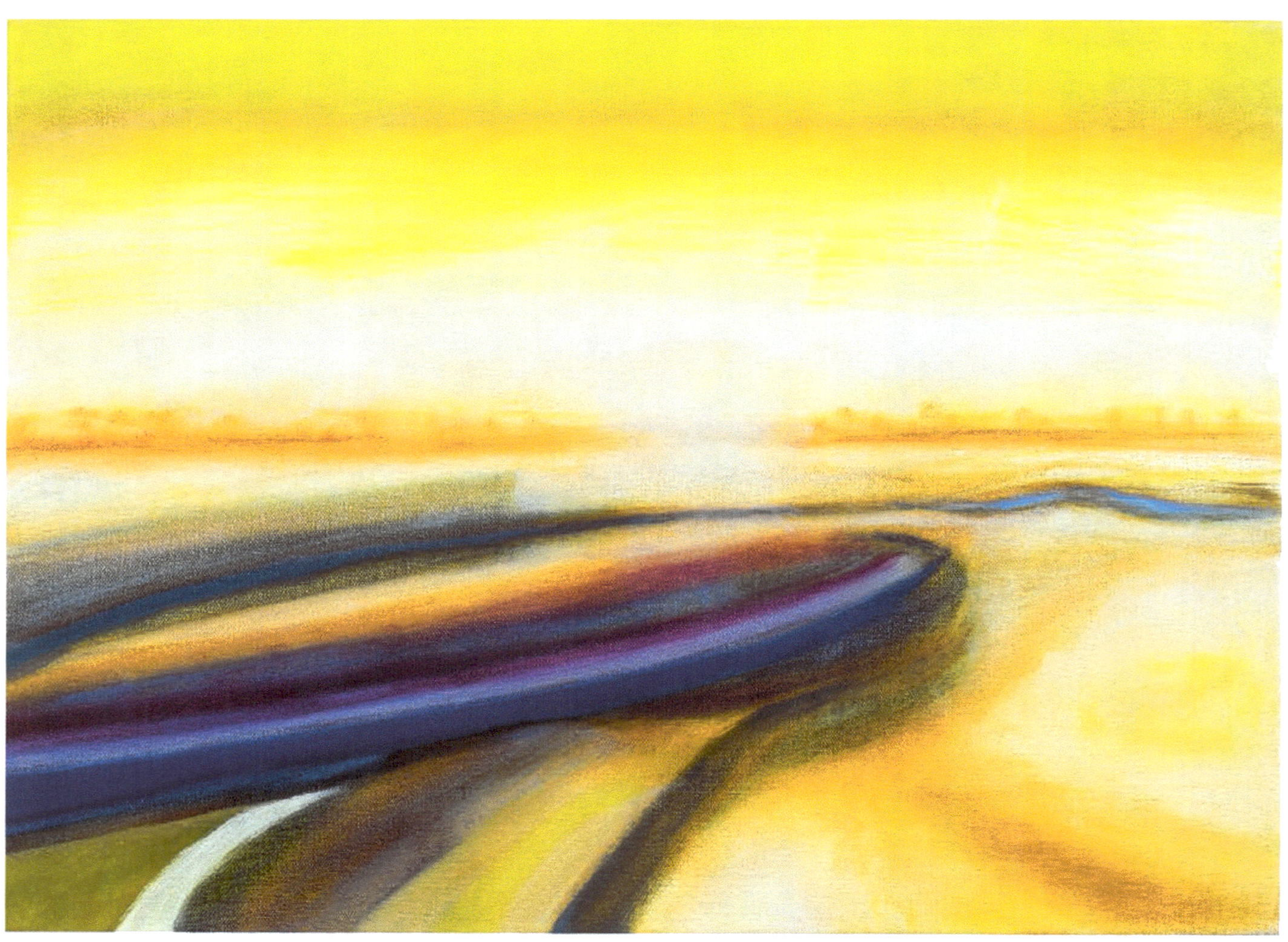

Golden, oil on canvas, 14" x 19", 2019

Susan Maakestad was a recipient of a National Endowment for the Art fellowship from Arts Midwest in 1988. She is the recipient of the 2013 Arts Accelerator Grant from Arts Memphis, purchase awards from the Urban Arts Commission in Memphis, and three individual artist grants from the Peoria Area Arts and Sciences Council. She has been a fellow at the MacDowell Colony and the Virginia Center for the Creative Arts. Her work has been included in the national publication, New American Paintings, and the Painting Center in New York's online Art File. Her watercolors are included in The Drawing Center in New York's online Viewing Program. Her work has been exhibited nationally including at Groveland Gallery in Minneapolis; Sazama Gallery, Chicago; Steinway Gallery, Chapel Hill; and The Rockford (IL) Art Museum. Public collections include the Tennessee State Museum, Memphis Brooks Museum of Art and the City of Memphis. She is currently represented by The Rymer Gallery in Nashville.

"I am a bird watcher and a sky watcher.

I long to be outdoors but if I'm inside, I look out the window.
If there is no landscape to view out the window, I look for one online.
Nature is a solace.
And yet the reports about nature are grim. For example, since 1970 nearly three billion birds have disappeared in North America. This is a sad commentary on how humans have altered the landscape. The collective will to fix the planet is not strong enough. I want to be an informed citizen but it is exhausting to stay current when the news is so bleak.
And so I paint. I make paintings filled with exaggerated color and space that reflect the awe I feel when I am in nature looking at the sky, feeling the wind, listening to the birds. Rather than express my feelings of sadness, I celebrate nature and the arts. Landscape abstraction is my means to represent what's good about being alive right now on this broken planet.
Painting is a solace."

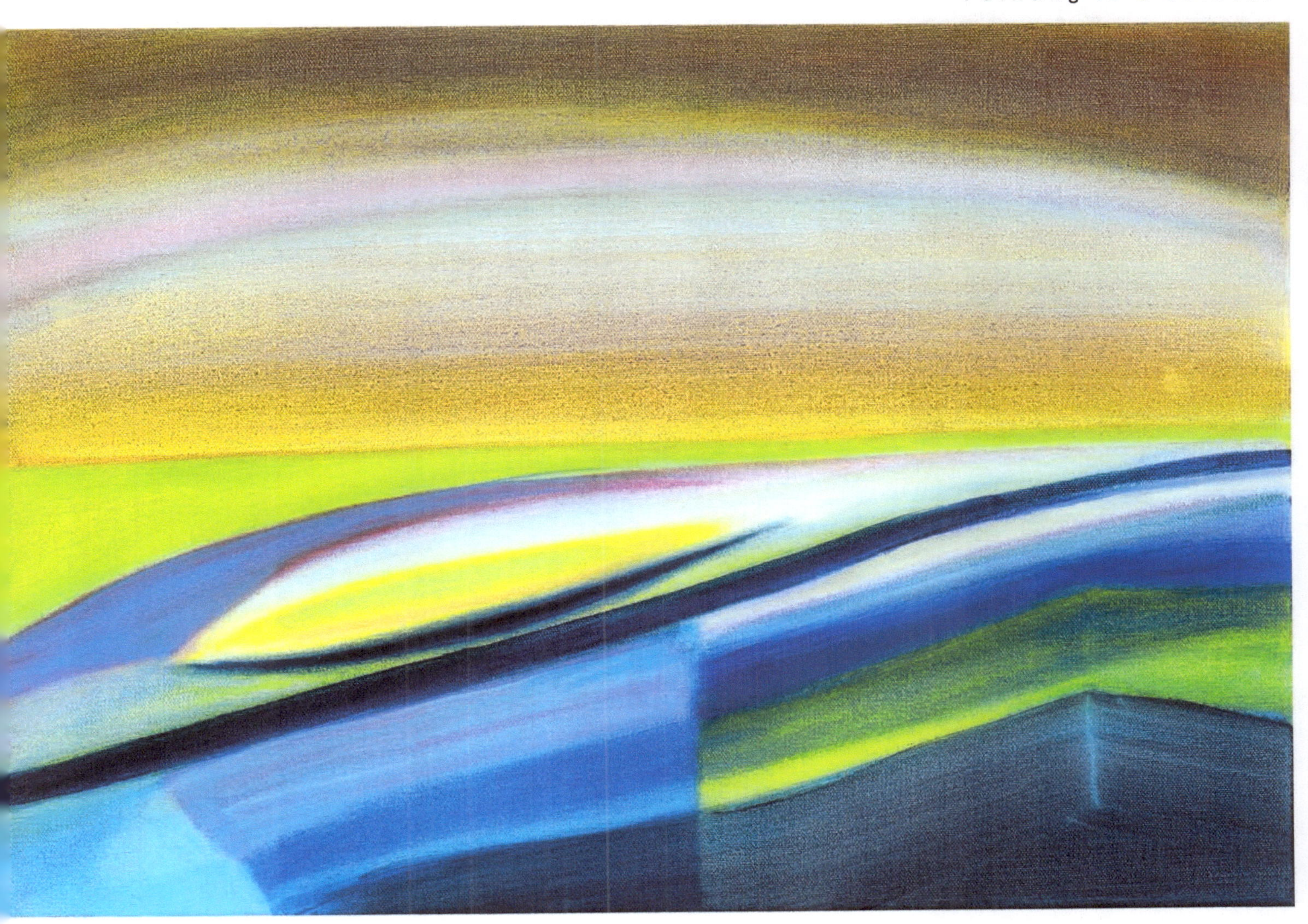

Spring, oil on canvas, 13 x 18", 2019

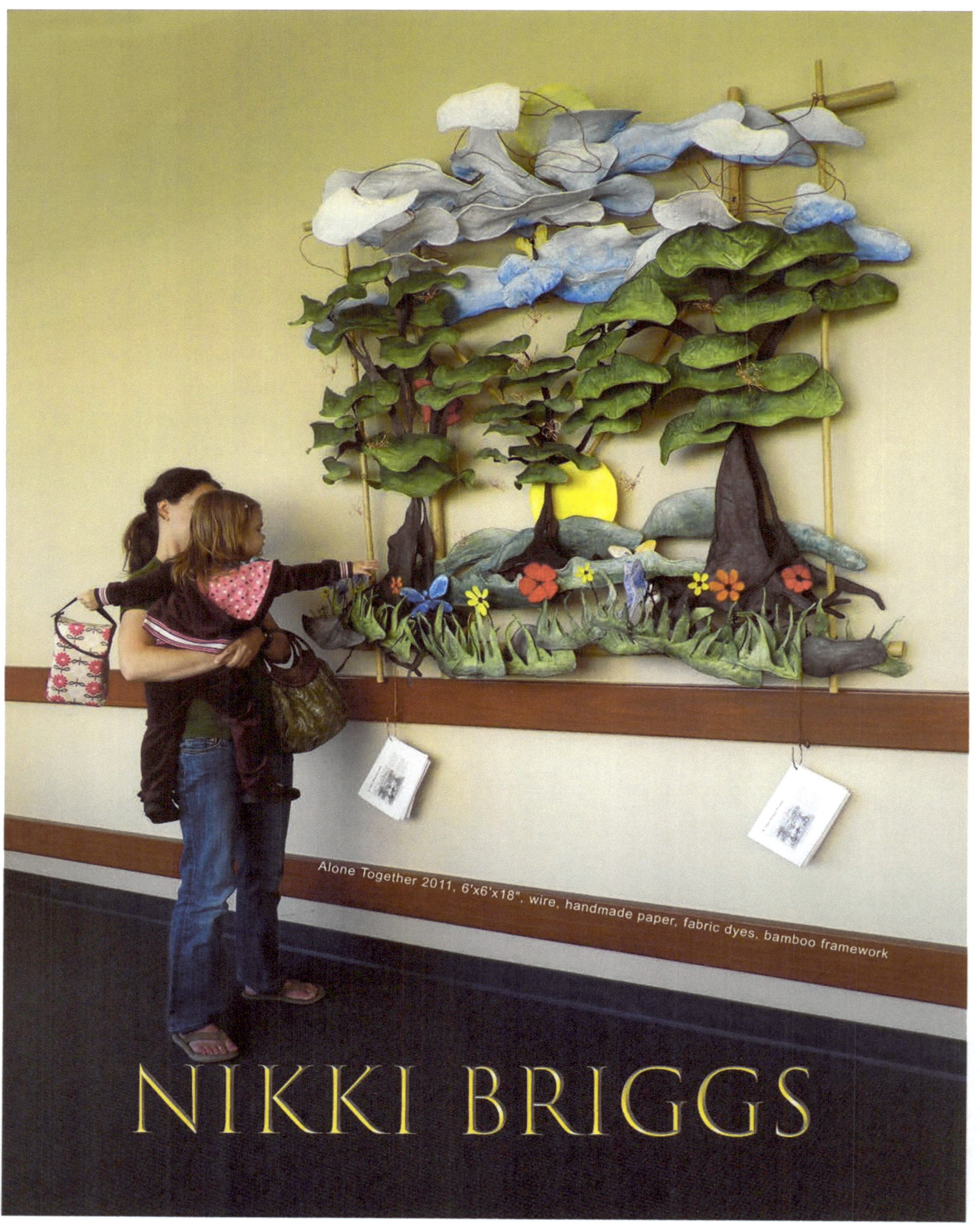
Alone Together 2011, 6'x6'x18", wire, handmade paper, fabric dyes, bamboo framework

NIKKI BRIGGS

@paper_wire_art

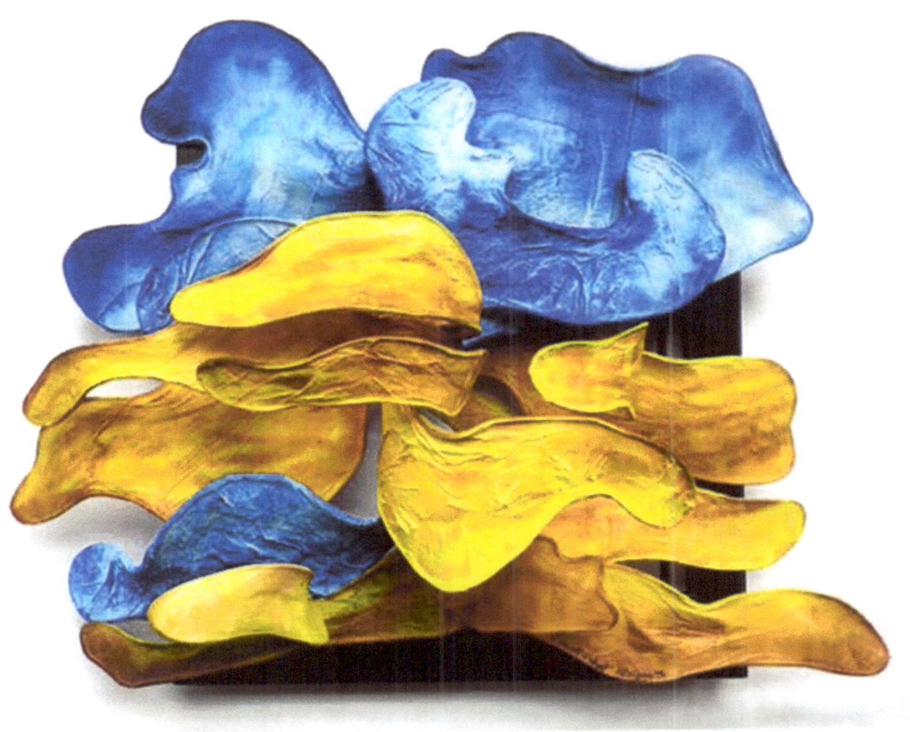

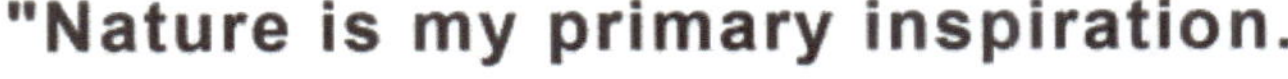

Homage to Van Gogh's Wheatfields, 2006, 20"x20"x8", wire, handmade paper, fabric dyes

"Nature is my primary inspiration. It continually reintroduces me to my own self. The connection that I share with others through my work, as well as the emotional and psychological benefits I derive from it are what motivates me to create. I like to push the boundaries of what is considered art by attempting to create in ways that have not yet been conceived, and I hope this inspires similar efforts in others."

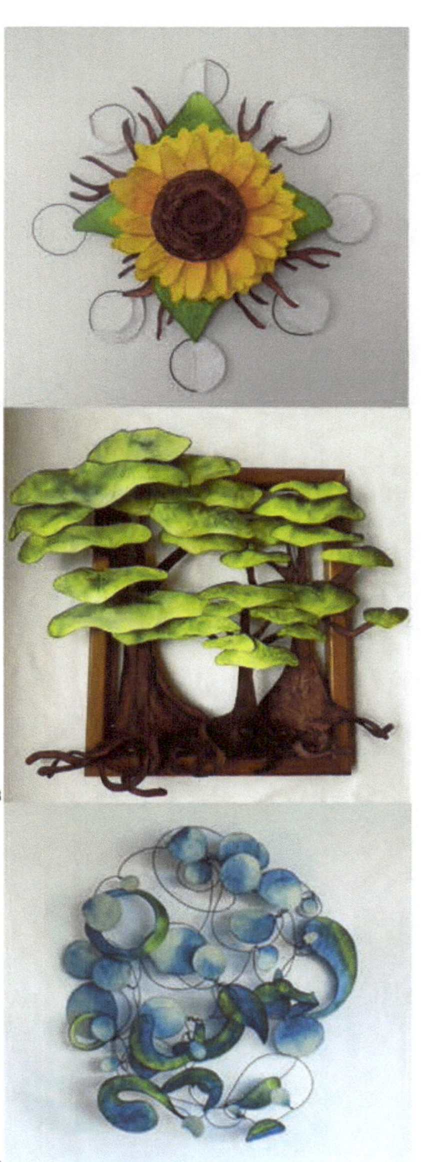

A

B

C

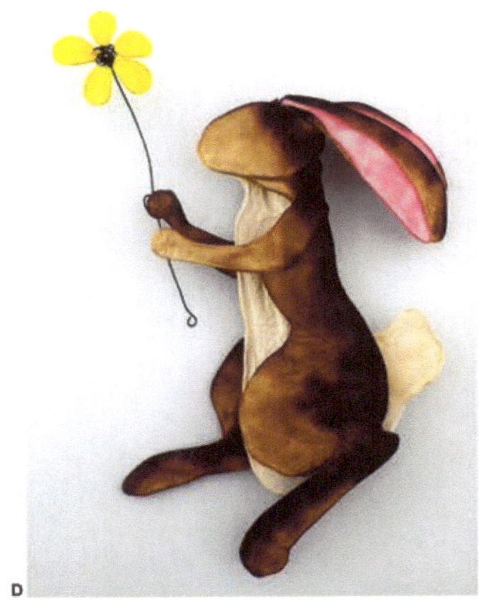

D

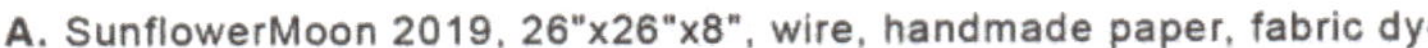

A. SunflowerMoon 2019, 26"x26"x8", wire, handmade paper, fabric dyes

B. Family, 2011, 32"x32"x10", wire, handmade paper, fabric dyes, custom walnut frame

C. General Sherman 2004, 30"x30"x8", wire, handmade paper, fabric dyes

D. Bunny Rabbit 2009, 20"x15"x4", wire, handmade paper, fabric dyes

JOYBELLA MCCRAY

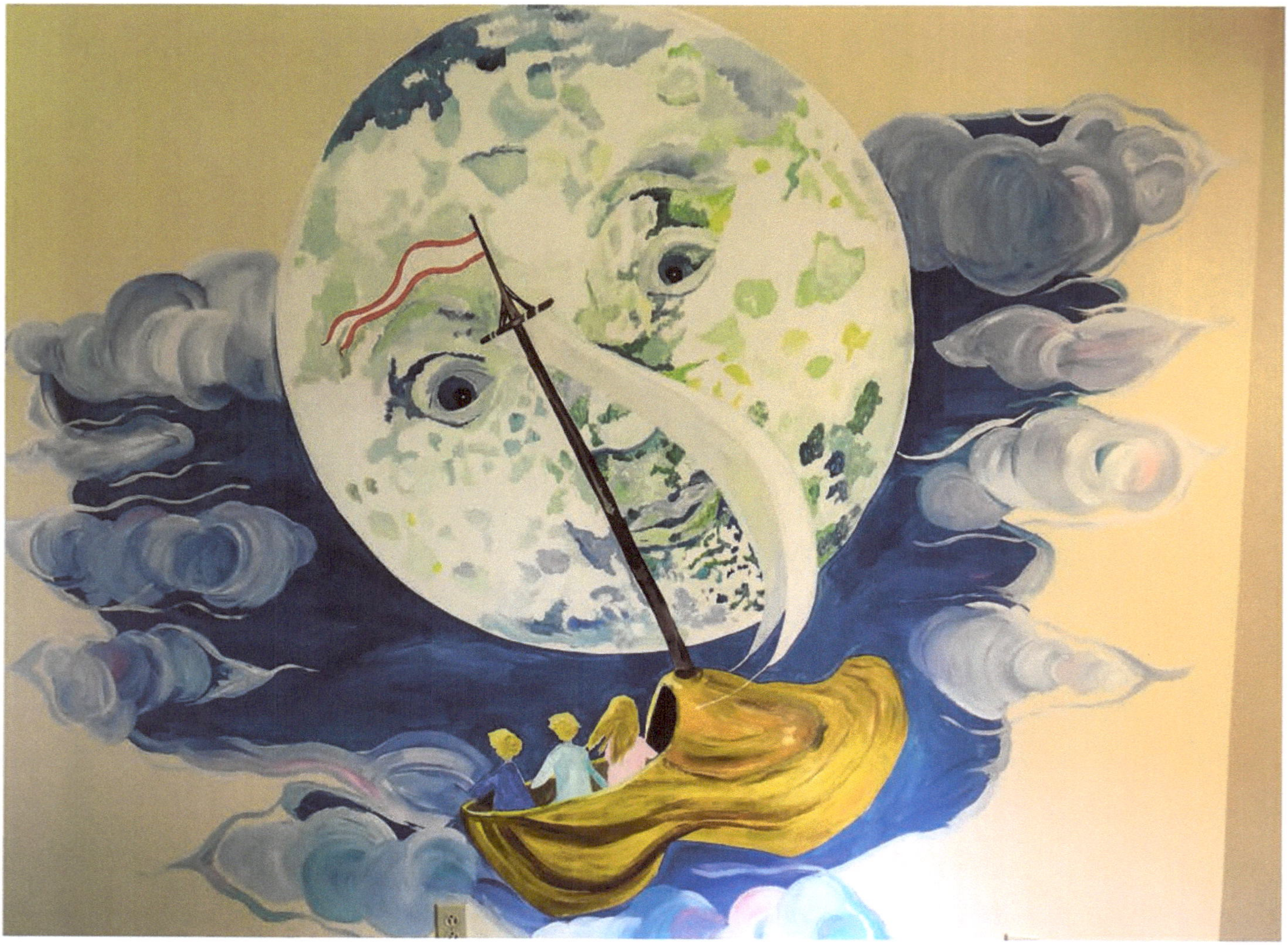

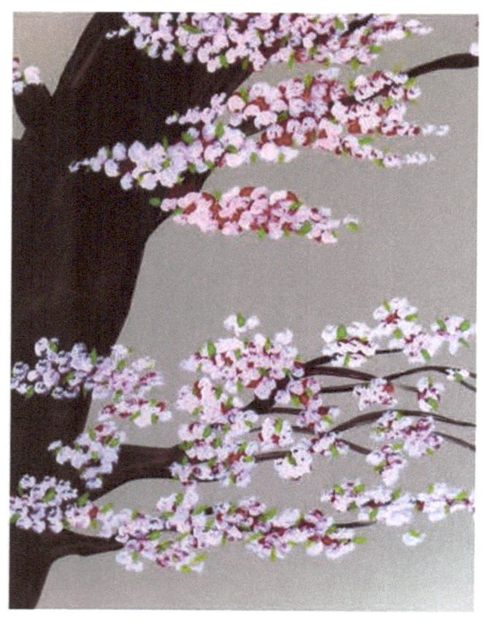

I USE A LOT OF WHAT I LEARNED DURING MY TIME AT MCA TO THINK OUTSIDE THE BOX AND CONCEPTUALIZE ALTERNATIVE SOLUTIONS.

JOYBELLA MCCRAY

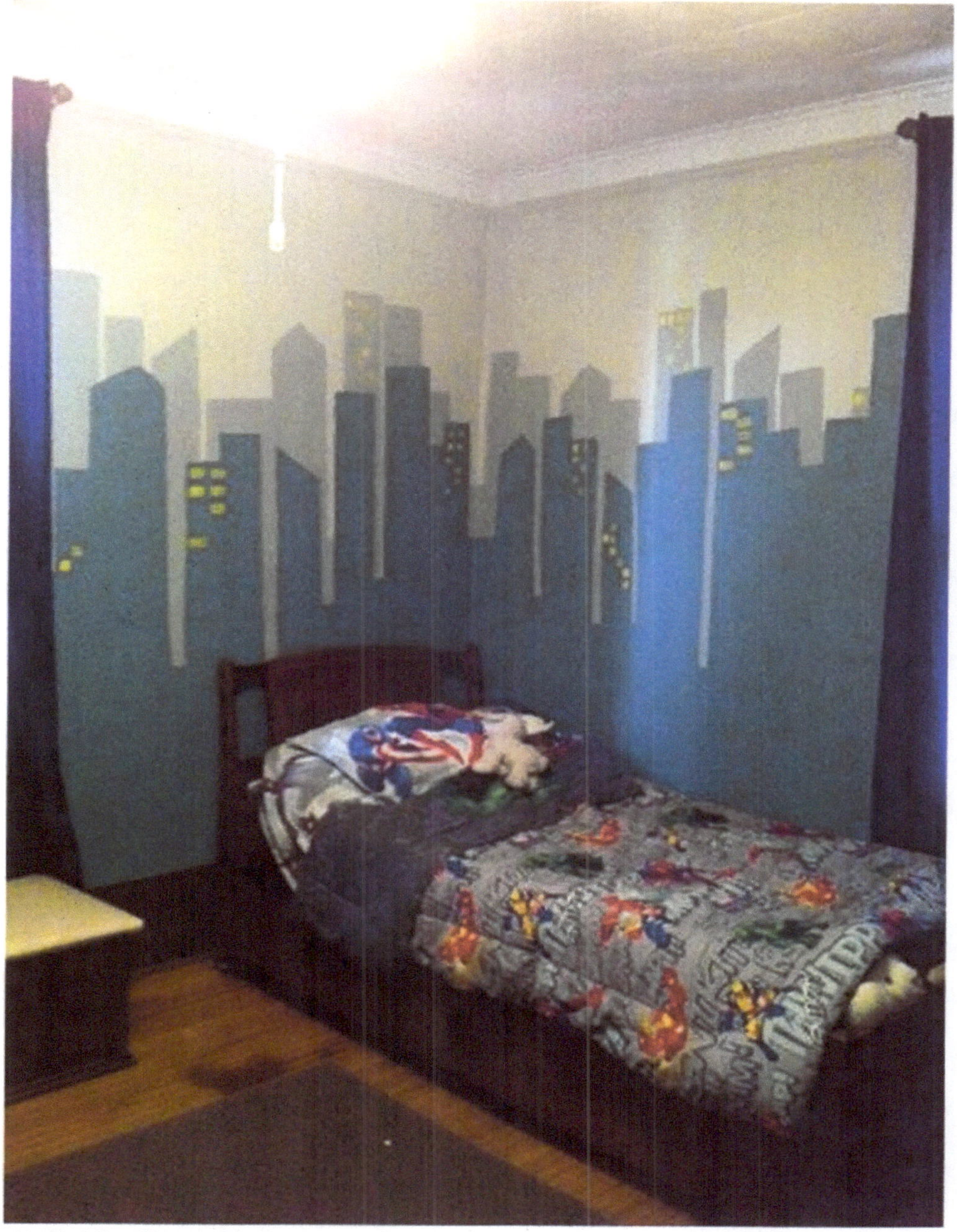

MURALS WITH MEANING

I LOVE DOING

COMMISSIONS FOR

FAMILY AND FRIENDS

BECAUSE IT MEANS

SOMETHING TO THEM.

"Untitled Mural" **2008-2019** Acrylic on bedroom walls

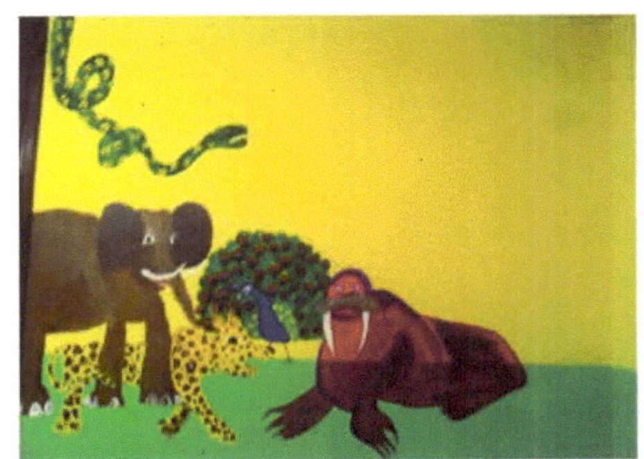

"mural detail" **2008-2019** Acrylic on bedroom wall

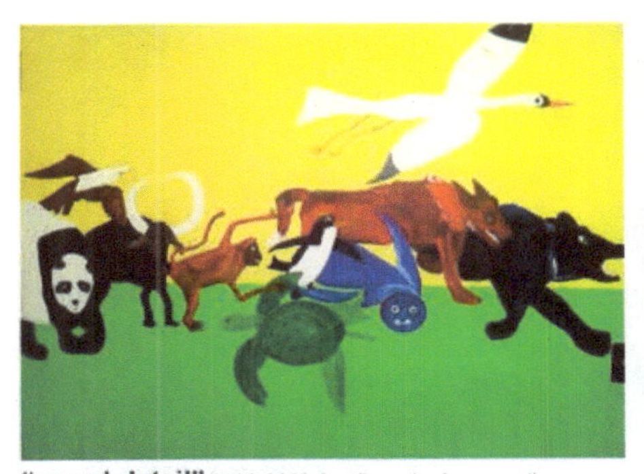

"mural detail" **2008-2019** Acrylic on bedroom wall

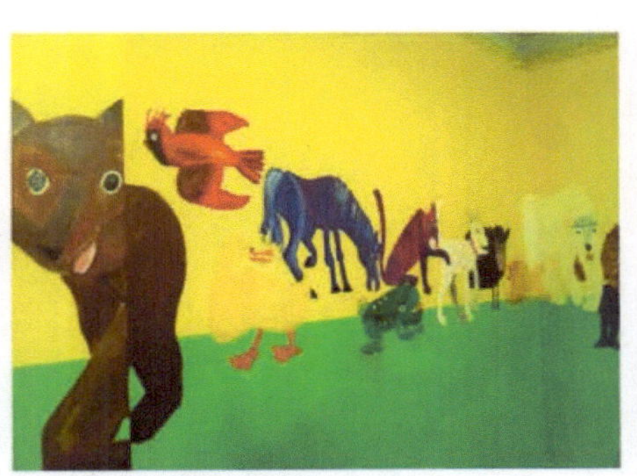

"mural detail" **2008-2019** Acrylic on bedroom wall

BRIAN MADDEN

www.maddenbrian.wordpress.com

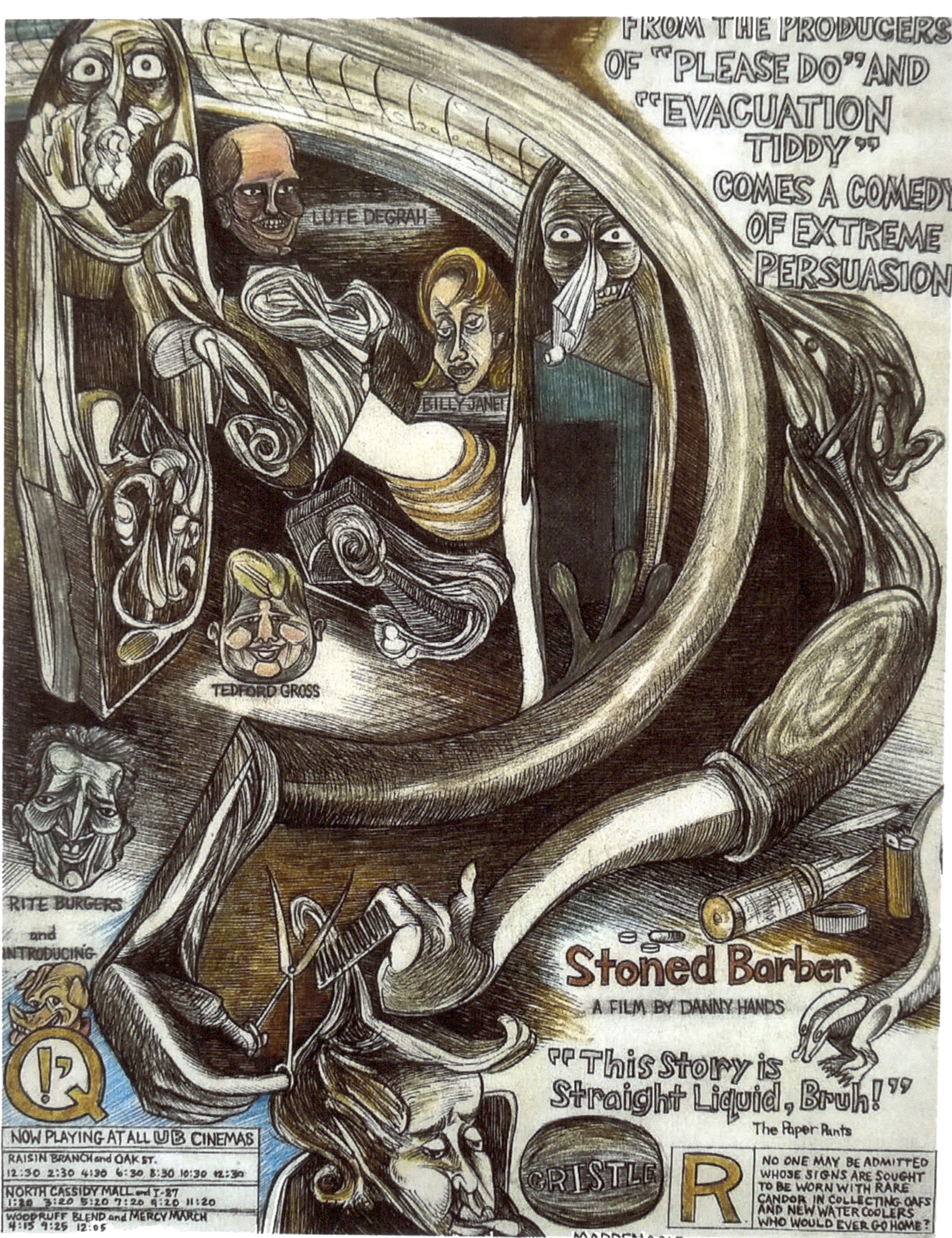

The Stoned Barber, 2015 drawing, 9" x 12"

BRIAN MADDEN

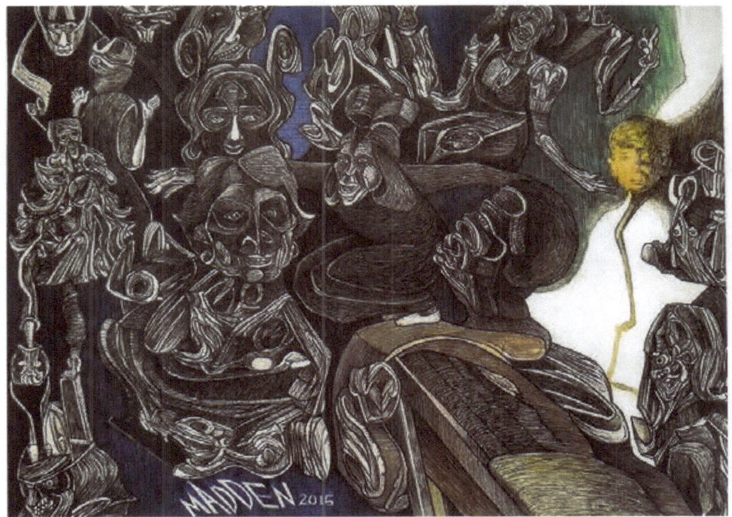

Blue Futures, 2015 drawing, 9" x 12"

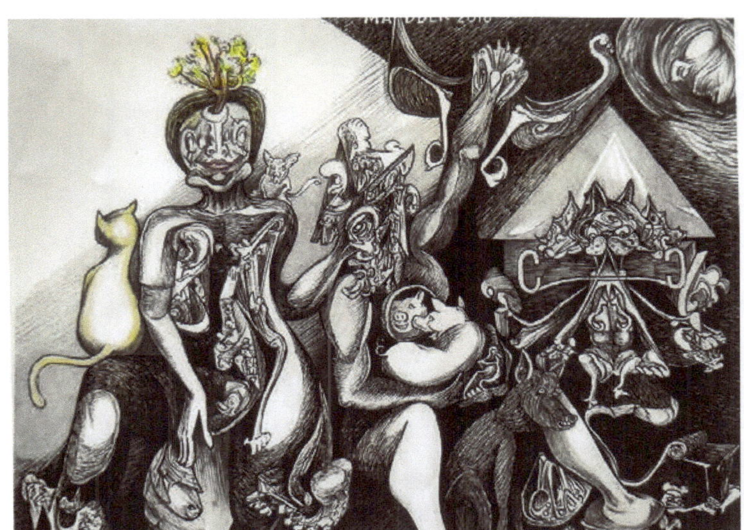

A Man is a Cat is a Pig is a Turtle, 2018 drawing, 9" x 12"

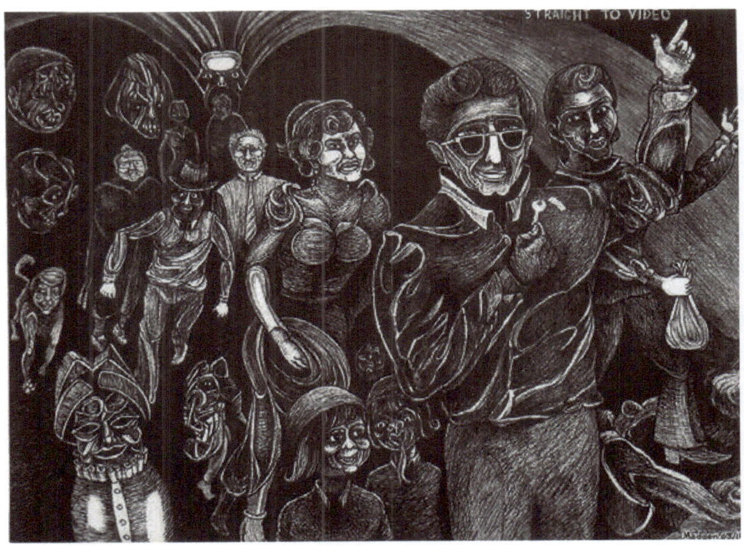

Straight to Video, 2014 drawing, 9" x 12"

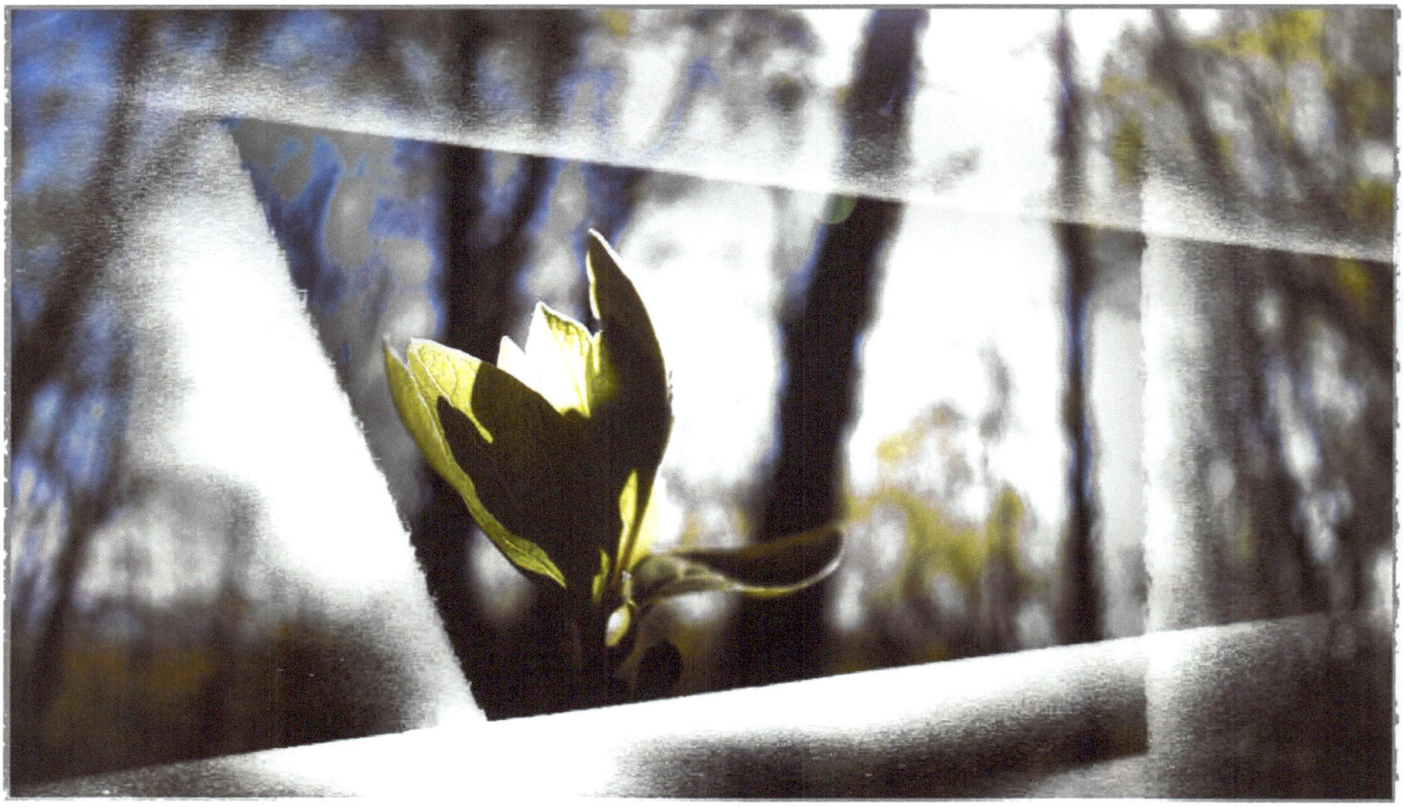

Growth 2010 28" x 22" Giclée Print on Metallic Luster Resin Coated Media

Tamika D. Williams, MFA 2000

tdwms@mac.com

I am an artist, a designer as well as a design educator. My love for a variety of mediums has allowed me to put together a body of work, that has its viewers appreciating it, as well as asking three questions: "What is that? Where is that? How did you do that?" My goal with each image is to offer an engaging and enlightening exploration into my mind, where my curiosity, observations, and discoveries challenge the perception of how each of us view reality. Every image I take has a story and every piece I create is its very own adventure.

When I am not photographing the world, I am developing designs and projects for clients and students. I am always accepting new students and clients.

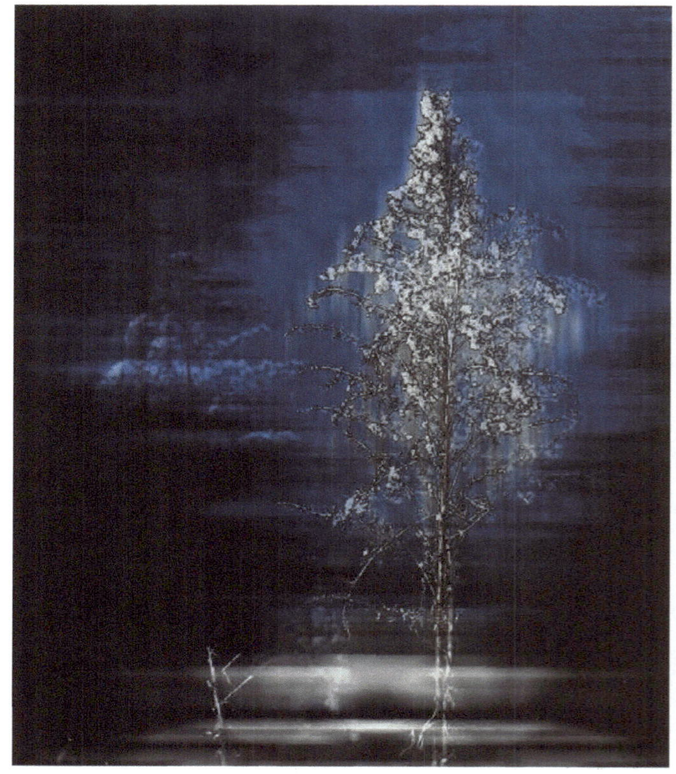

Soft Dreams 2007 22" x 28" Giclée Print on Metallic Luster Resin Coated Media

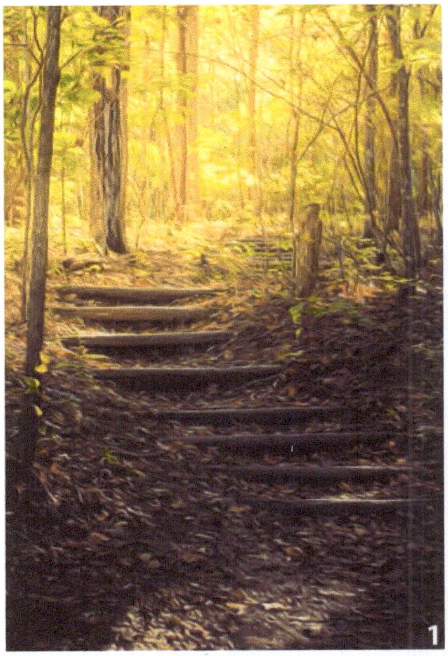

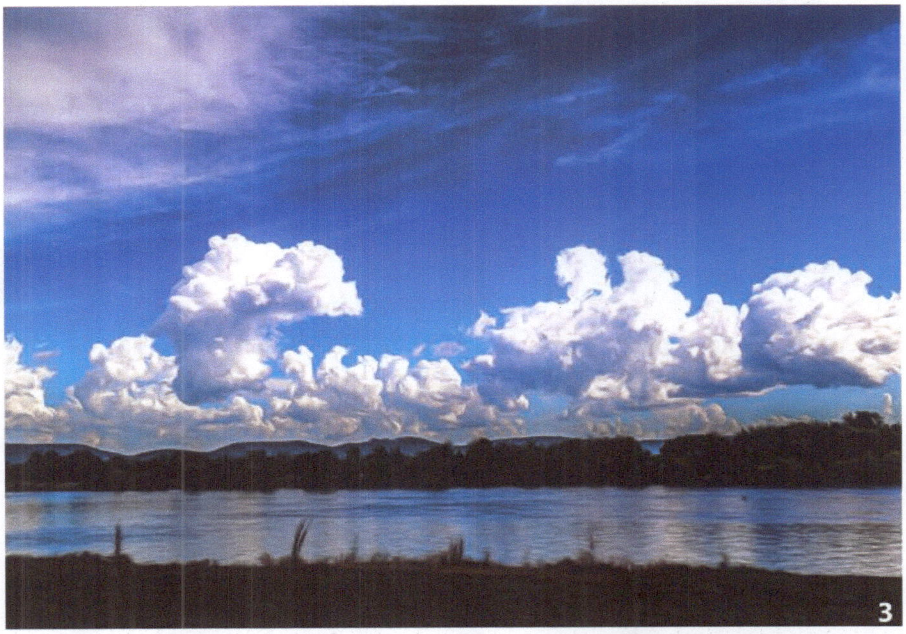

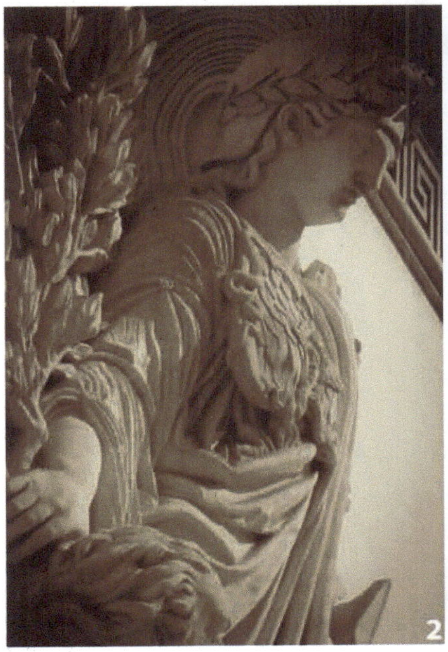

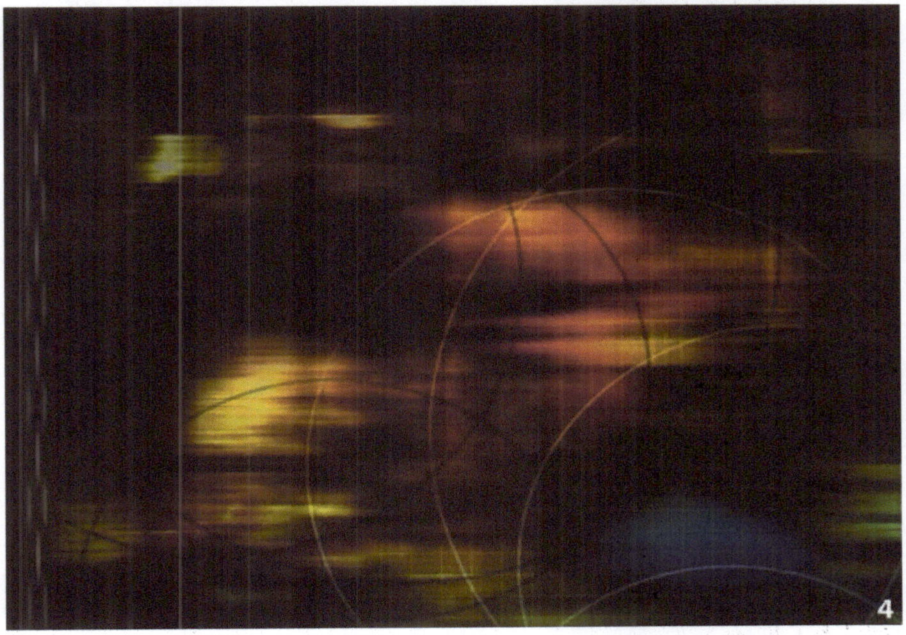

1. **Green Mountain Trail, 2019** 24" X 36" Giclée Print on Premium Satin Gloss Canvas Poly/Cotton Blend

2. **Arc de Triomphe Detail , 2017** 24" x 36"Giclée Print on Premium Satin Gloss Canvas Poly/Cotton Blend

3. **Ditto Landing, 2019** 36" X 24" Giclée Print on Premium Satin Gloss Canvas Poly/Cotton Blend

4. **Binary Motions, 2009** 24" X 18" Digital C-Print on Semi-Satin Media

Visit me on the web:
www.tdwms.com
www.wmsstudios.com

Let's stay connected, follow me on Social Media. Whether its Facebook, LinkedIn, Twitter or Instagram, you can follow me using **@tdwms**

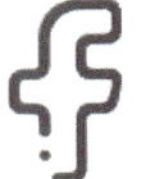
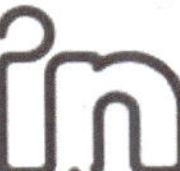

Art Hullender

Memphis College of Art 1998
BFA in Graphic Design

It took a long time to find my voice after art school. I traveled a lot, which included living in Japan twice. After bouncing back and forth between teaching at tattooing for a few years, I finally ended up staying in higher education. I finished my PhD in Applied Linguistics in 2014. In 2017 I began painting again and haven't looked back. Most recently, I completed my first Artist Residency in France in December 2019.

Currently teaching Graphic Arts
@ Southwest Tennessee Community College

fastercreature.com
Instagram.com/fastercreature
art.hullender@gmail.com

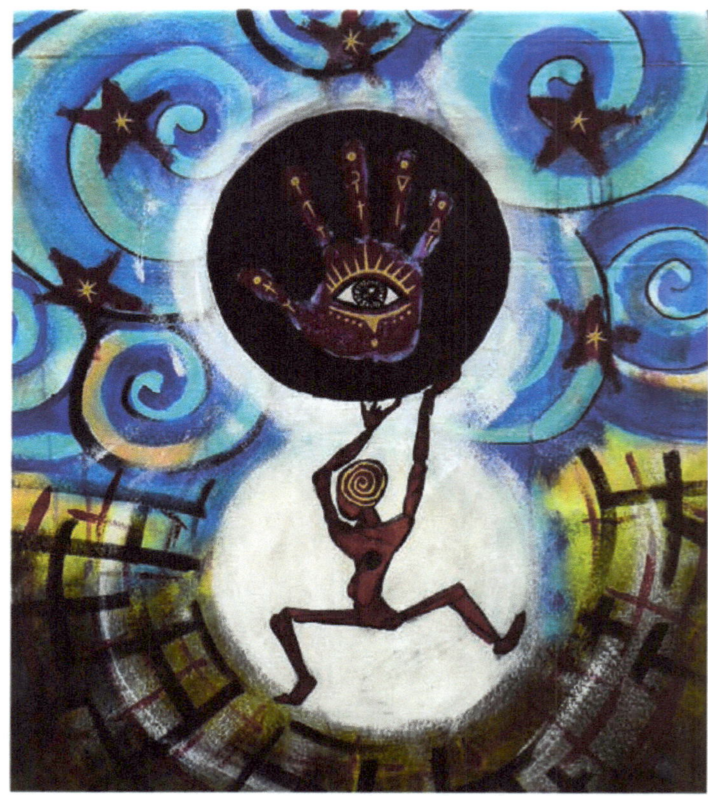

"Celestial Alchemy". 24"x30". Mixed Media. 2018

"Serpent in the Garden". 55"x55". Acrylic on Masonite Panel. 2020

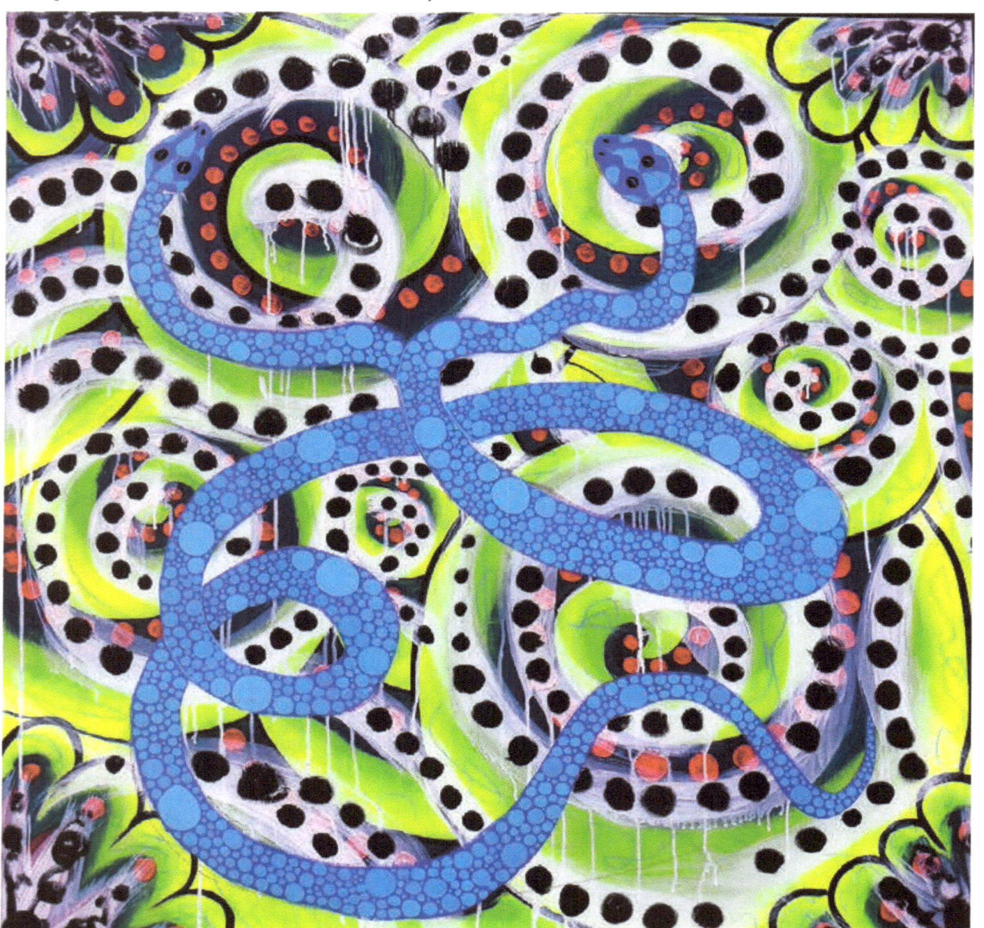

It is my general goal to create a visual environment that is dreamlike and influenced by my sleep disorder, but unlike that of traditional surrealism. I try to work in a style that is abstract, design influenced, and both representational and nonrepresentational without falling fully into any one category. I have lived a very unique life, which provides visual and philosophical influences of everything from living in Japan to studying linguistics and cognitive sciences.

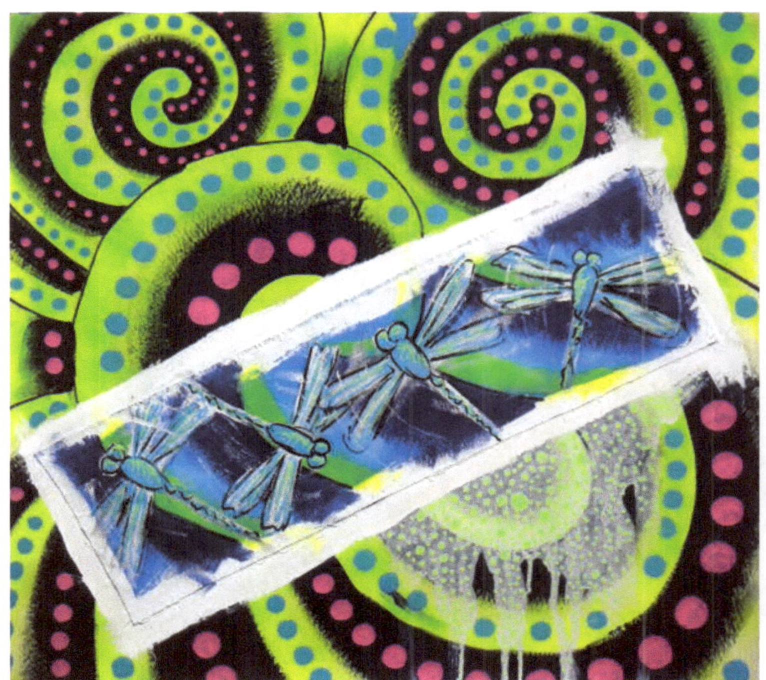

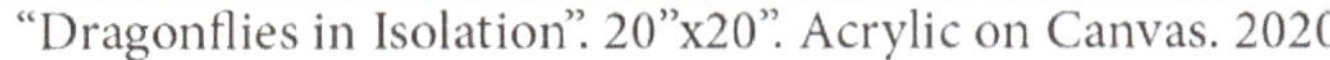

"Dragonflies in Isolation". 20"x20". Acrylic on Canvas. 2020

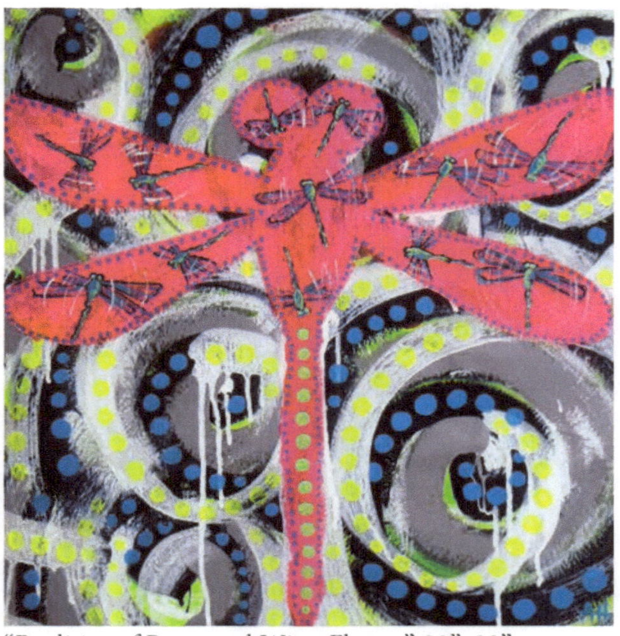

"Realities of Perpetual Wing Flutter". 22"x22". Acrylic on Canvas. 2020

"Dragon on the Wind". 45"x45". Mixed media on Masonite. 2019

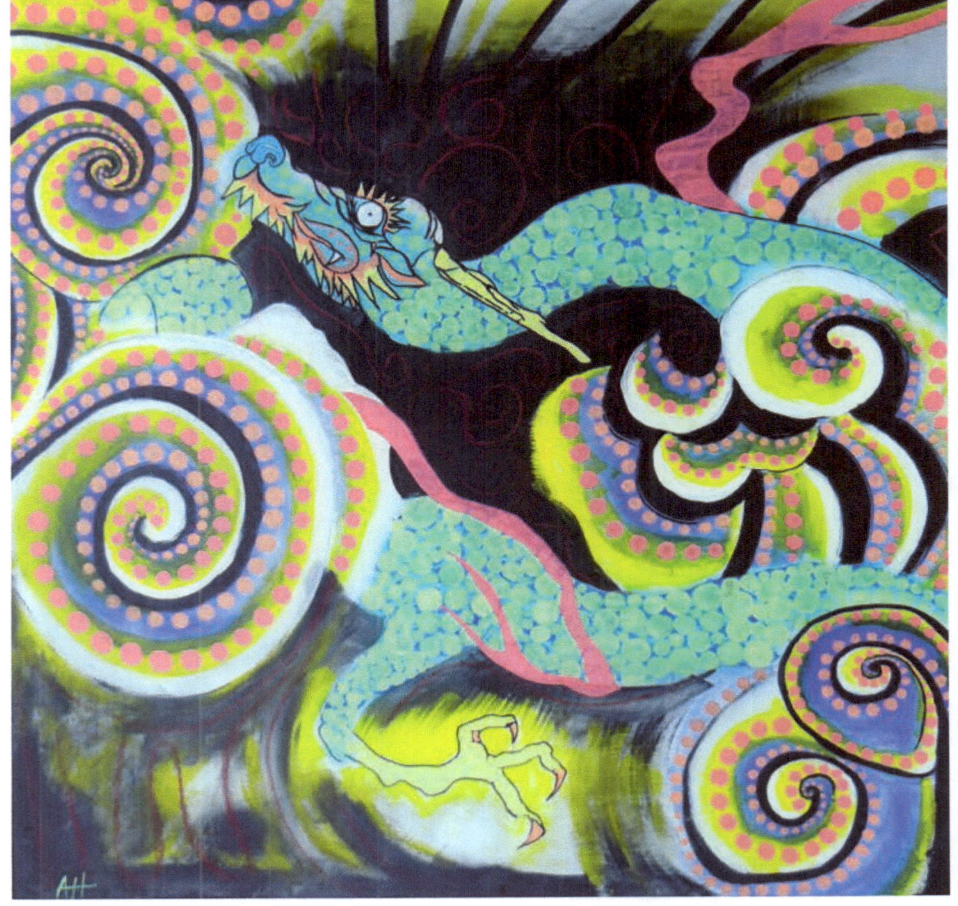

My use of Color is influenced by my brief time in the tattoo industry in the early 2000s. I got used to using a closed palette. Although I made a conscious effort to no longer be tied to the lined based drawing style that is engrained into how you are trained when doing tattoos, I like keeping colors bold and pure with minimal mixing. I often go as far as mixing discarded tattoo ink with gel medium to get a good bold color. I find the bright colors contribute to an overall energy and play off the expressionist mark making well.

JINA ANNE

sushiandrobots.com

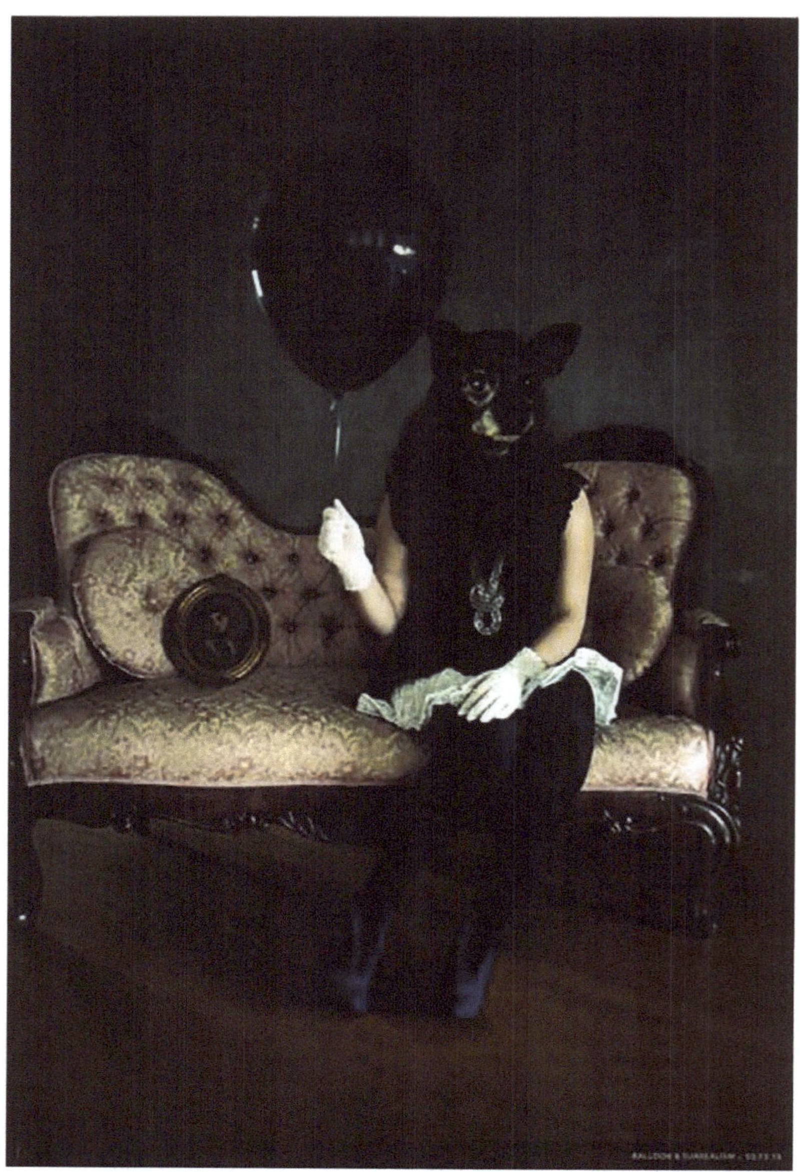

"photo manipulation" 2012

JINA ANNE
sushiandrobots.com

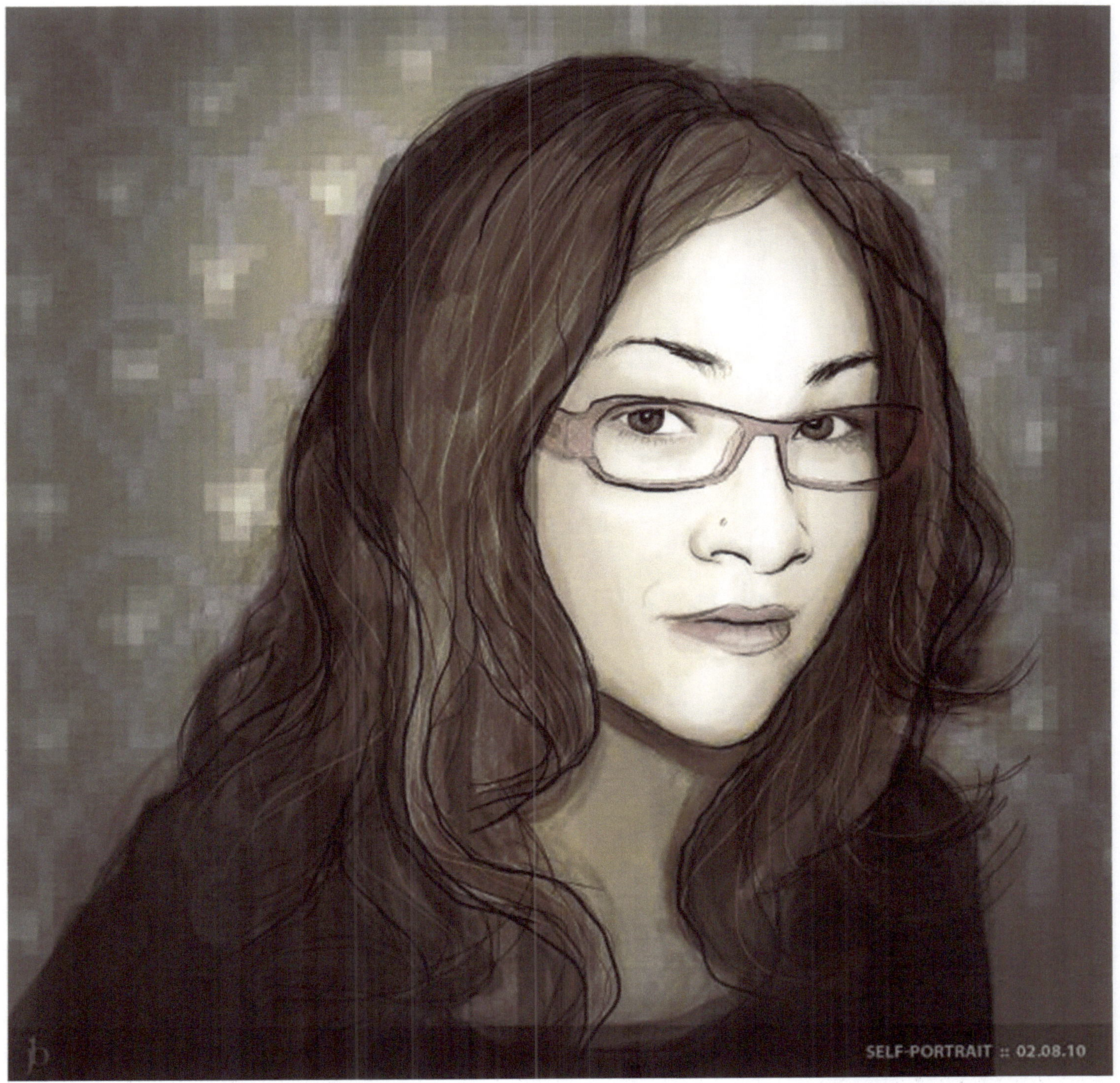

"self-portrait on wacom tablet" 2010

DAVID HALL

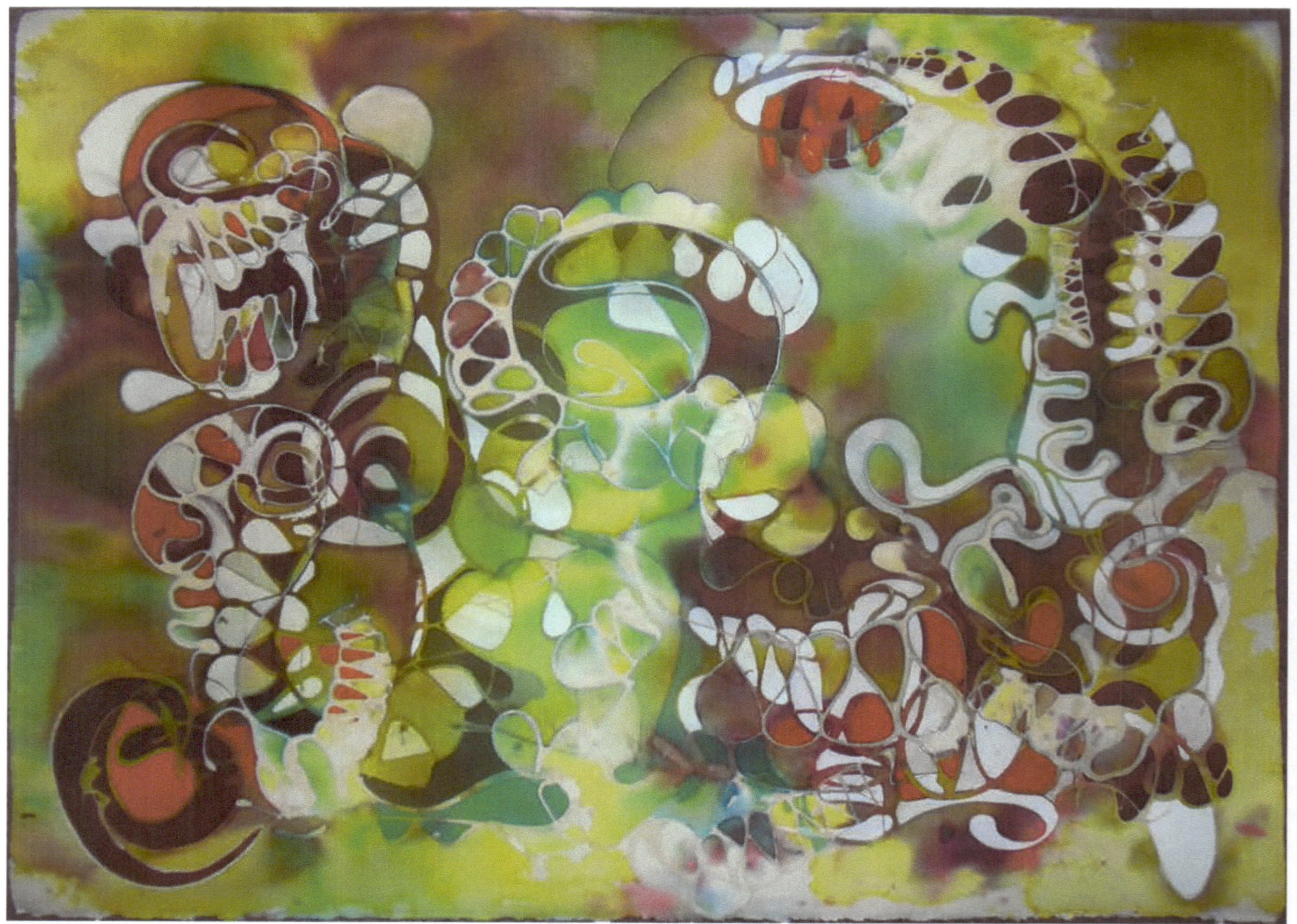

Illusory Dancer, 2020, mixed media, 22" x 30"

The instinctive impulse is primary to my working process. I revel in the moment when mind meets matter. The generation of image is sequential, in cycles of formation and dissolution, between ethereality and solidity of form. Once in the zone of creative euphoria, I channel improvisation and invention, problem solving and visual retort into the work.

DAVID HALL

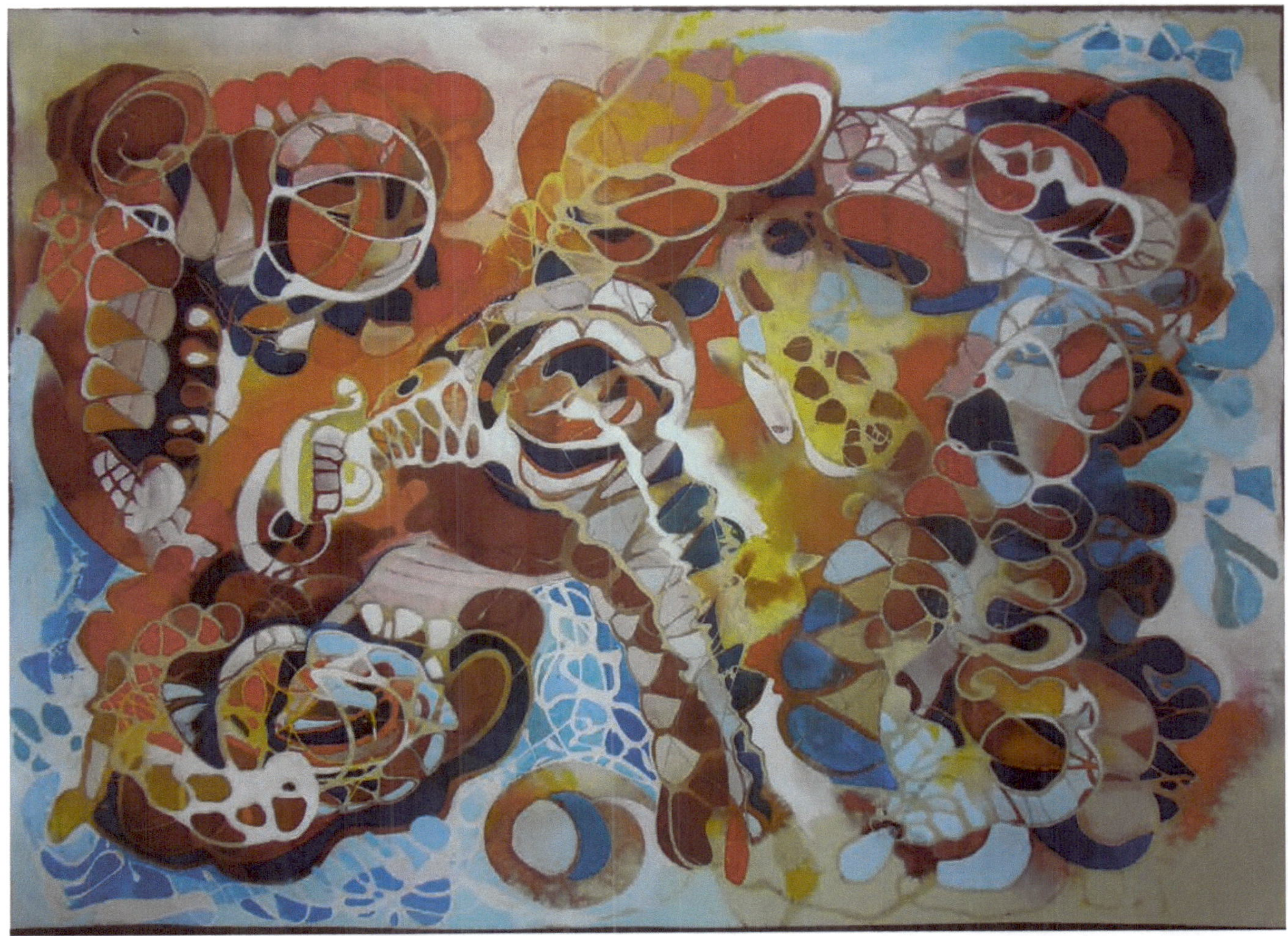

A Braid Unravelled, 2020, mixed media, 22" x 30"

There are numerous variables that move me, but a constant is the idea of unleashing a process, a sequence of events mediated upon a sheet of paper, a block, or plate. Materials and processes imbue their own distinct essences, and I am ever mindful to let them speak. I think through the material—like a wordsmith mining keen ruminations from initially nebulous stirrings. The thought and the act are a single taste.

My highest aspiration in life is to live in the present moment, attentive to my mind stream and to proceed with contemplation and wonder. I am guided by the sense that the plane upon which I am working is a tableau of infinite potentialities, and that setting forth with deliberate and eventful actions amounts to conjuring. One of my teachers once said, "Energy follows intention"—this simple principle is one that I cultivate, and it permeates my studio practice.

MARYLONGART.com

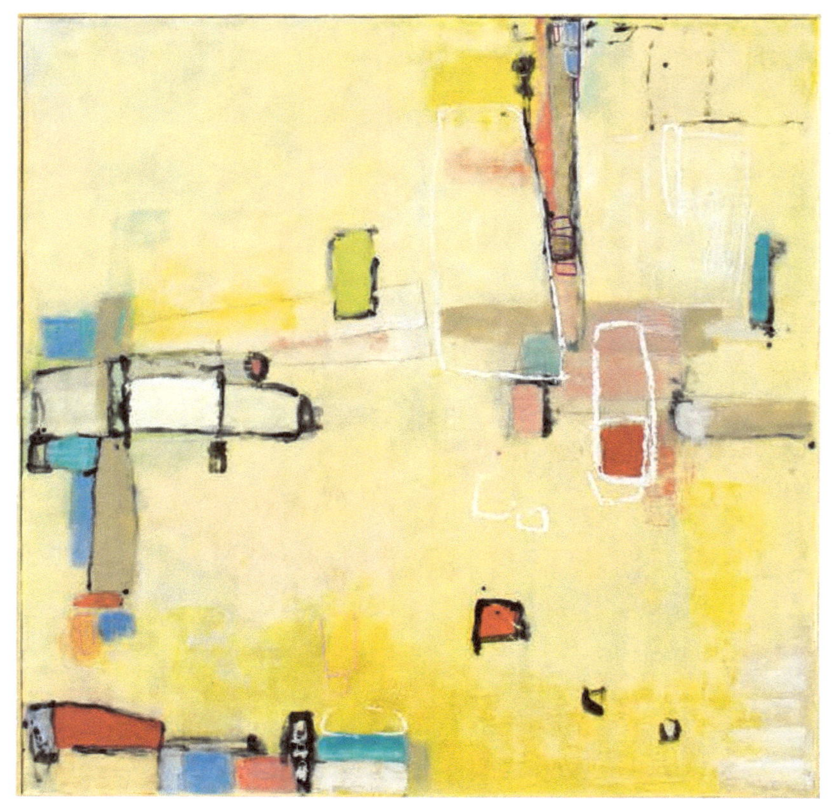

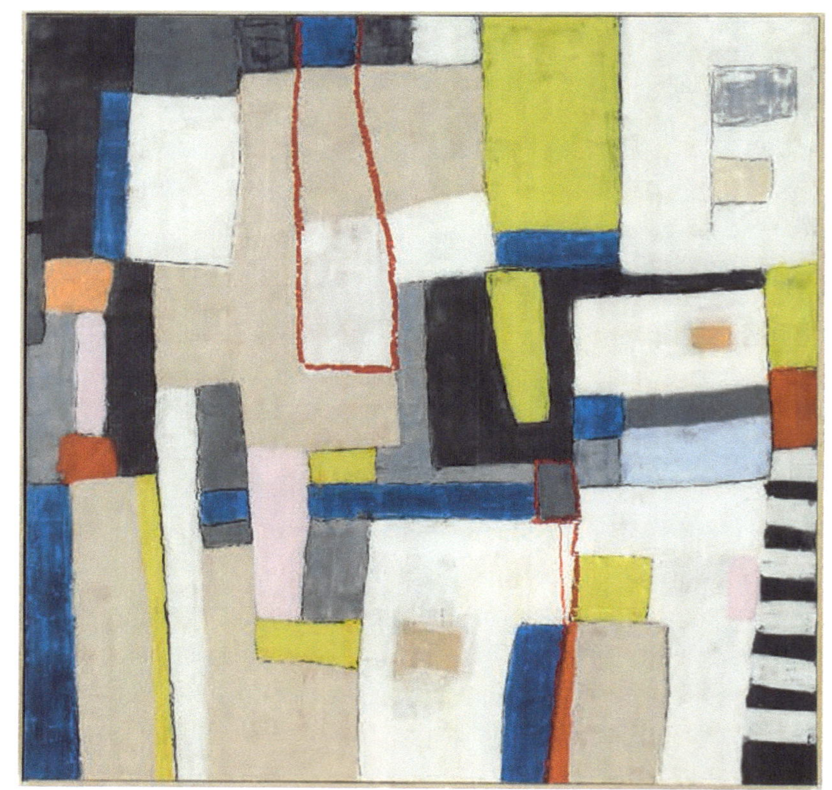

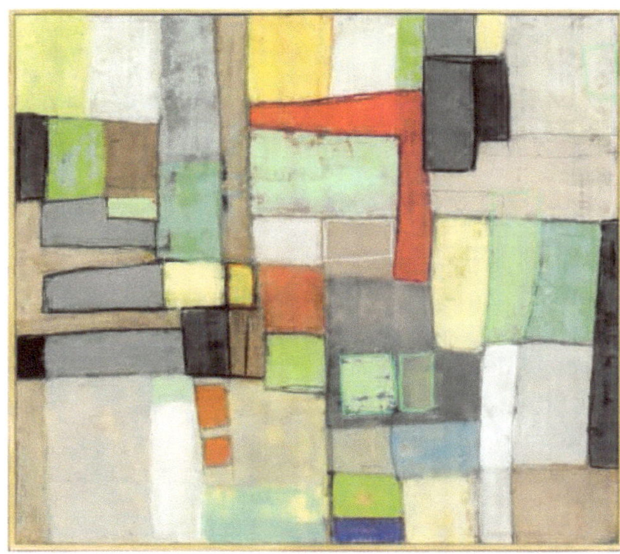

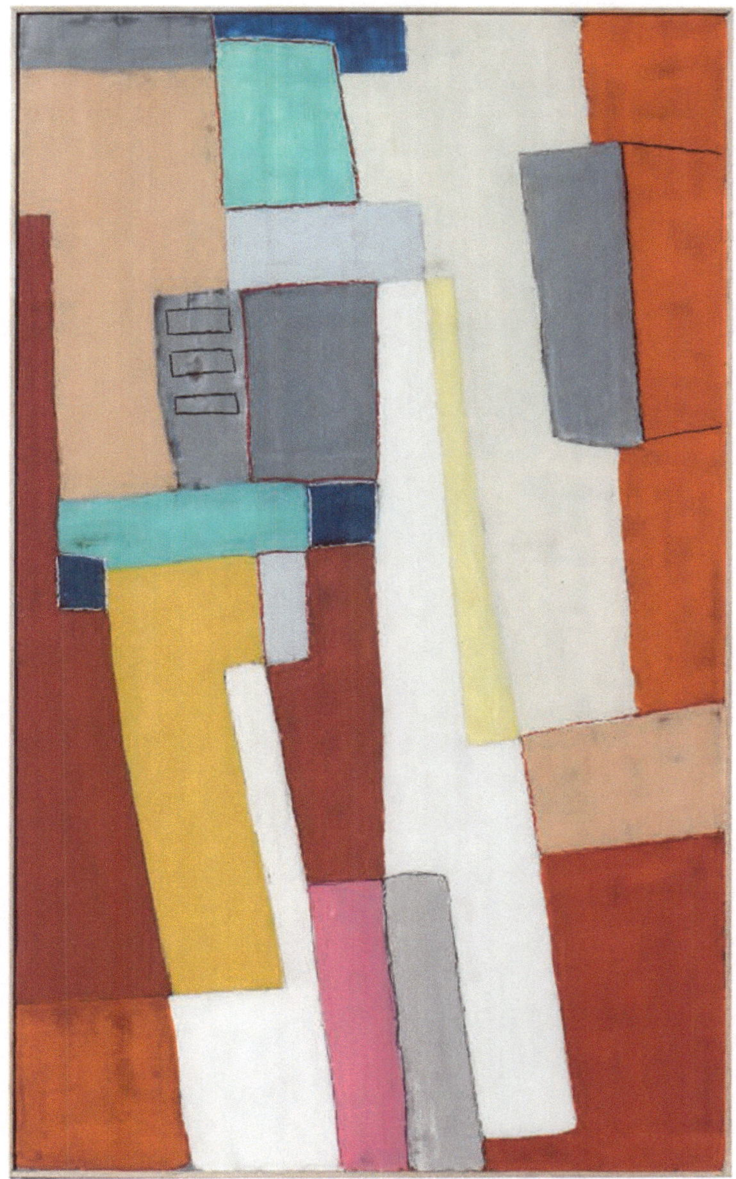

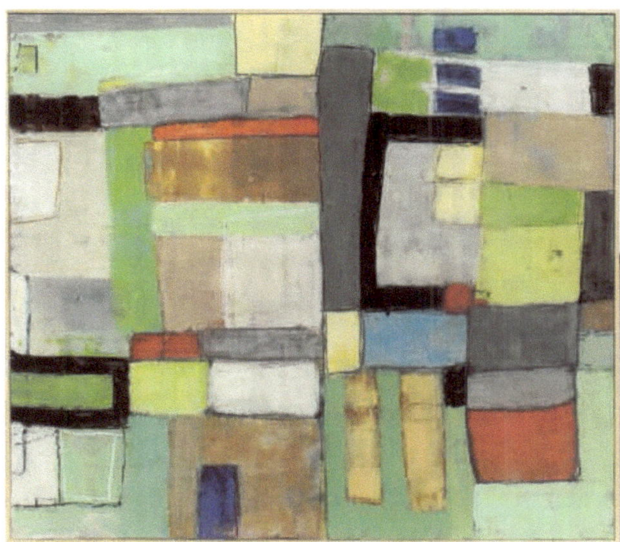

Mary Long
Wax Encaustic on Panel
"Blowout" 61"x61" 2015, "Game Day" 48.5"x48.5" 2019, "Carolina 2 & 3" 33"x37" ea. 2017, "Red River" 61"x37" 2020

Mary Long was born in Ohio and has lived in Tennessee since the mid-1990s. Following studies in graphic design and painting, she began working in encaustic in 2001.
"I grew up near Canton, where there is a crazy-quilt patchwork of rural farms and factories. It's a juxtaposition of architectural grayness against expanses of happy saturated colors that inspires my work to this day," she says. Long often begins her paintings with marks drawn in oil stick, over which she applies many layers of wax combined with oil paints. "I scrape down in between the applications, revealing some of the marks, while leaving others faded or hidden in little worlds that have an element of history to them. The paintings begin in what I call a chaotic, adolescent phase and grow as layers of color and additional lines weave the elements together." In the latest work I am decompressing, exploring more of the spaces in between. They don't simply represent topographical maps but also time and space, the painting acts as a 'slice' or a 'snapshot' of something continuous," says Long.

Thomas Matthew Pierson

www.mattpiersonart.com

Follow me on   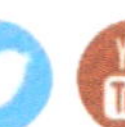 

@mattpiersonart

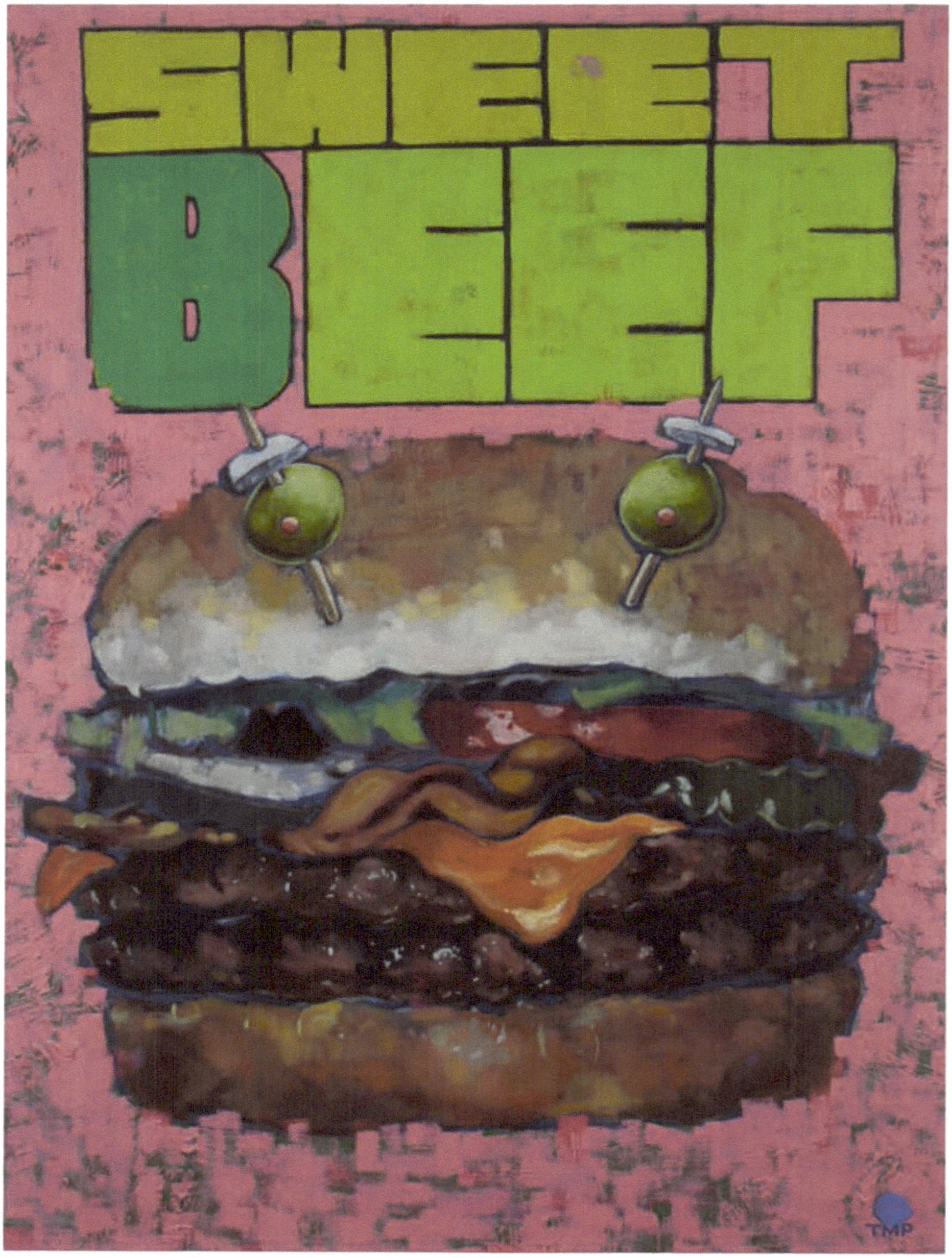

Sweet Beef
Oil on Canvas
22"x30"
2018

Thomas Matthew Pierson
www.mattpiersonart.com

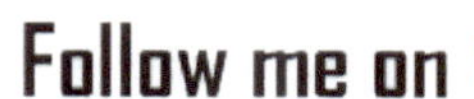

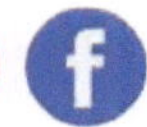

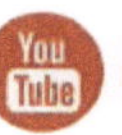

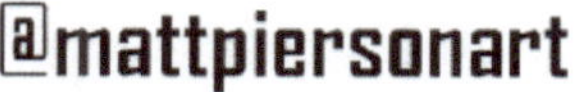

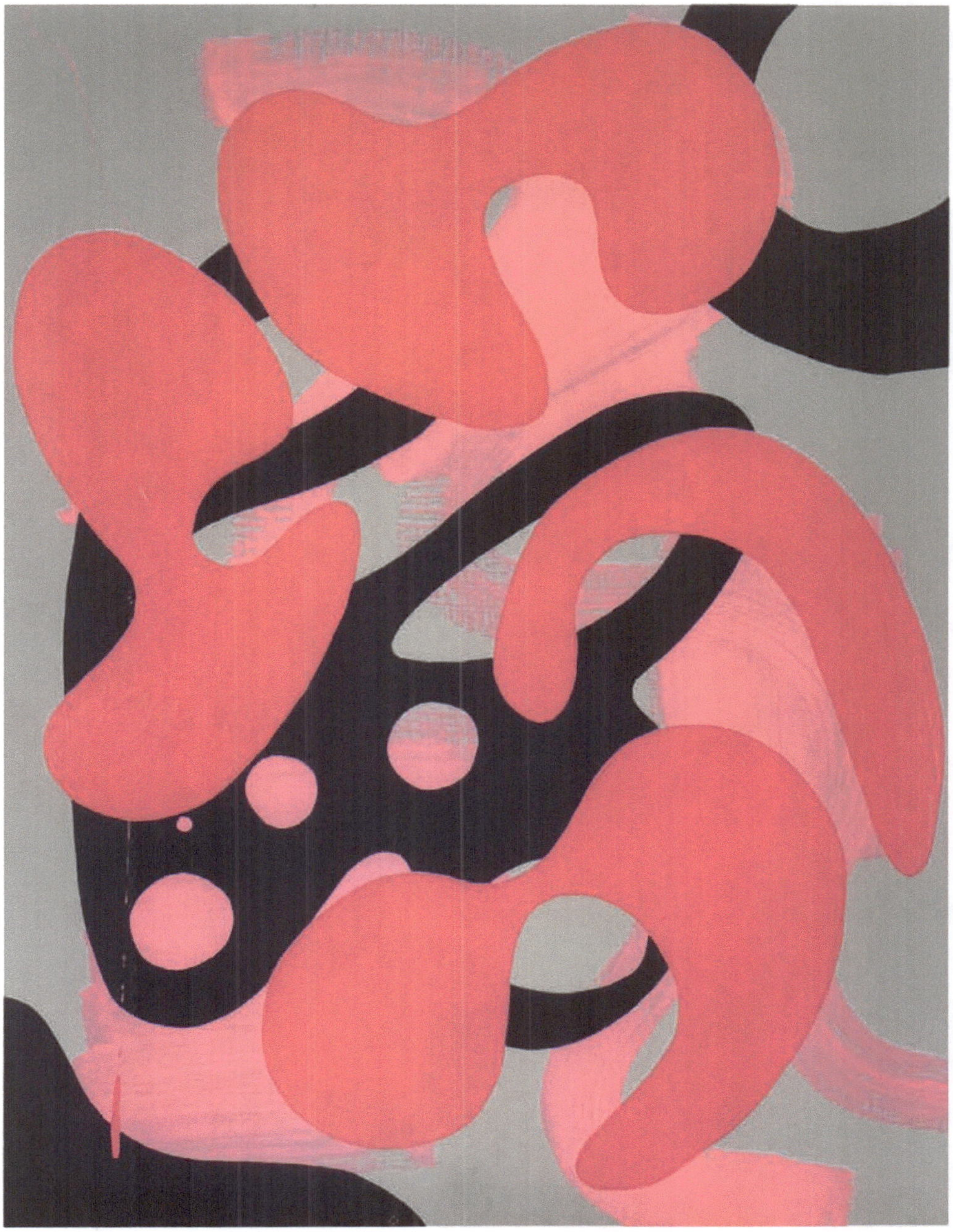

Amoeba Fractal 9
Acrylic on Hardboard
18"x24"
2020

ERICA QUINN

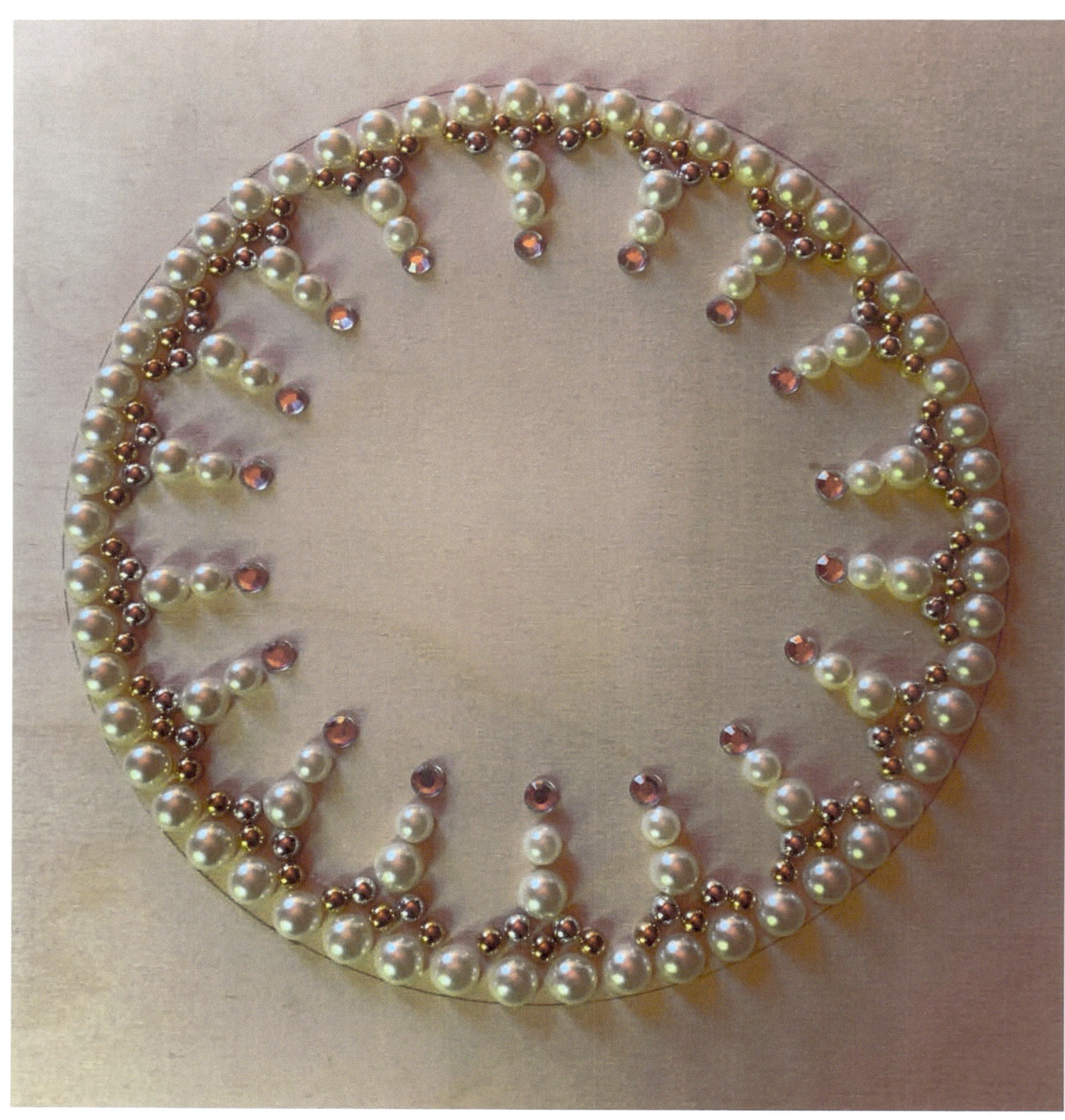

Gold, 2020, mixed media, 10" x 10"

ERICA QUINN

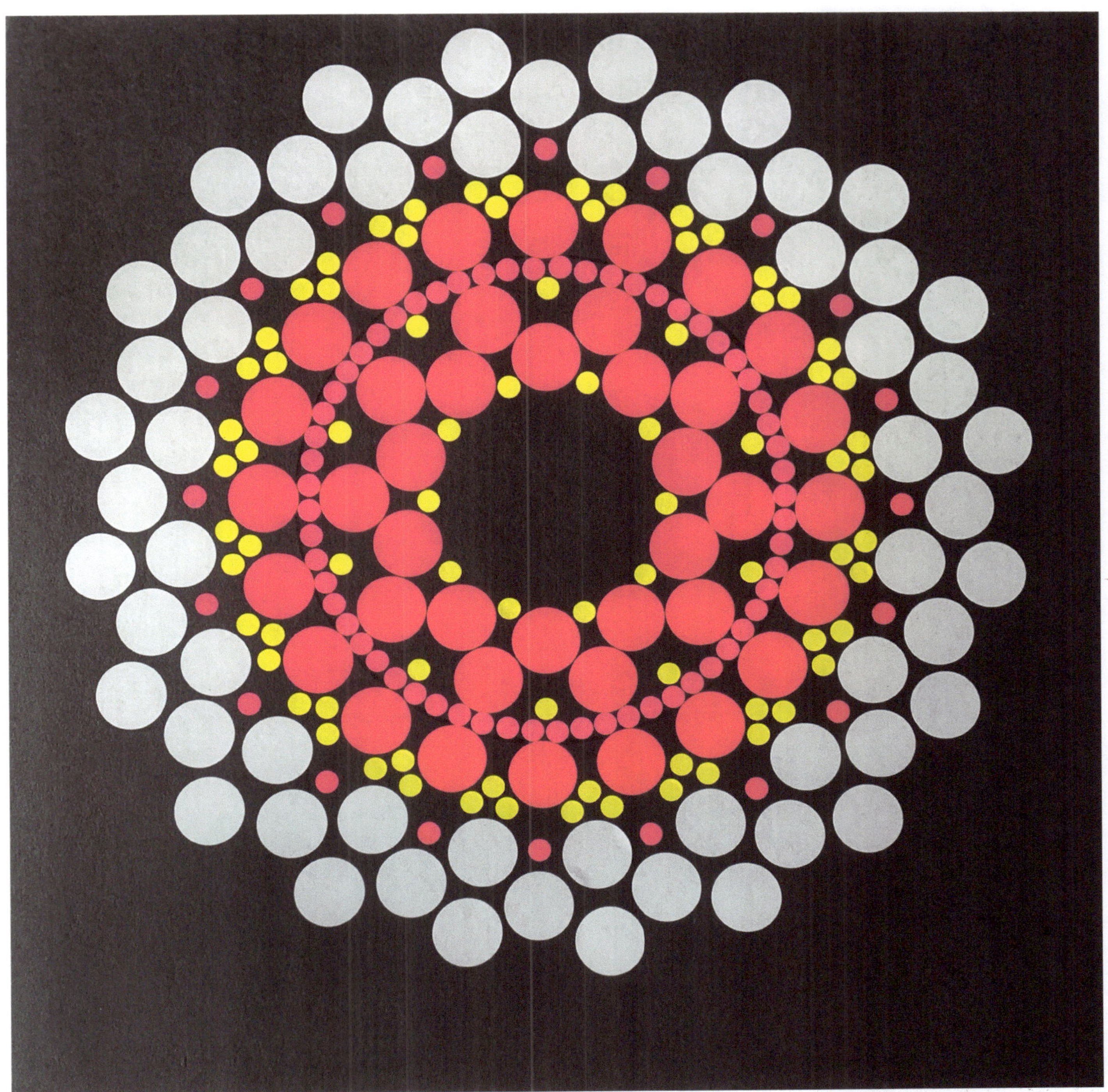

Flower Girl, 2020, mixed media, 12" x 12"

Josh Miller

Memphis College of Art 2001
BFA in Printmaking

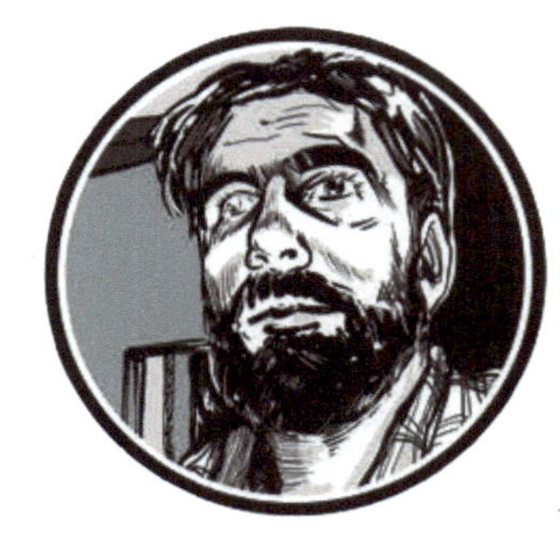

***Since** graduating from Memphis College of Art in 2001, I have focused mostly on working in the print and design field. In 2016 I began my own T-Shirt printing company named Yellow Dog Print Company. In between work and family over the past 20 years, I've managed to scatter in some moments of trying my hand at painting and drawing, mostly of people and characters. These are some of the results.*

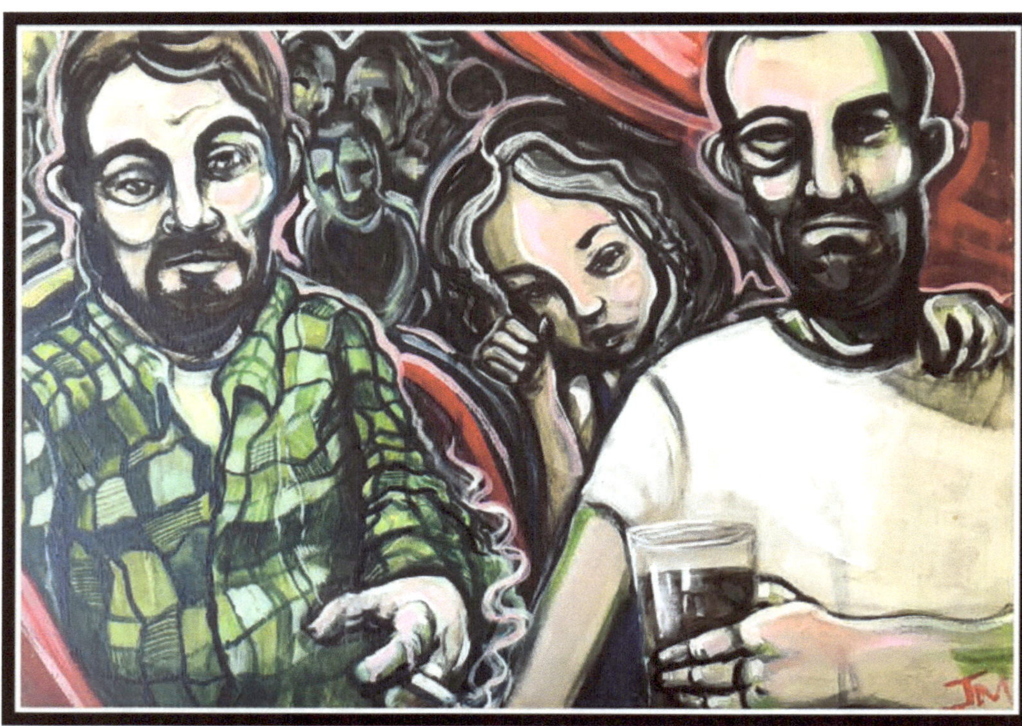

The Drinkers 18"x 24" Acrylic on canvas

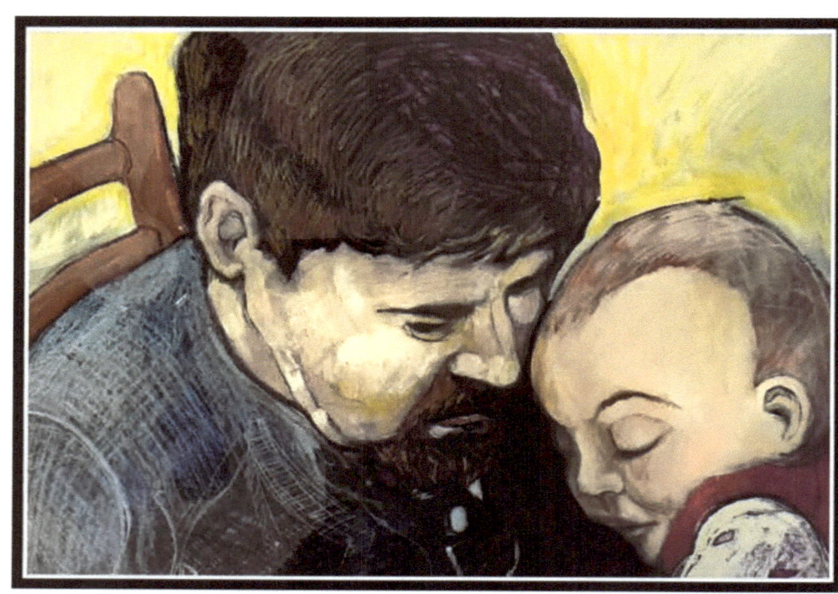

Jason and Wyatt 24"x 36" Mixed Media on Paper

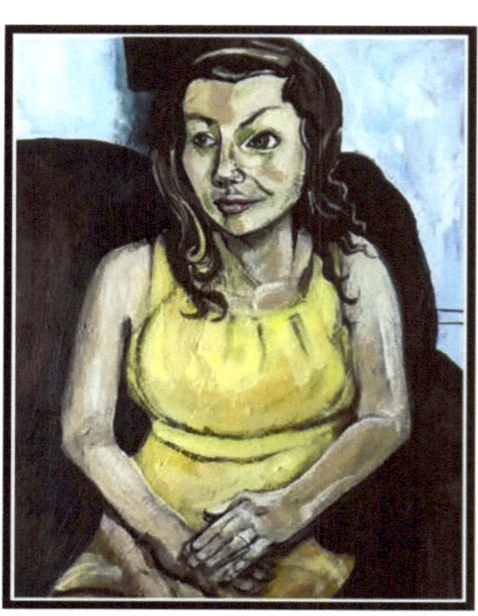

Priscilla 16"x 20" Acrylic on canvas

Josh Miller

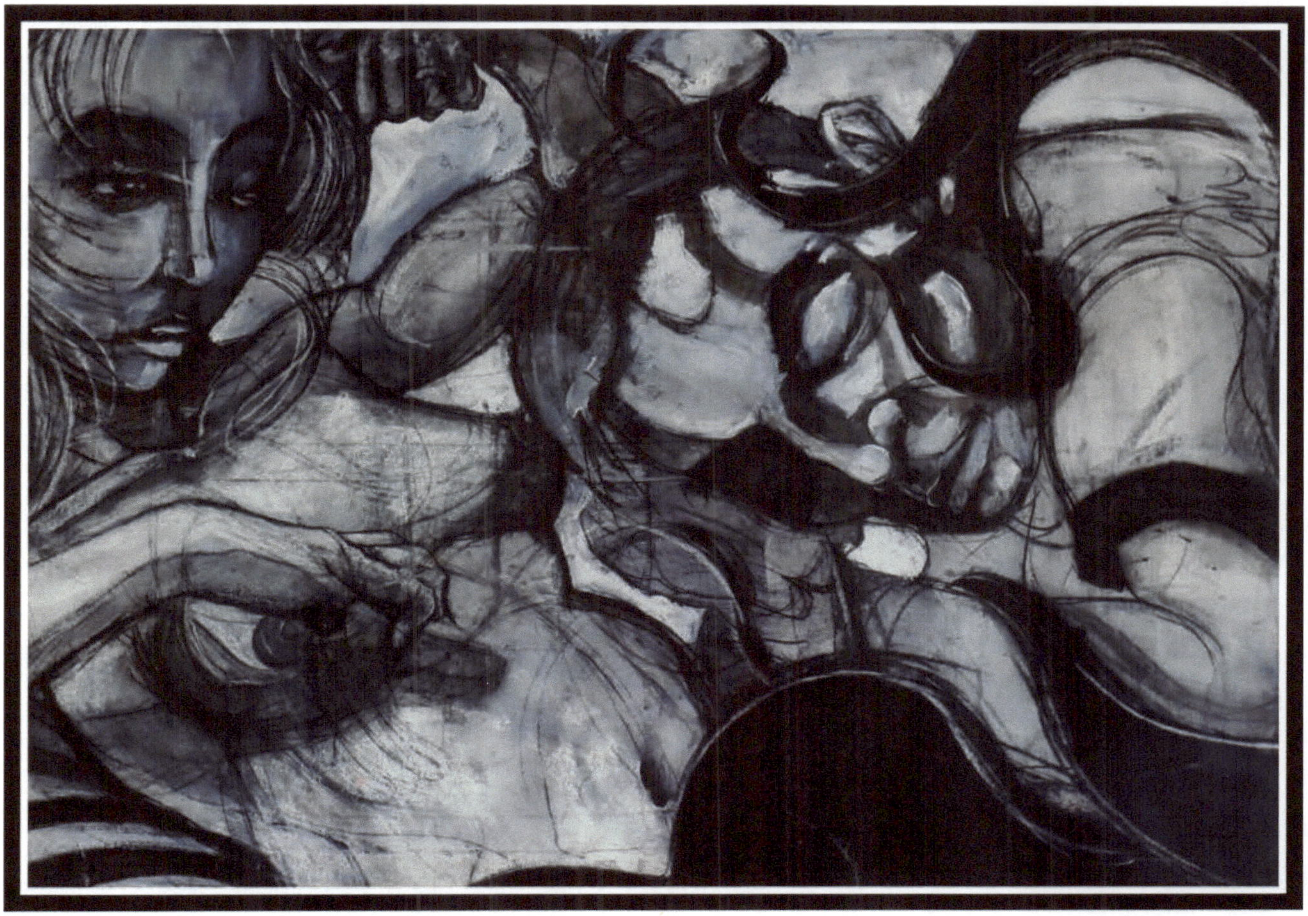

Strange Dreams *24"x 36" Mixed Media on Paper*

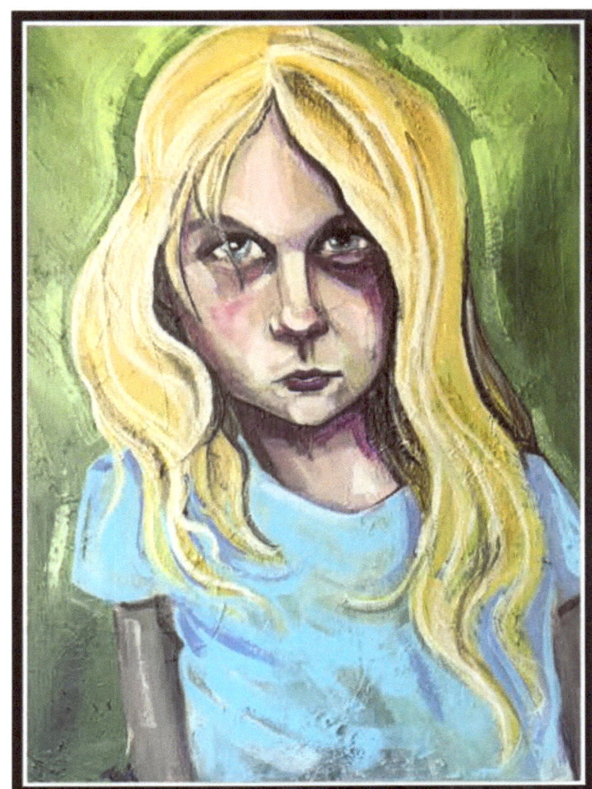

Marlee *16"x 20" Acrylic on Canvas*

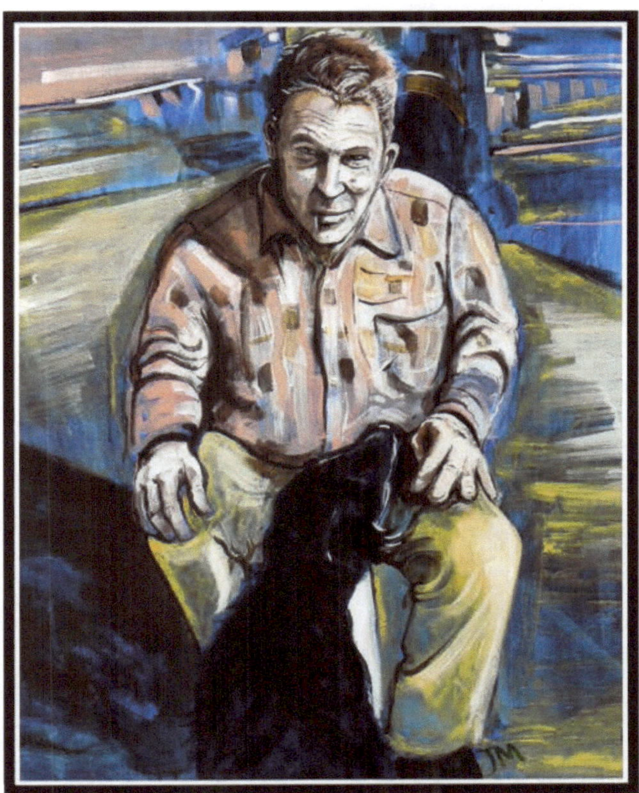

Bobby and Josie *24"x 36" Acrylic on Canvas*

Laura Summerford

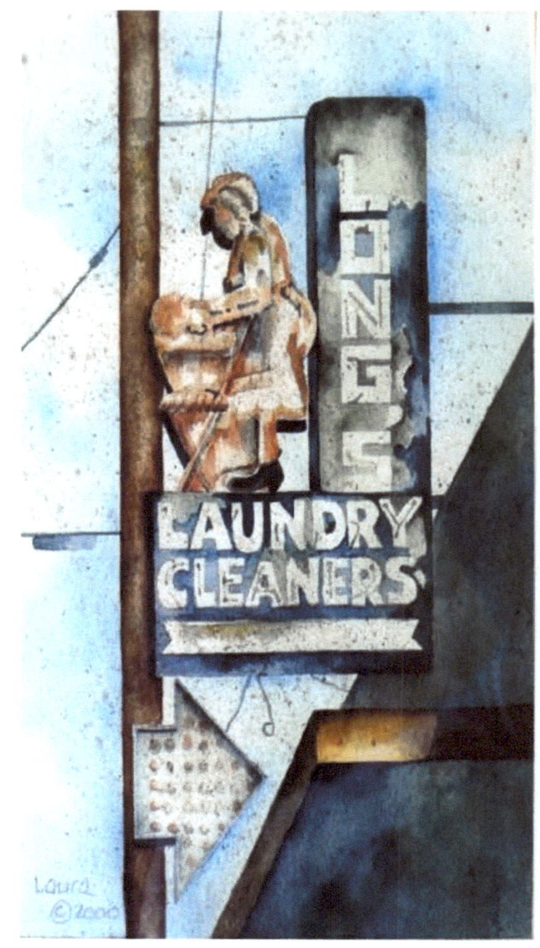

Long's Laundry, 2000

My watercolors are a reflection of my fascination with old advertising. During college, I was introduced to watercolor. The softness of the medium and light washes allow for multiple layers of color to show through my paintings. The layers enhance my subjects as most are in various stages of decay. For many years, I traveled the South documenting vintage buildings, neon and metal signs, and brick wall ads with a Polaroid "One Step" camera. I attended juried shows while working as a graphic artist at in-house agencies as well as printing companies. Later, I began working as a Senior Product Designer for Wang's International, Inc. in Memphis where I designed gifts, tabletop, seasonal items, and more. At this time, I am once again documenting the South as I see it.

tomyrislaura@gmail.com

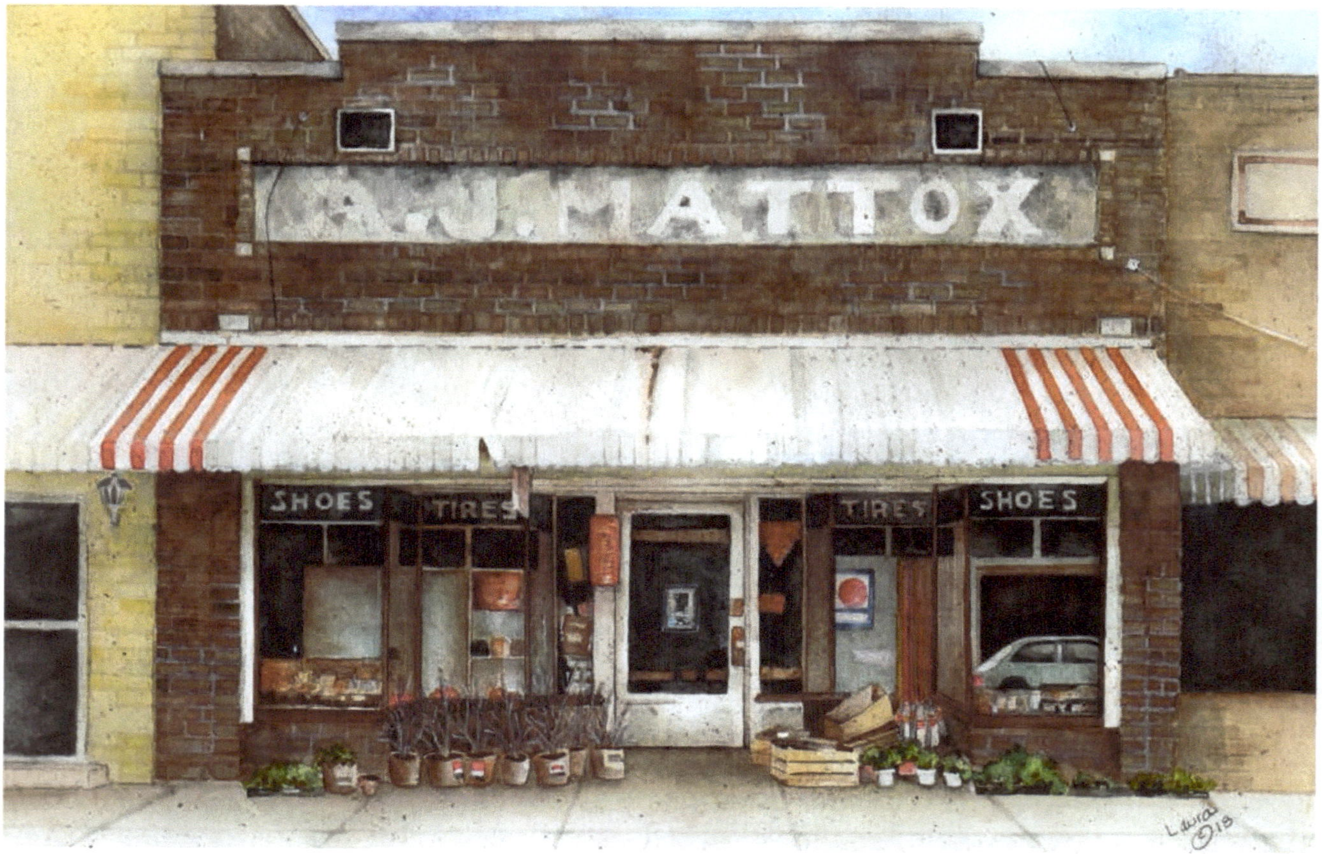

A. J. Mattox, 2018

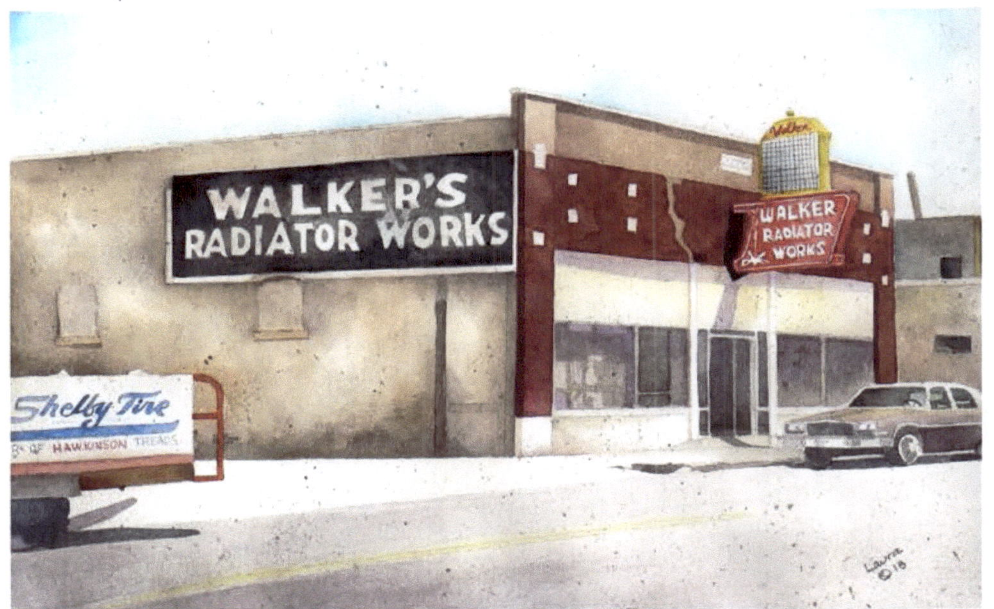
WALKER'S
RADIATOR WORKS
WALKER
RADIATOR
WORKS
Shelby Tire
Laura ©18

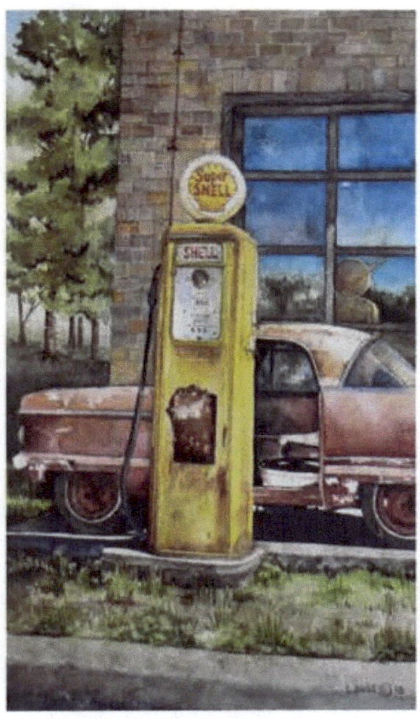
SHELL

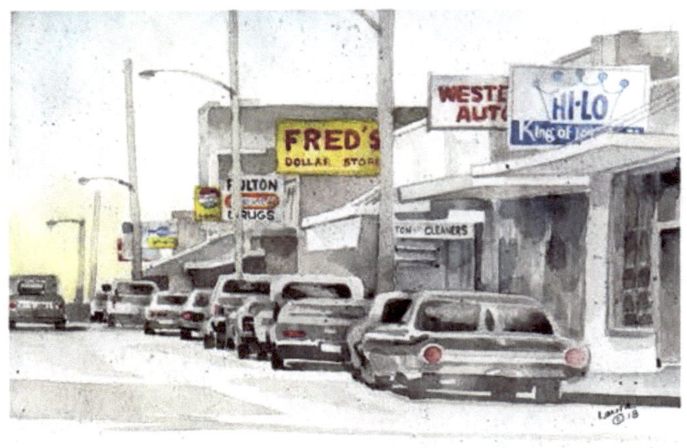
FRED'S
DOLLAR STORE
HI-LO
FULTON
DRUGS
CLEANERS

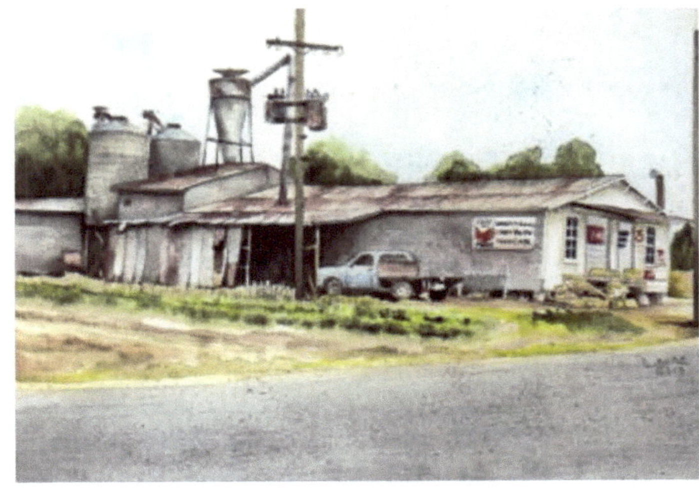

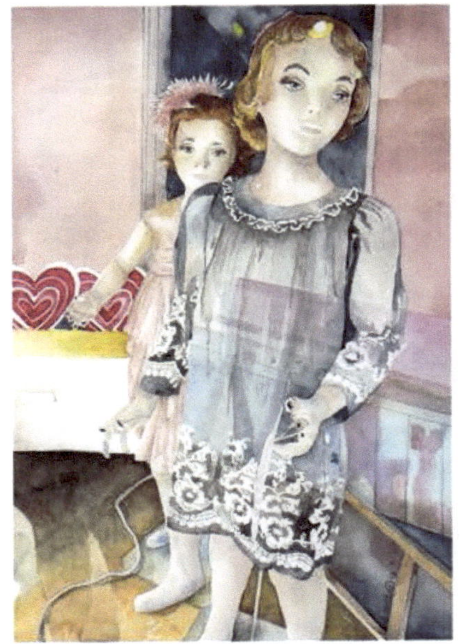

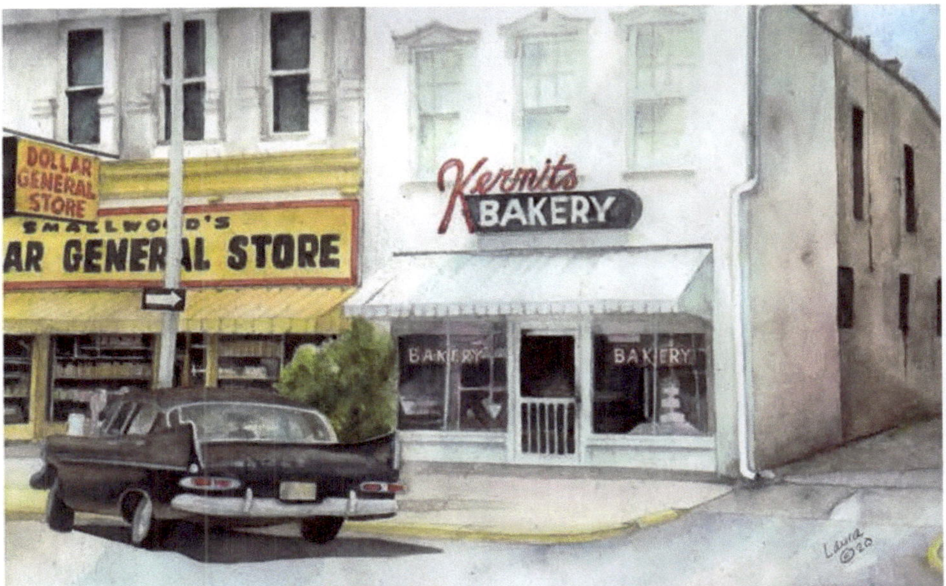
DOLLAR
GENERAL
STORE
SMALLWOOD'S
AR GENERAL STORE
Kermit's
BAKERY
BAKERY
BAKERY
Laura ©20

VANESSA GONZALEZ

VANESSAGONZALEZART.COM

MEMPHIS COLLEGE OF ART

BFA PRINTMAKING 2015

MFA FINE ARTS 2017

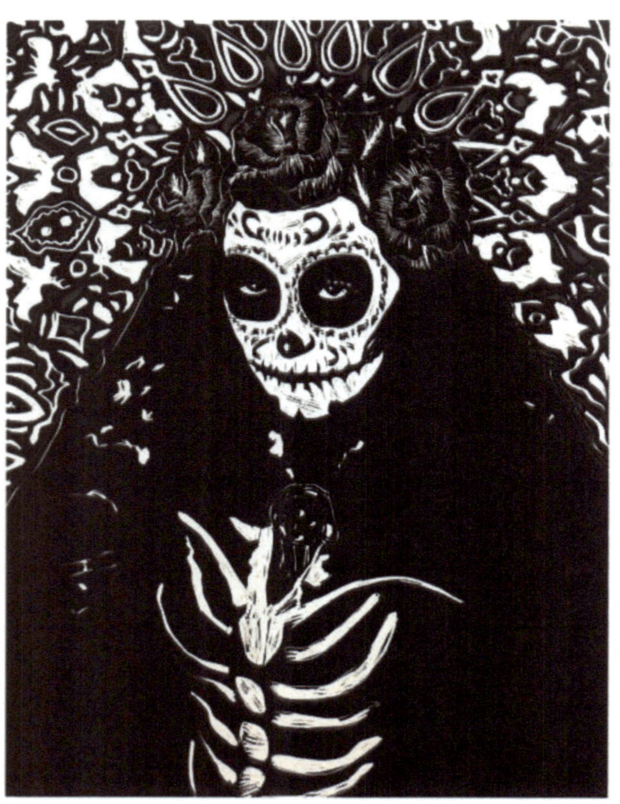

"Catrina" 22x30 Linocut 2015

I explore the sense of cultural dislocation and dissociation, based on my experience of moving from Mexico to the United States. Although I was born in Texas, I was brought up in Mexico and did not return to the United States until the age of 17. As such, my work explores the feelings inherent in the experience of feeling like an outsider who constantly needs to explain and justify my cultural identity despite residing in the country of my birth. My images are meant to represent identity, confusion and acceptance, which makes me explore the questions what is required to be part of a nation and what it means to be an Mexican American. Using the term "Mexican-American" as a constant influence rather than just a migration moment, reflects the significance of the diaspora I live in. I constantly use images that certifies my identity and nationality a representation of my two homelands, but they also show how I constantly cross an emotional border.

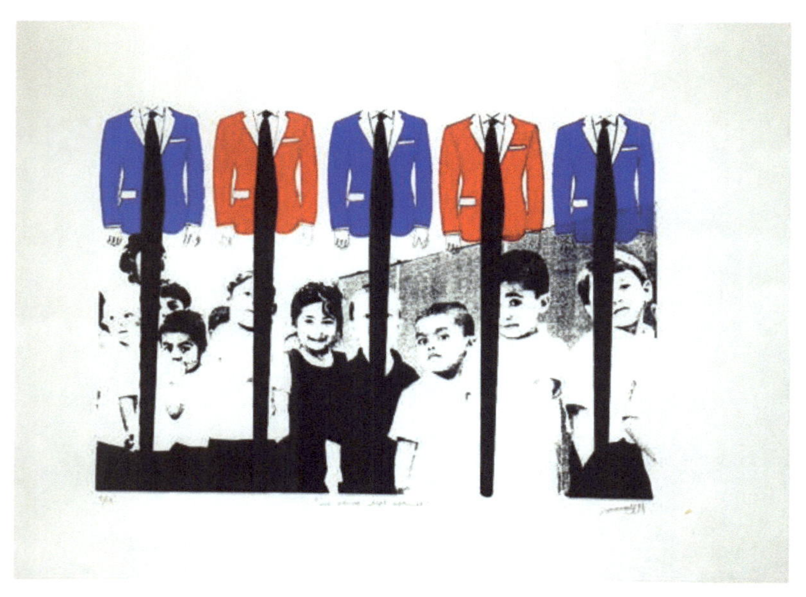

"No Child Left Behind" 22x35
Digital Illustration 2019

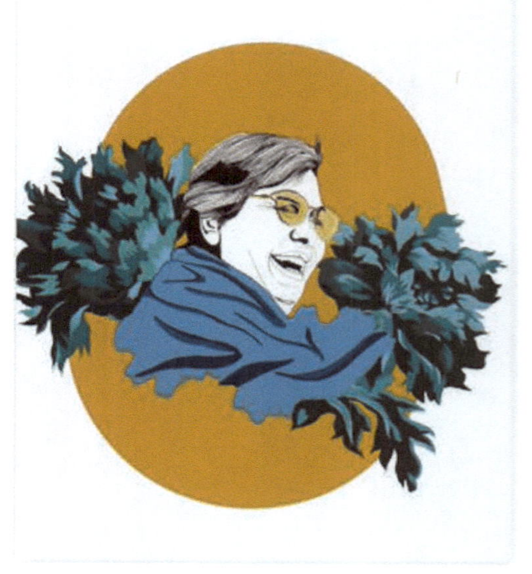

"Abuelita Antonia" 11x15
Digital Illustration 2020

Vanessa Gonzalez

Vanessa Gonzalez is a mix media artist. Raised in Leon Mexico, currently living in Memphis TN. Gonzalez was always exposed to Latino art and culture, which inspired her to become passionate to the rich cultural traditions. Vanessa's work has been exhibited locally, regionally, nationally, and internationally. Currently rpresented by the Agora Gallery NY

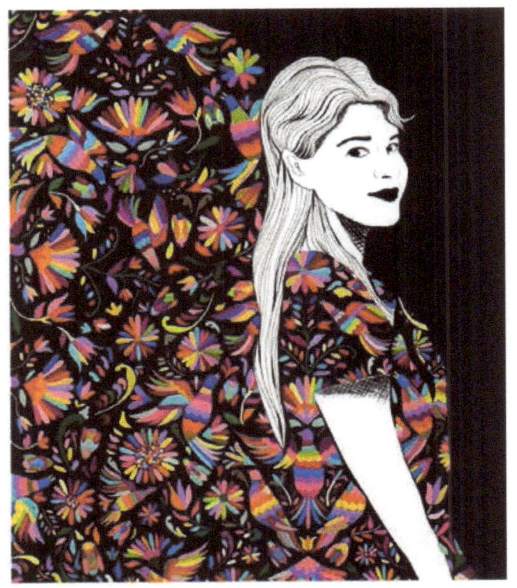

"Orgullo #1" 11x15 Digital Illustration 2020

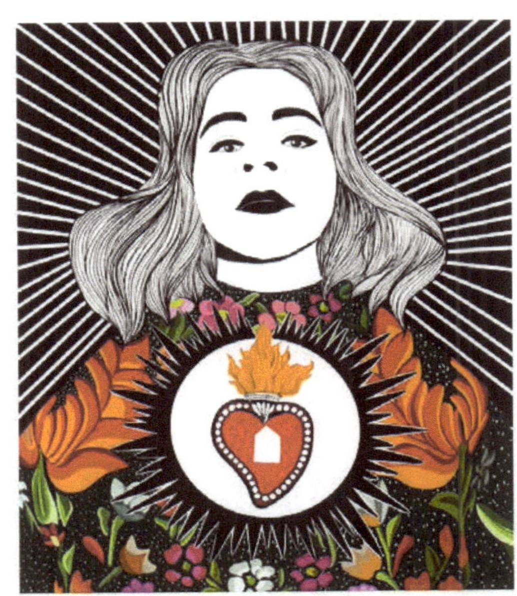

"Orgullo #2" 11x15 Mix Media 2020

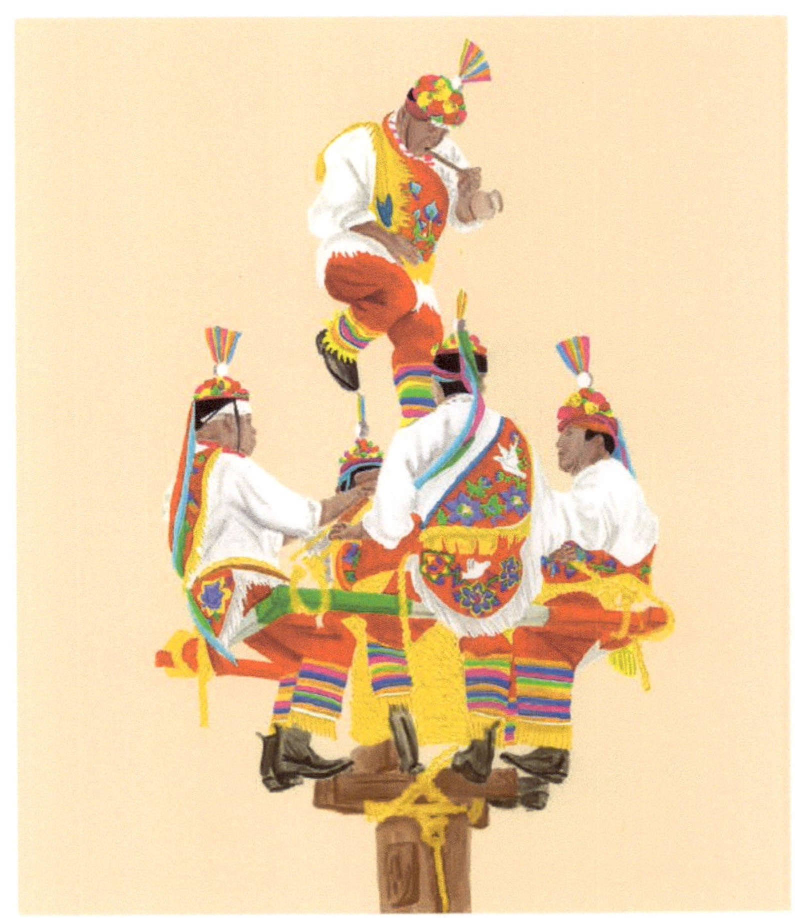

"Voladores" 12x16 Digital Illustration 2018

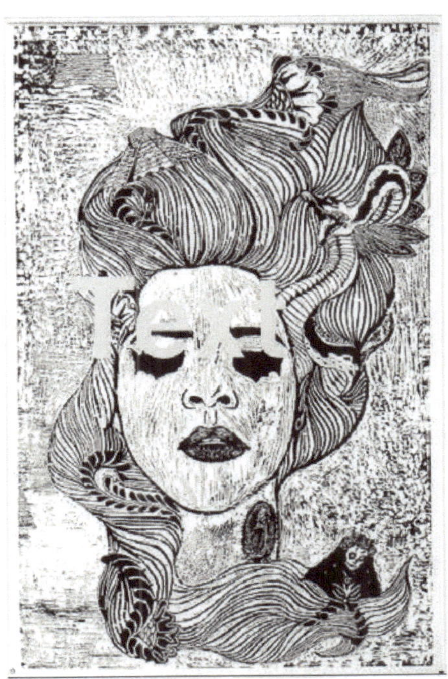

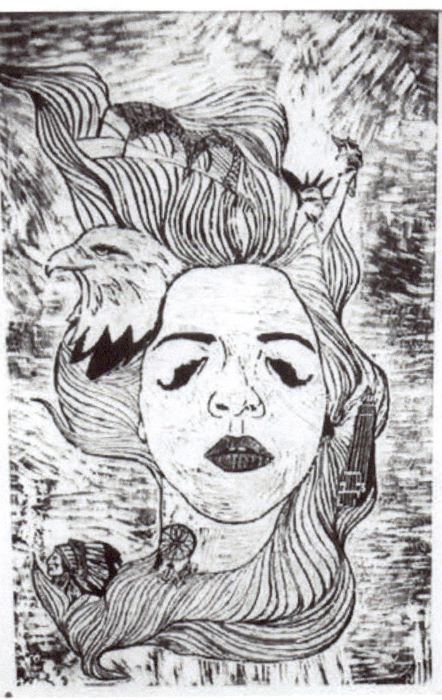

"Loss of Identidad" 34x50 Woodcut 2015

@ LAURITZEN WRIGHT

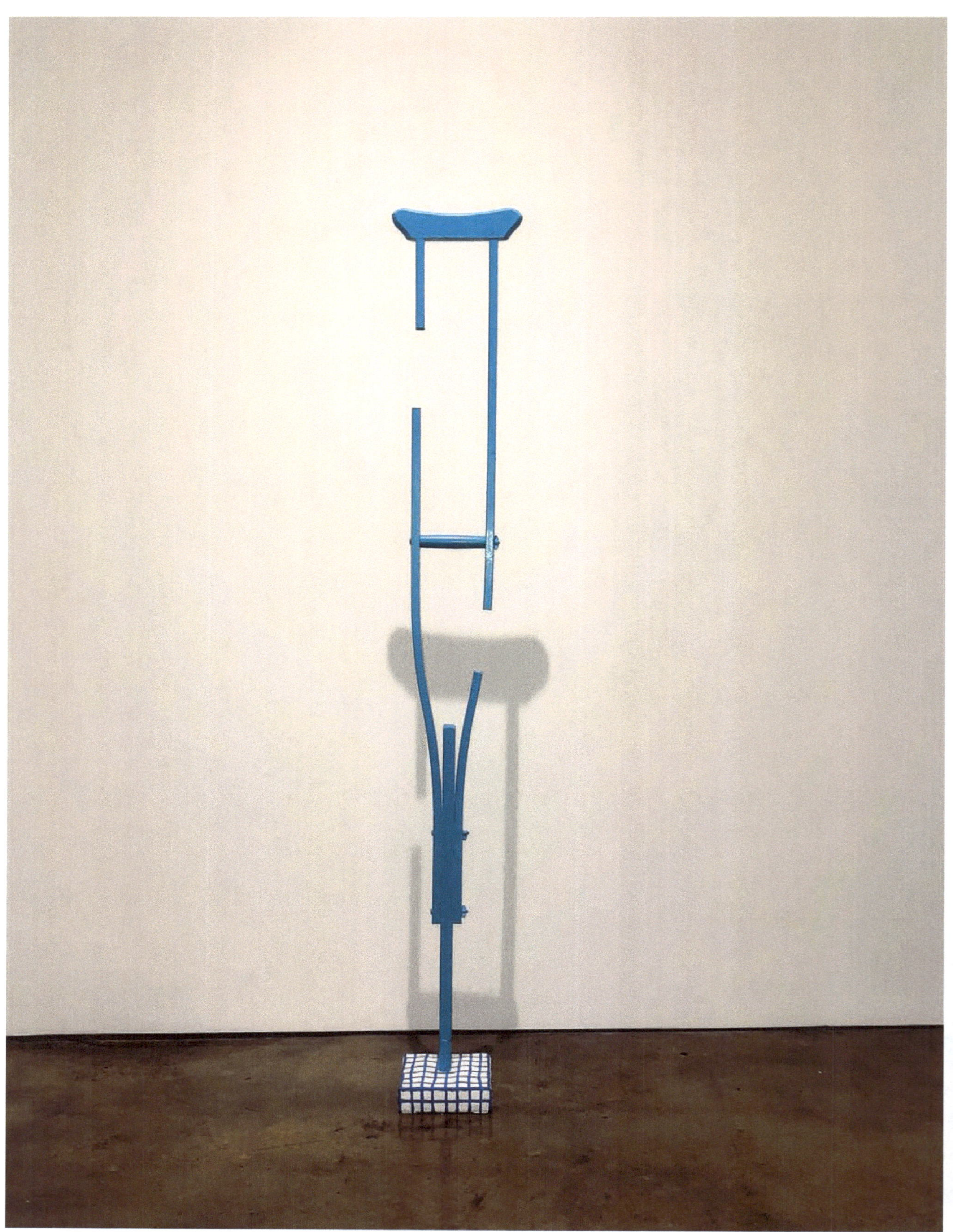

A Masterpiece of Introspective Nostalgia, 2019

TAD LAURITZEN WRIGHT.com

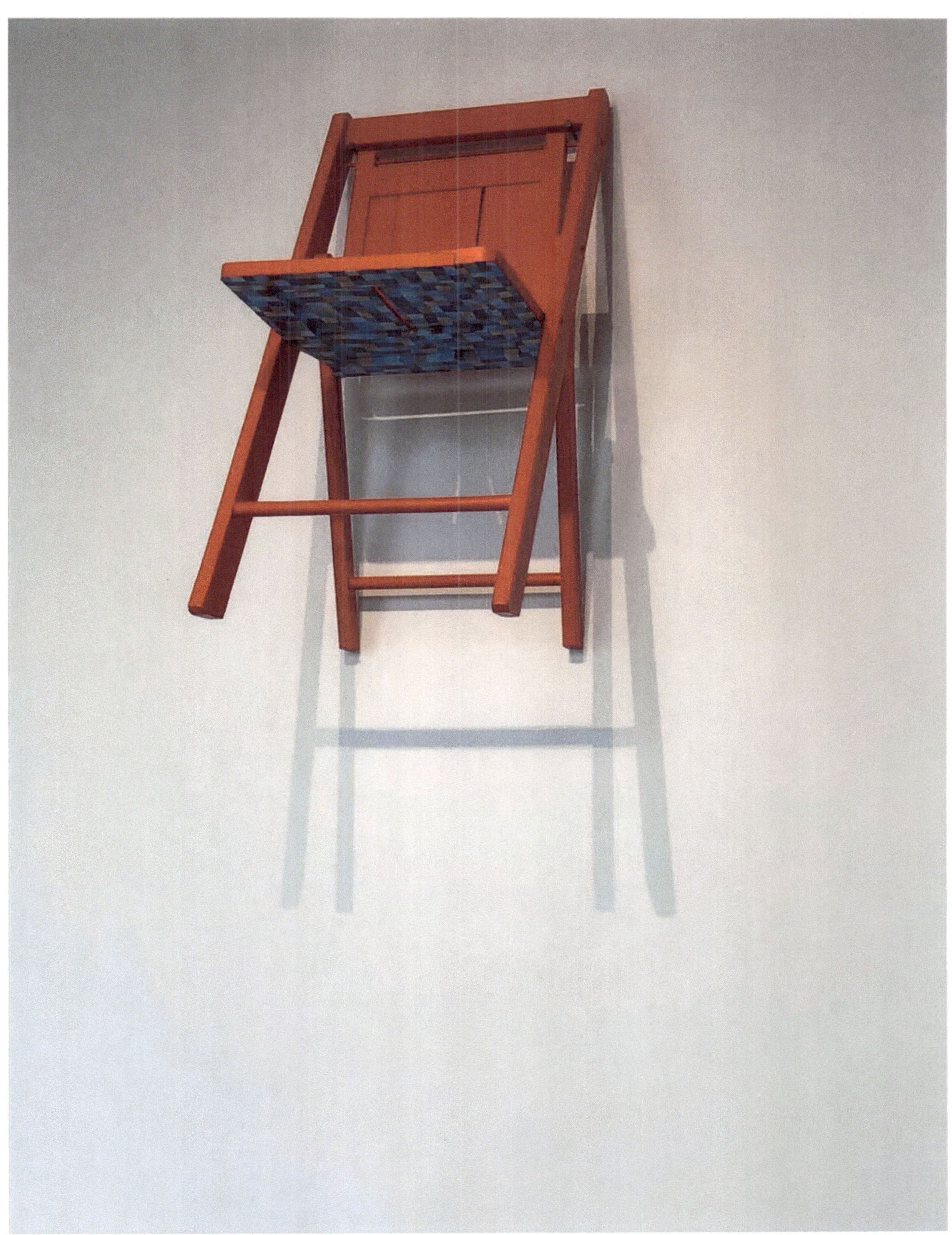

Everything I Remember About You, 2019

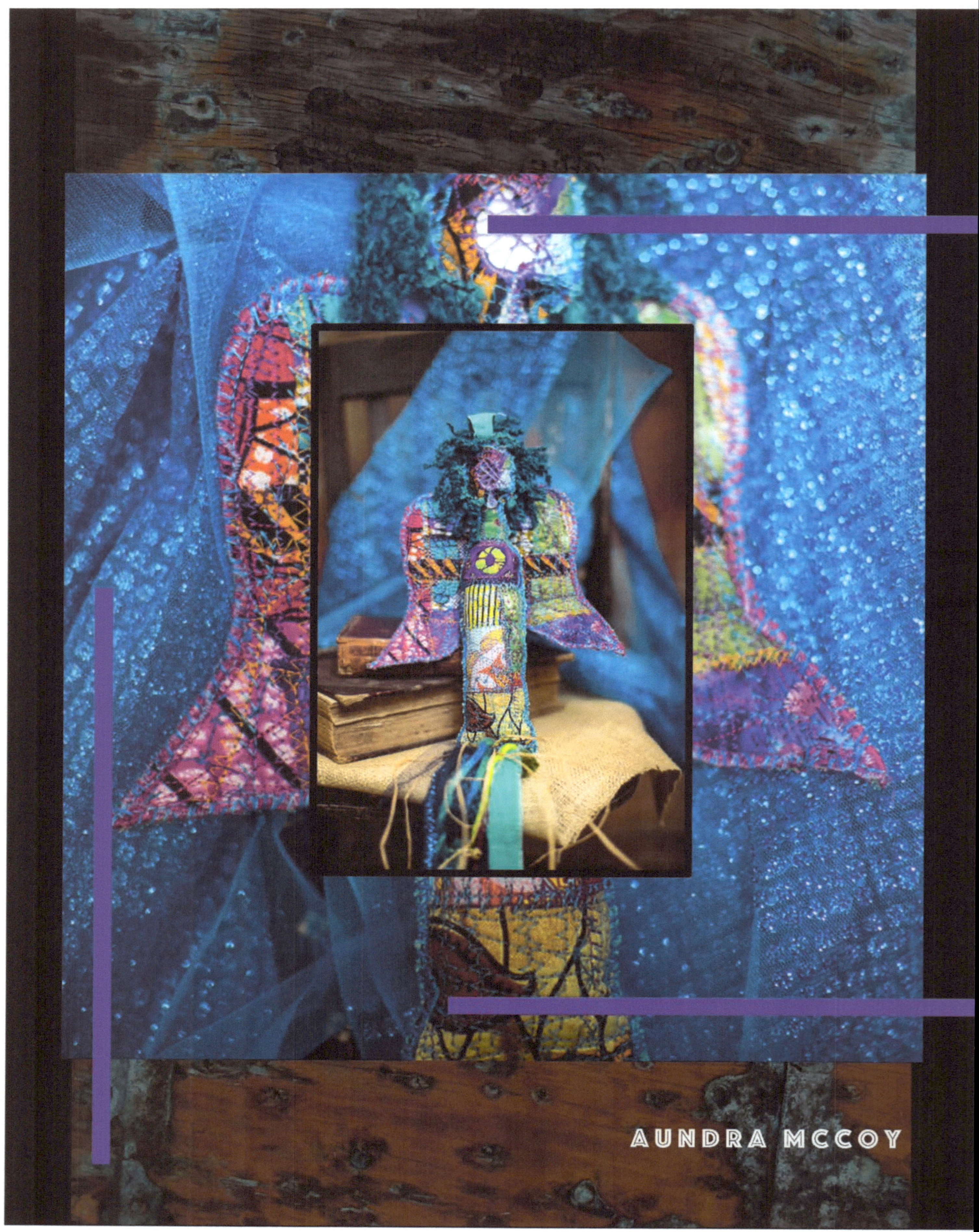

AUNDRA MCCOY

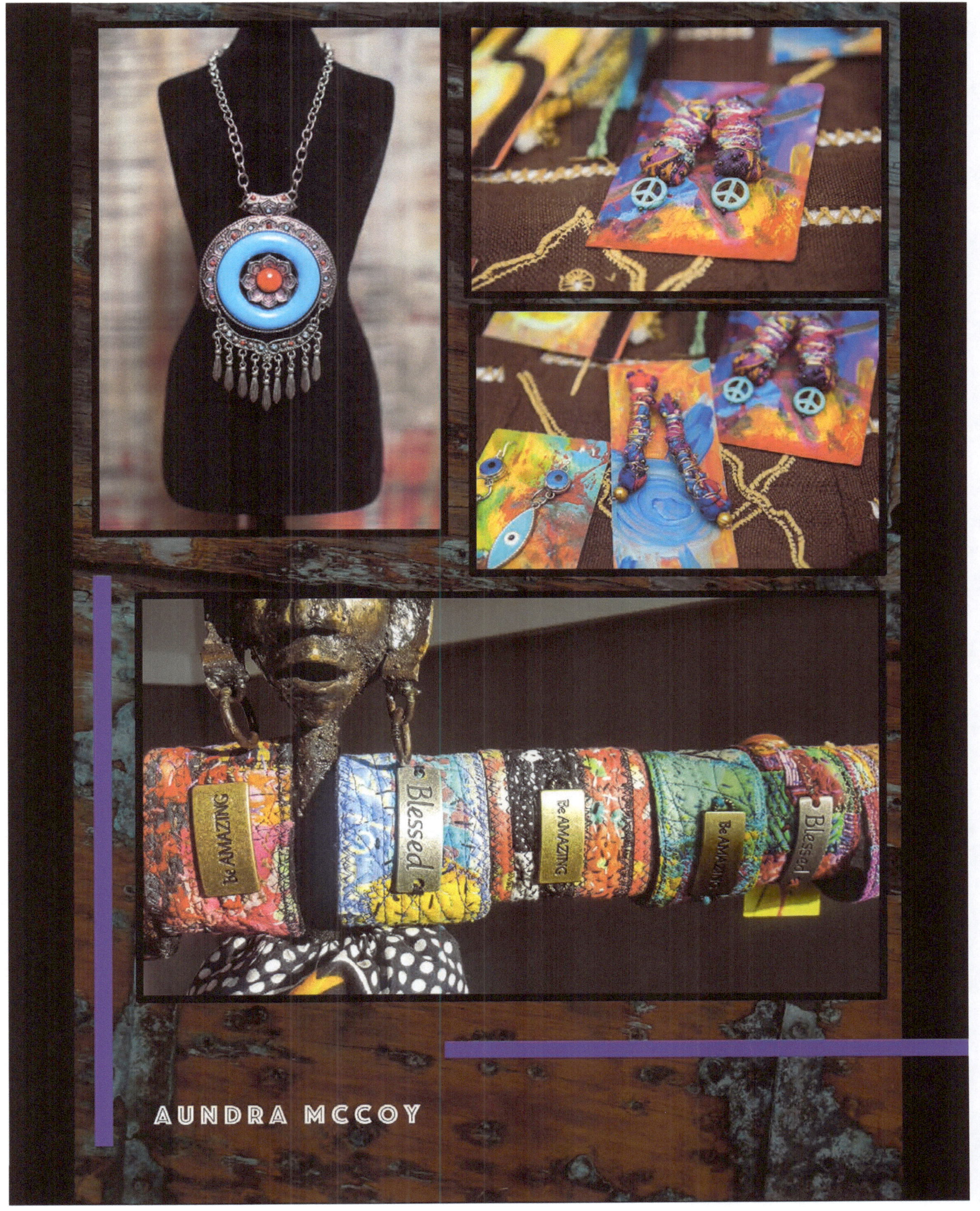
Be AMAZING
Blessed
Be AMAZING
Be AMAZING
Blessed
AUNDRA MCCOY

LISA TRIBO

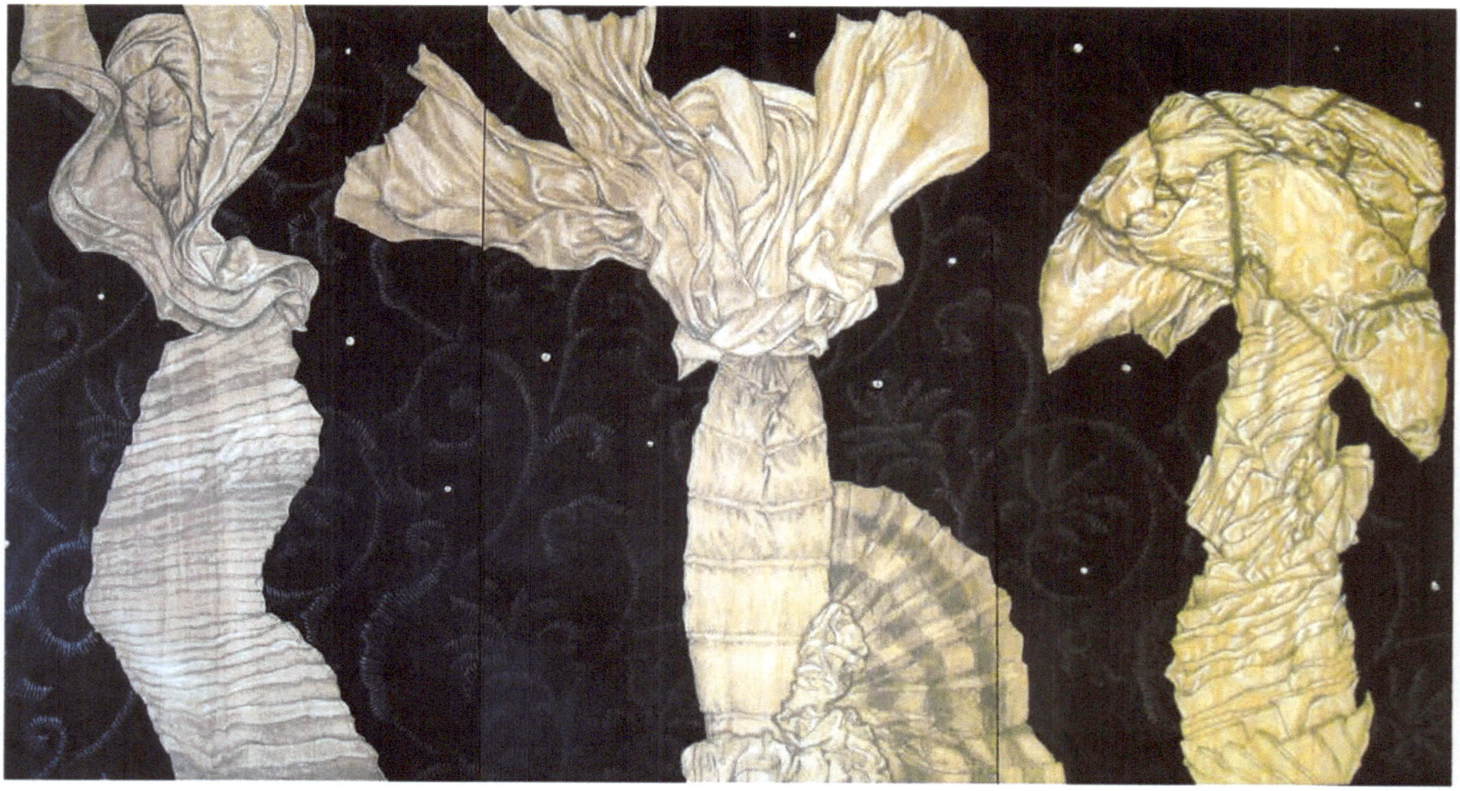

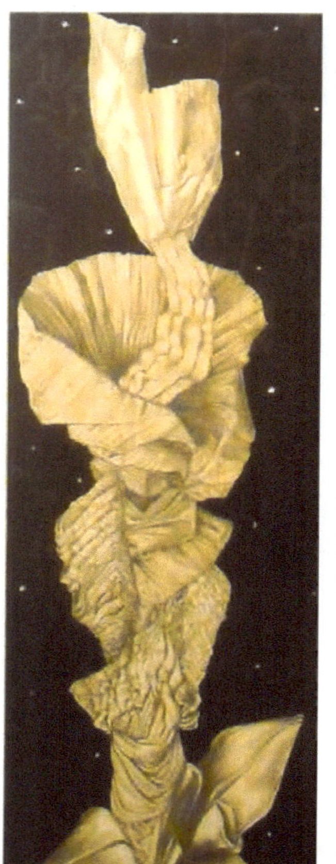

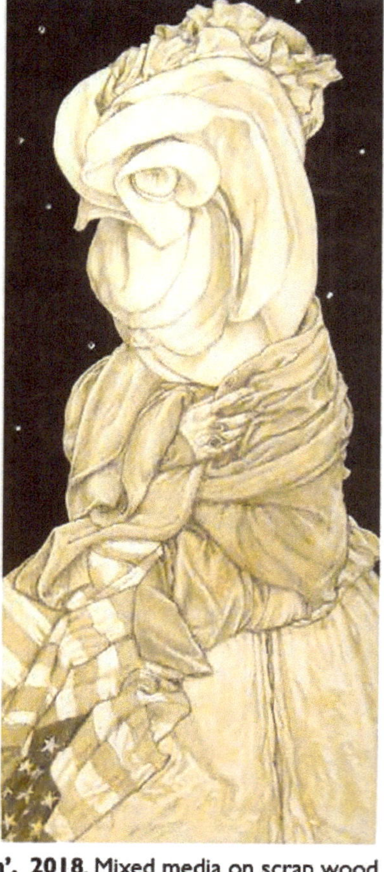

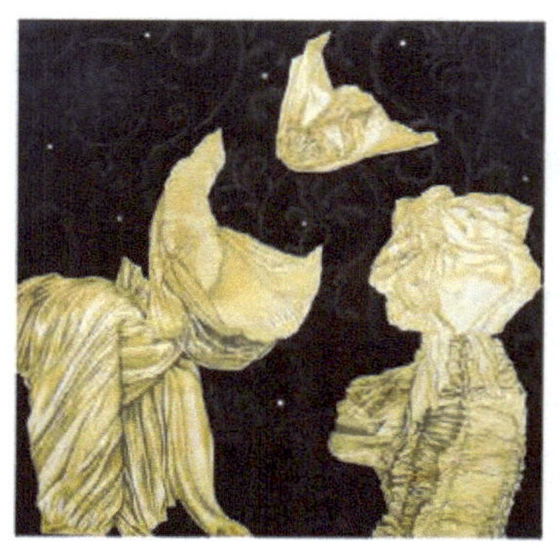

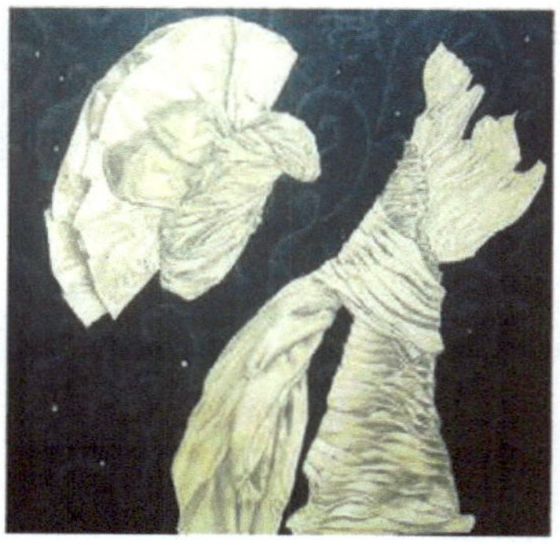

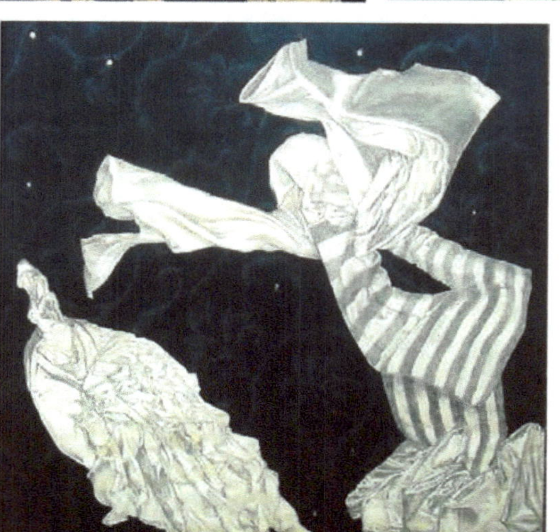

Details of 'The Night Garden', 2018, Mixed media on scrap wood

LISA TRIBO

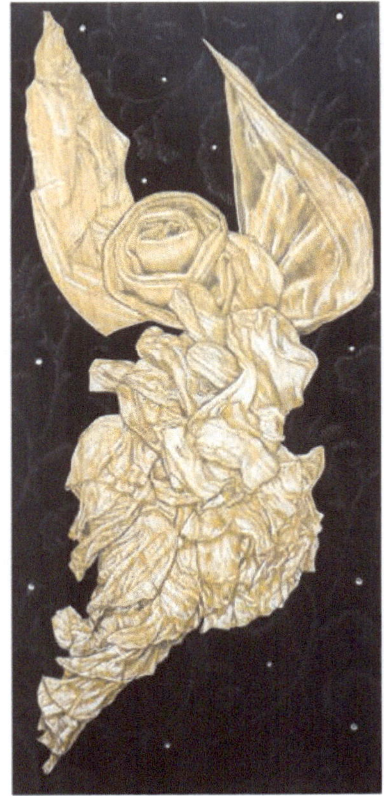

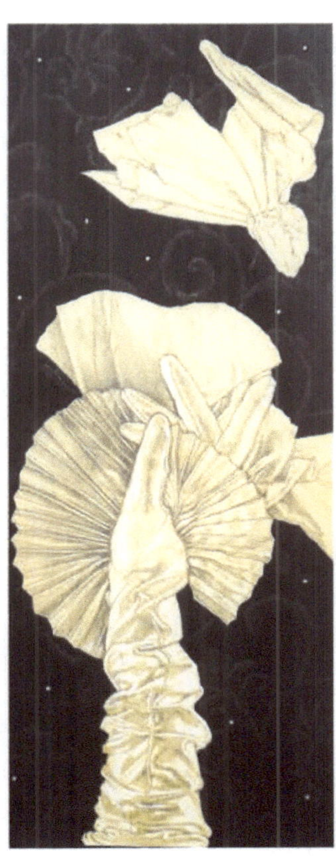

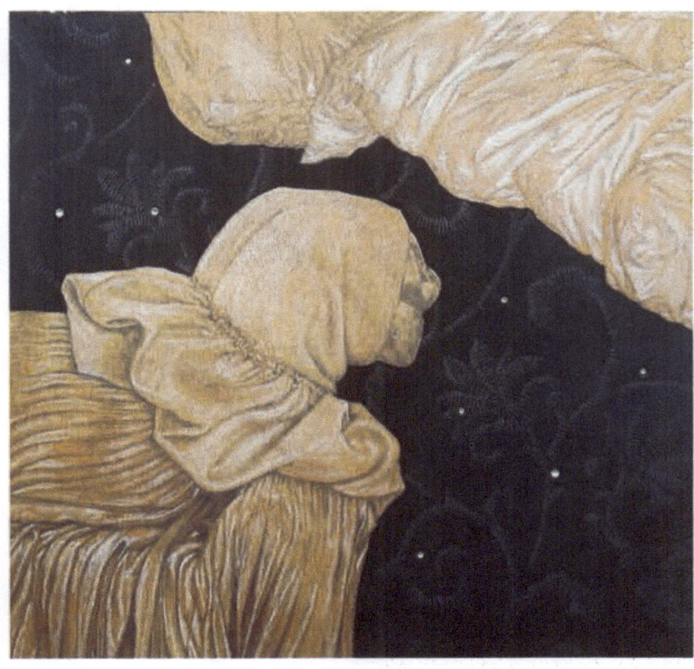

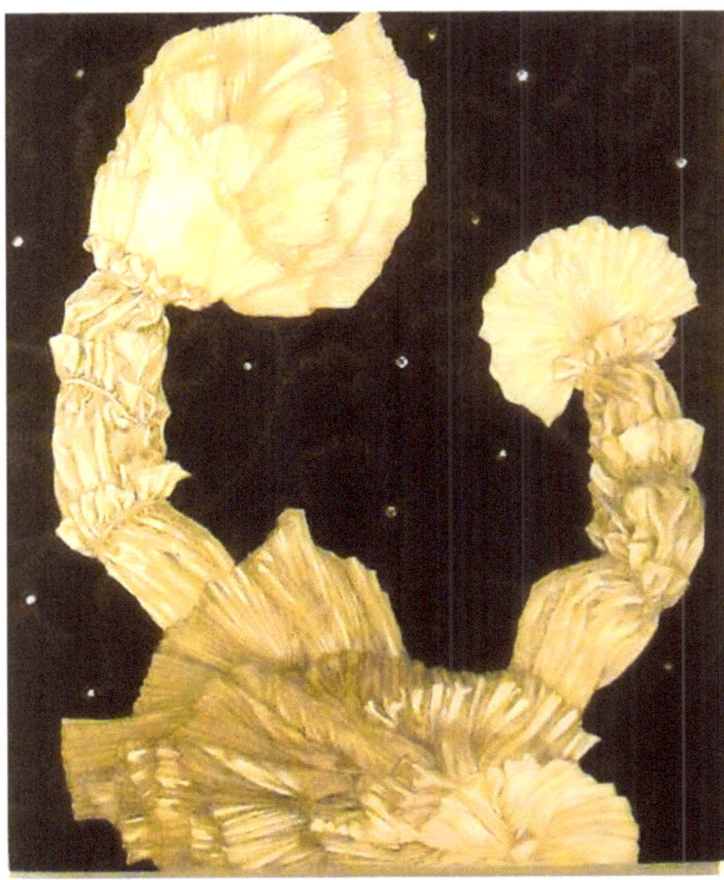

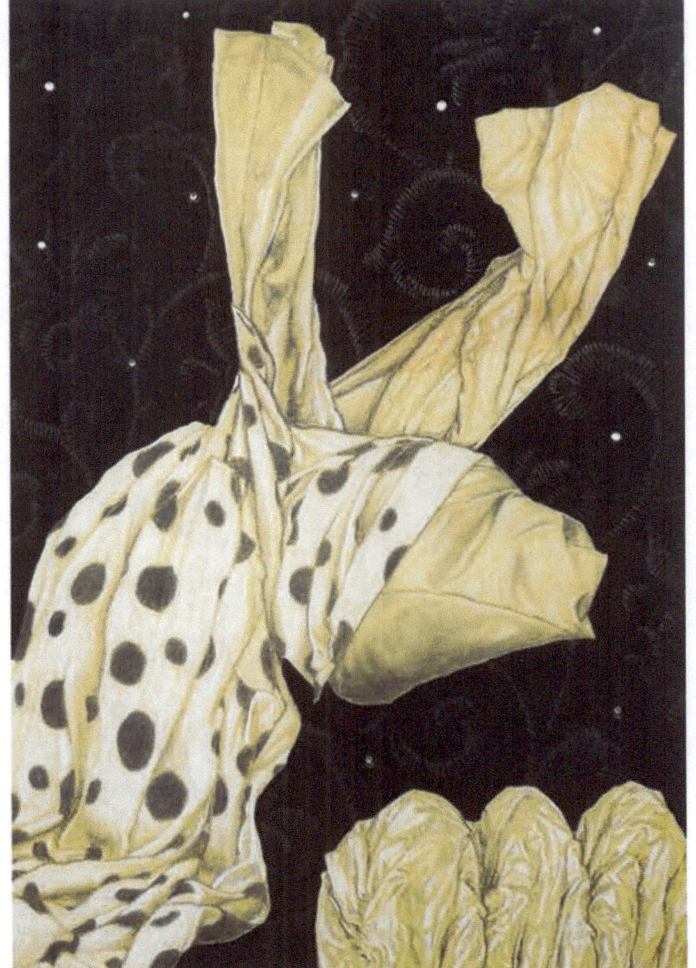

Details of 'The Night Garden', 2018, Mixed media on scrap wood

Rebecca Coleman

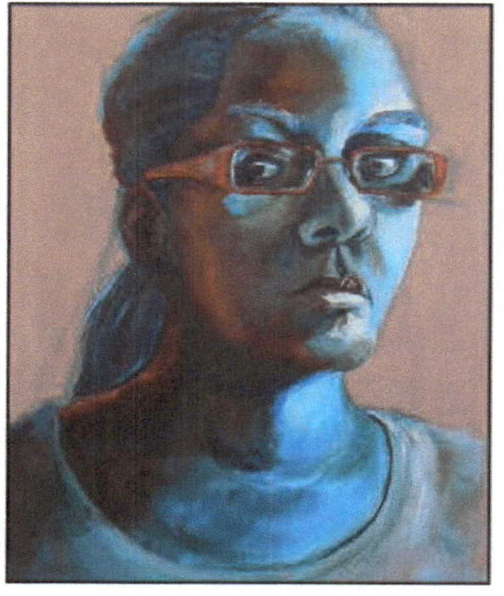

Self-Portrait
acrylic, 16" x 20"
2012

Rebecca Coleman, now Rebecca Coleman Wiley, earned her MFA in Studio Arts in 2013. Since earning her degree, she has taught at community colleges as an adjuct and full-time art instructor in Arkansas and Tennessee. She continues to work as a full-time instructor, mother, and freelance artist.

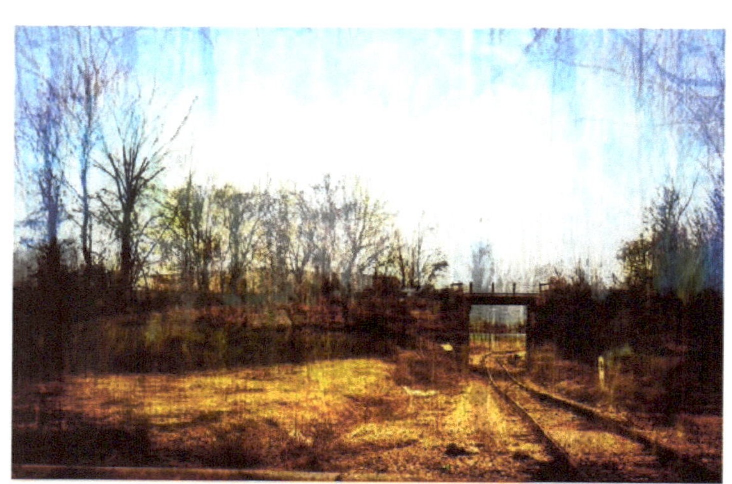

Memory Field: The Bridge
digital print, 30" x 20"
2013

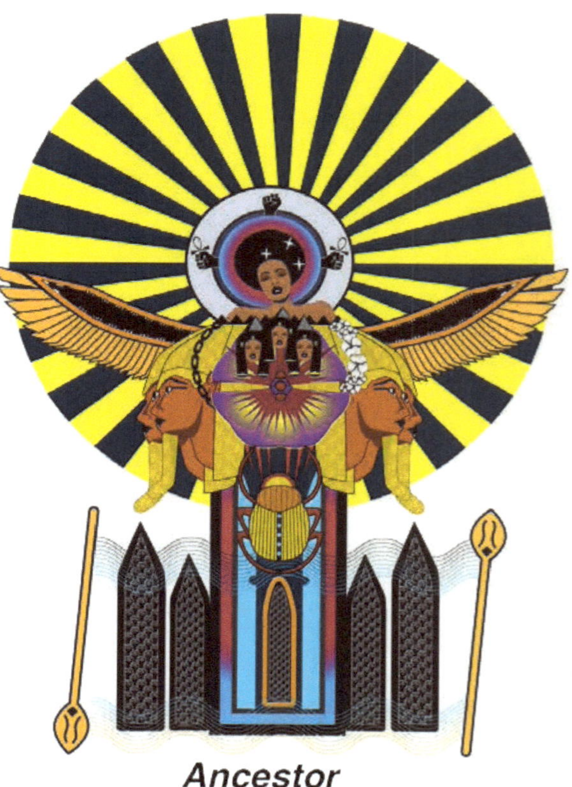

Ancestor
digital, 15" x 20"
2019

Rebecca Coleman

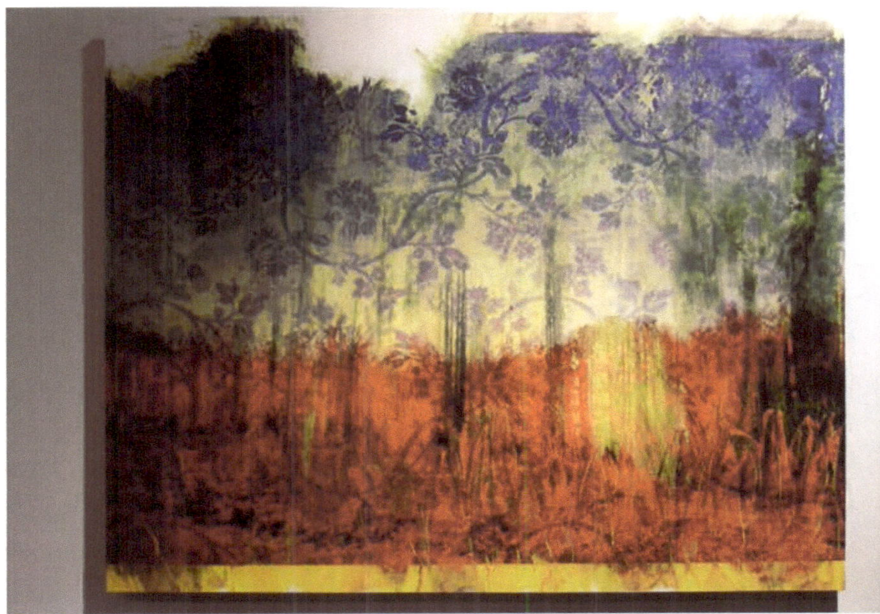

Home
digital print, 4' x 3'
2012

Working with digital imaging, I am exploring the tangibility of memory as it relates to family history. Although, I am working from personal memories of my family and the memories passed down to me, the importance to the viewer is not to know what the memories I am sharing are or who are portrayed, but the act of remembering and forgetting. The hope is that the viewer will realize how easily memories can be lost and experience the need to explore the works.

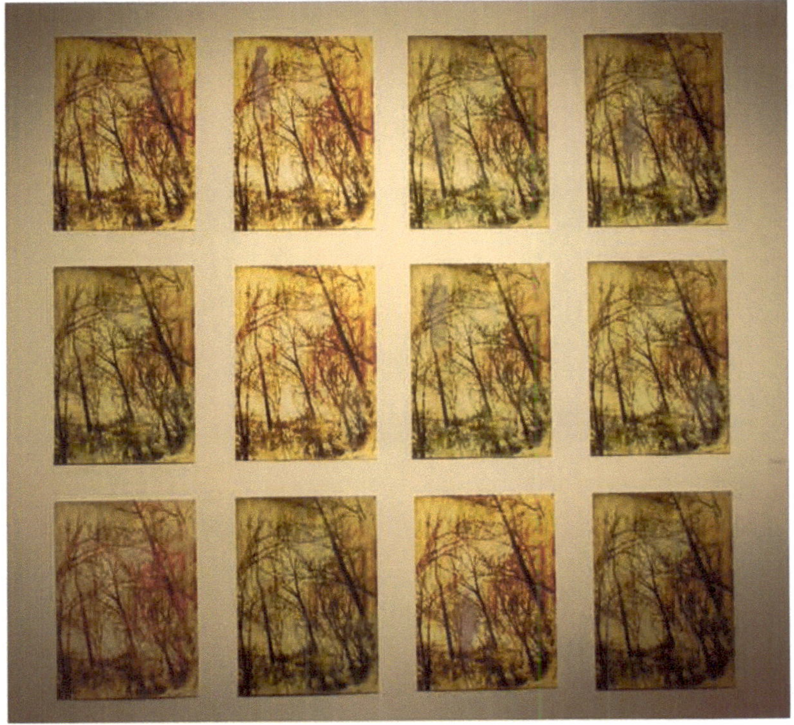

Impressions
collograph and digital print
15" x 21" (each)
2012

Cetin "Chet" Oguz

www.cetinoguz.com

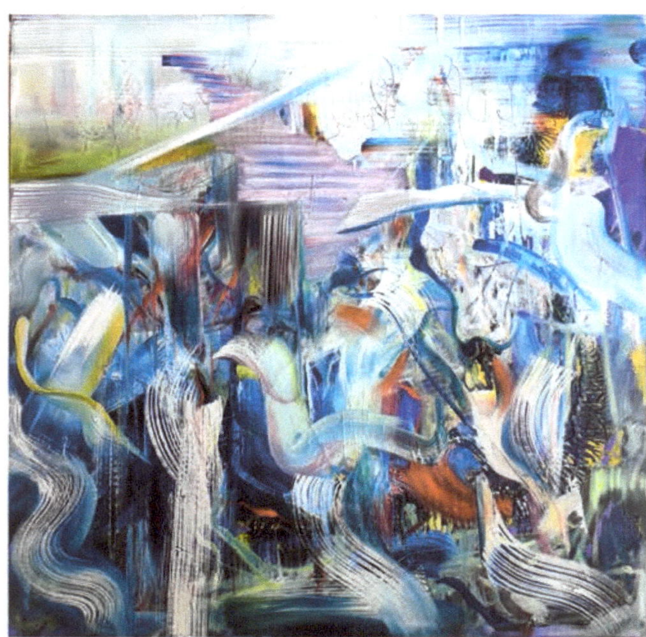

Jones Bayou 072119
Oil on canvas 36x36 inches

Blurry Clarity

My works are physical records of my connection with time, place, and memory.
I am attached to the present moment when I create art. I contemplate the possibilities and form the future by each layer, stroke, transition, and color. In my work, I reminisce of the places I've lived, and interpret the sceneries I witness. I know that everything changes through time, and my mind and senses aren't immune to this phenomenon. Through abstraction, I embed myself to the ever-changing aspect of time, place, and memory. I transform as time passes, as places change, and as memories fade. All of this takes place with an instant brush stroke or click of a button.

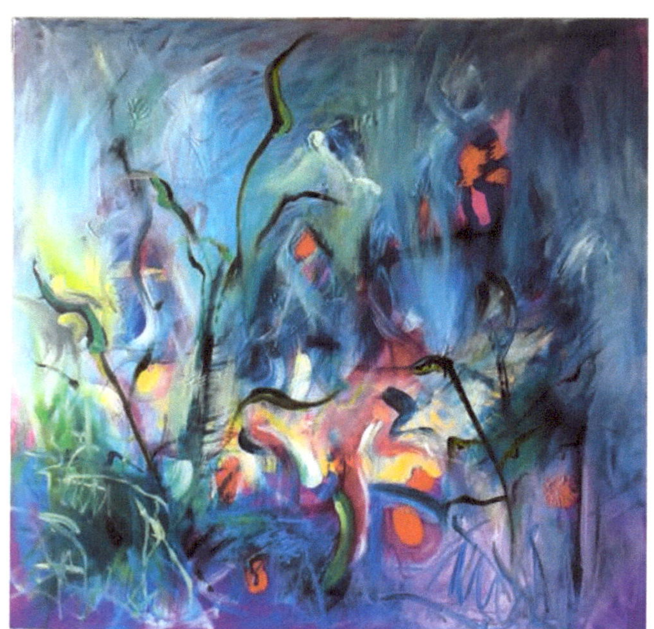

Jones Bayou 070119
Oil on canvas 36x36 inches

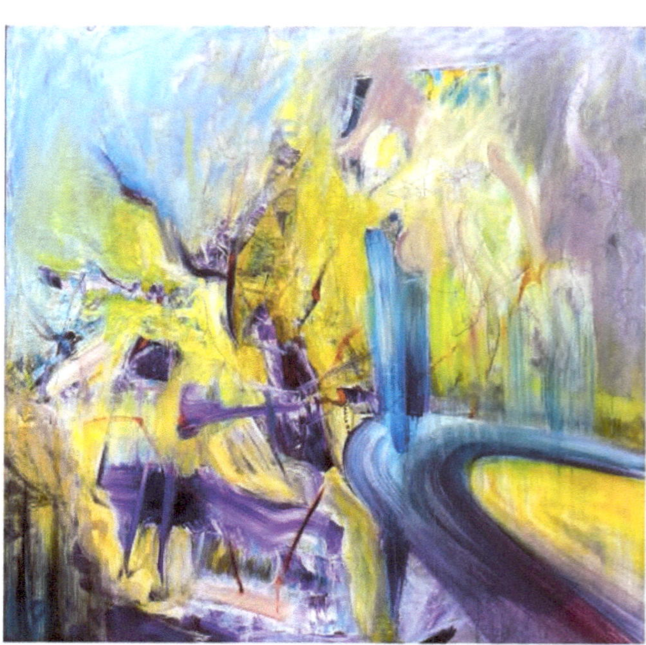

Jones Bayou 022020
Oil on canvas 36x36 inches

Professor of Art, Painting and Drawing
Faculty Senate President, 2019-2020
Delta State University, Department of Art
coguz@deltastate.edu

Cetin "Chet" Oguz

www.cetinoguz.com

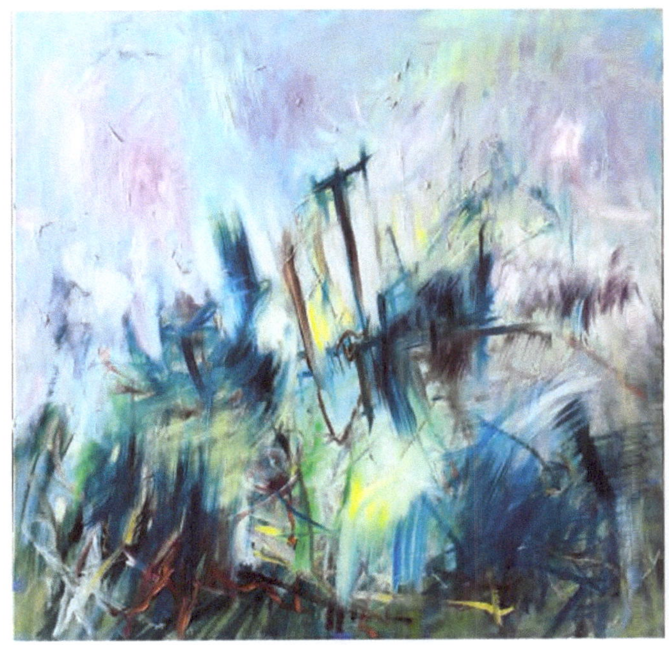

Jones Bayou 052219
Oil on canvas 24x24 inches

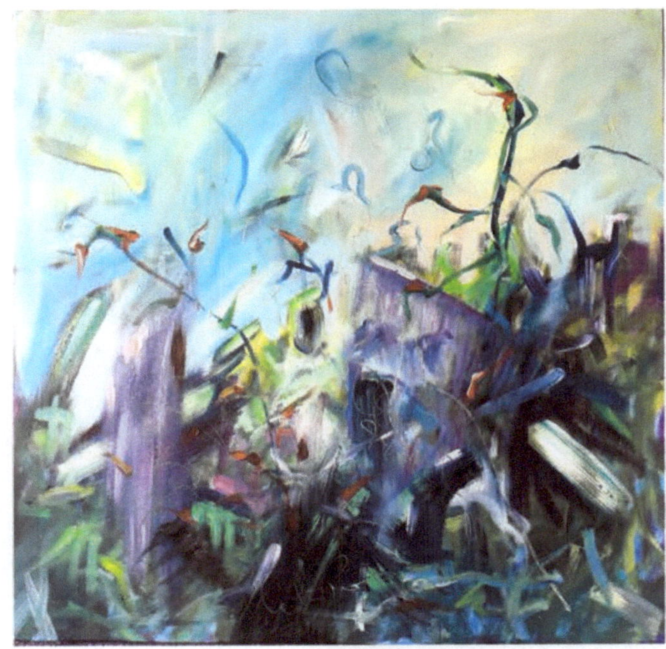

Jones Bayou 062119
Oil on canvas 24x24 inches

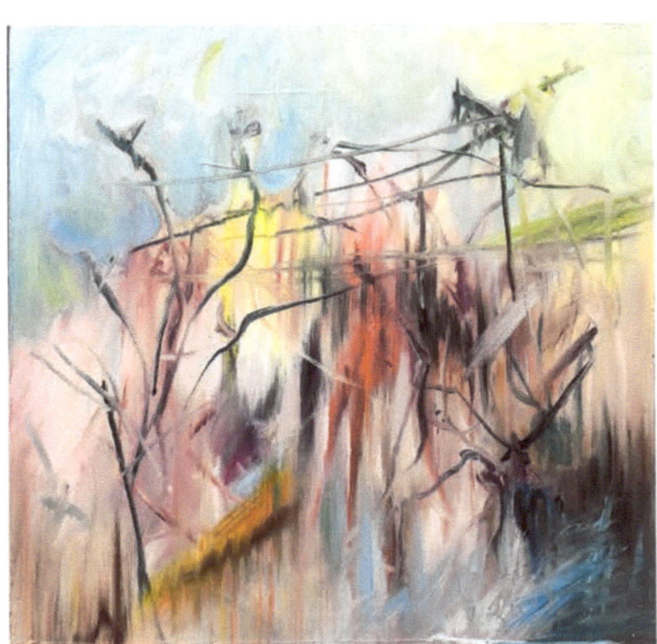

Jones Bayou 030919
Oil on canvas 16x16 inches

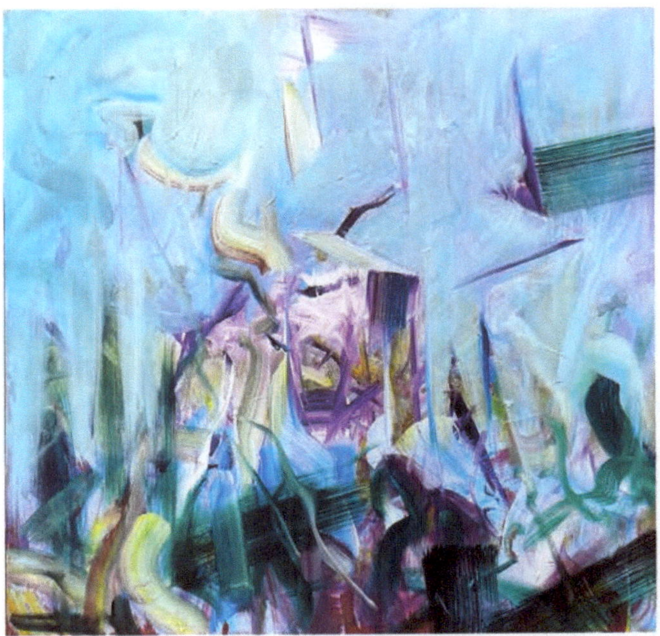

Jones Bayou 031420
Oil on canvas 36x36 inches

Professor of Art, Painting and Drawing
Faculty Senate President, 2019-2020
Delta State University, Department of Art
coguz@deltastate.edu

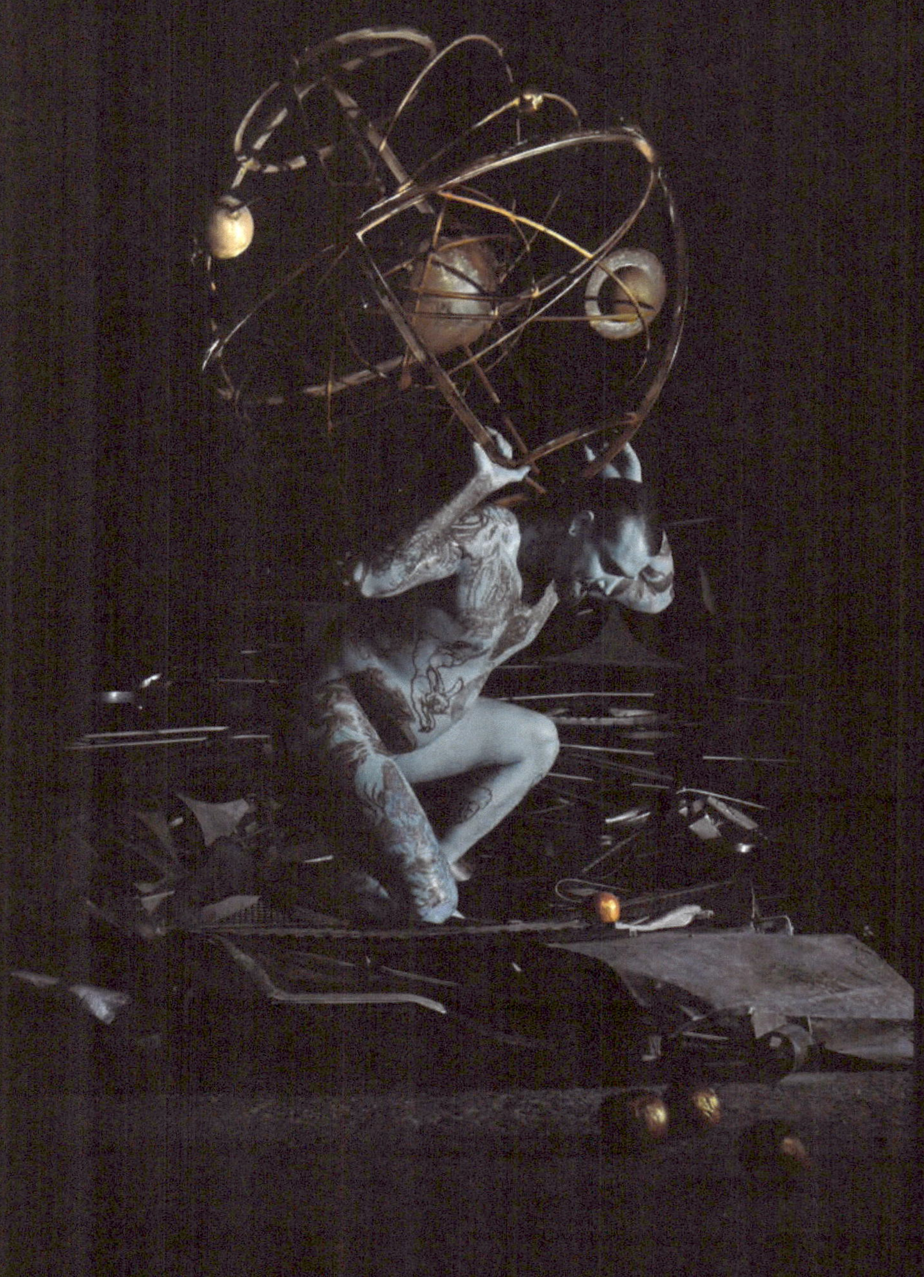

He would have to relinquish his grasp to reach for new wisdom.
Surrender would bring relief.

Atlas Reckoning, 2009.
pictured above: Robert Fortner

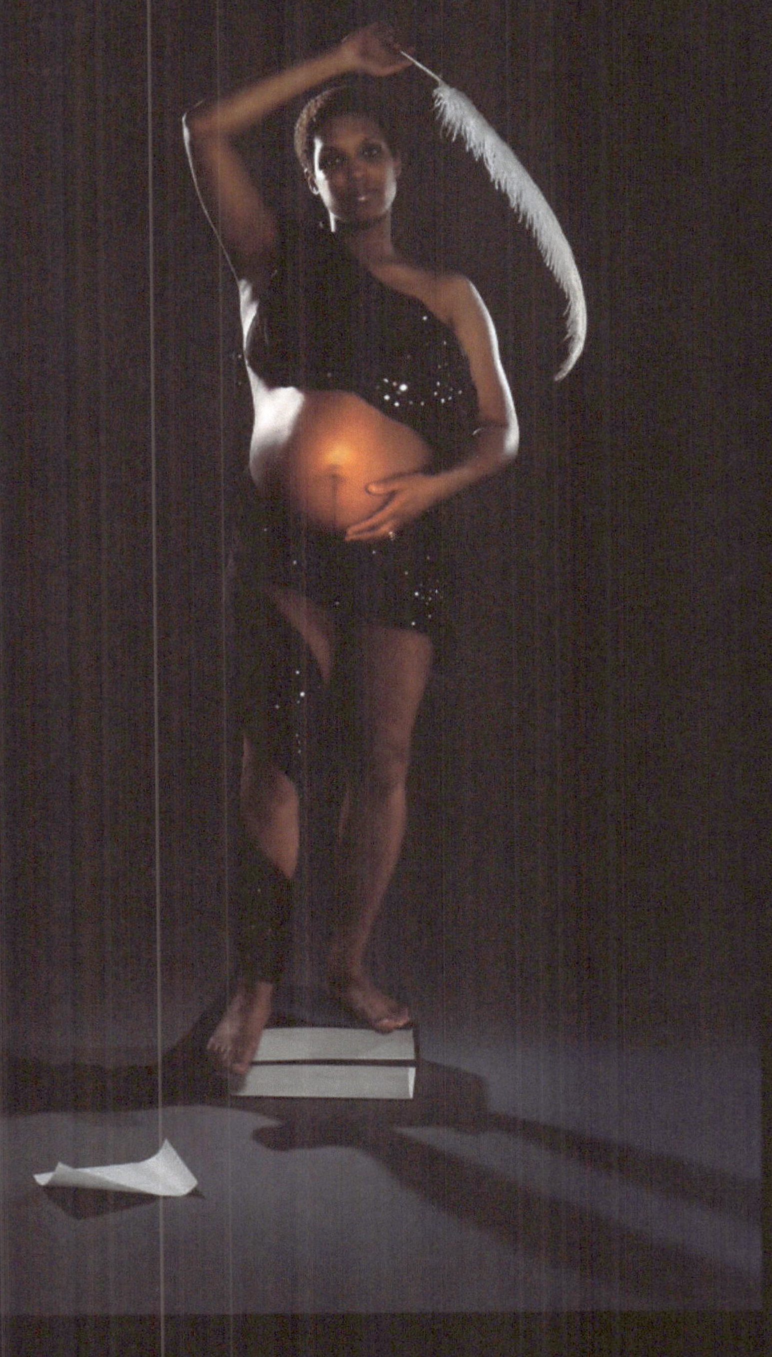

Aliyah, 2010.
pictured above: Niani Colom-Omotesa, *of Blessed Memory*

r salant MFA Memphis College of Art, 2003
rsalant.com robin@rsalant.com

art community performance

Andrea Prince

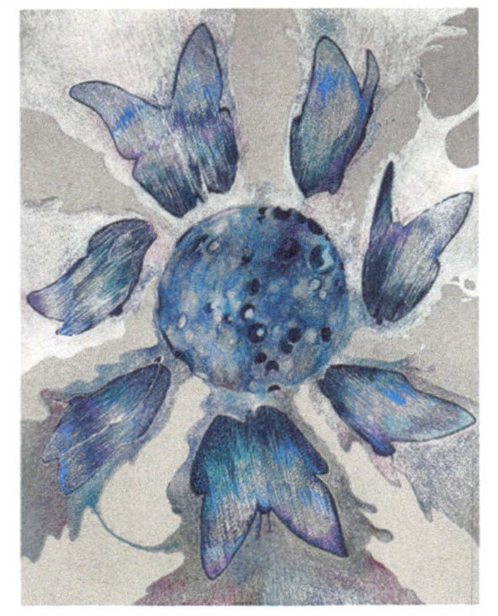

Twilight

11" x 14"

Ink, gouache and colored pencil

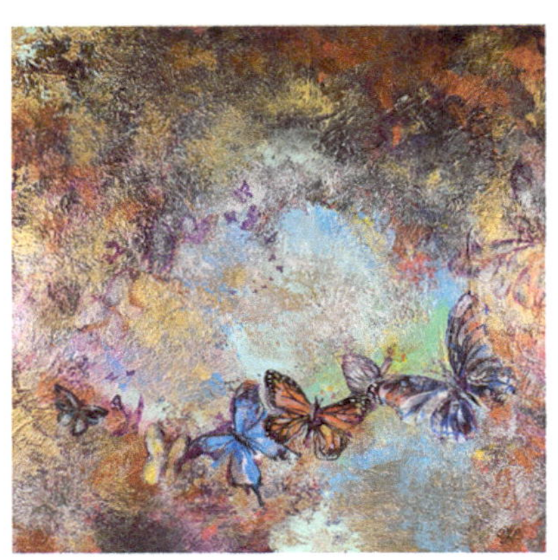

Patina Dream

11" x 14"

Acrylic on Panel

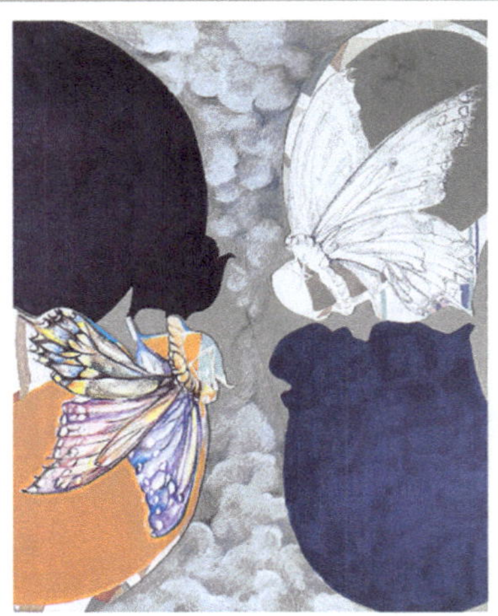

Reflect

11" x 14"

Ink, watercolor and colored pencil

bio

Andrea Prince completed her Master of Fine Arts from Memphis College of Art, her Bachelor of Fine Arts from Marshall University and will complete a Master of Arts in Teaching this year from Marshall University Graduate College. Prince works primarily in drawing and painting media, exploring site specific installation and sculpture when the work calls for additional investigations. Prince loves working in a sketchbook: documenting observational studies, writing about art and exploring ideas freely. The works selected for this exhibition in print were created in late 2019 and early 2020.

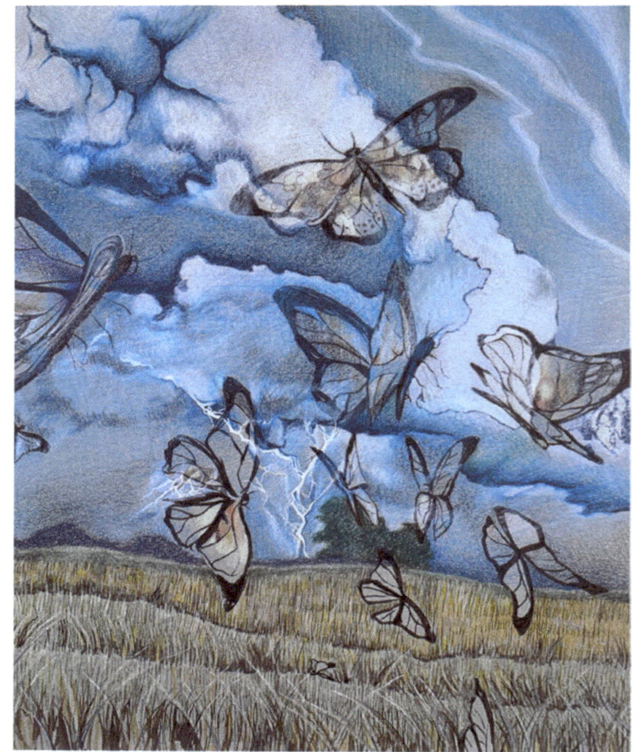

Weather the Storm

11" x 14"

Ink, marker, gouache and colored pencil

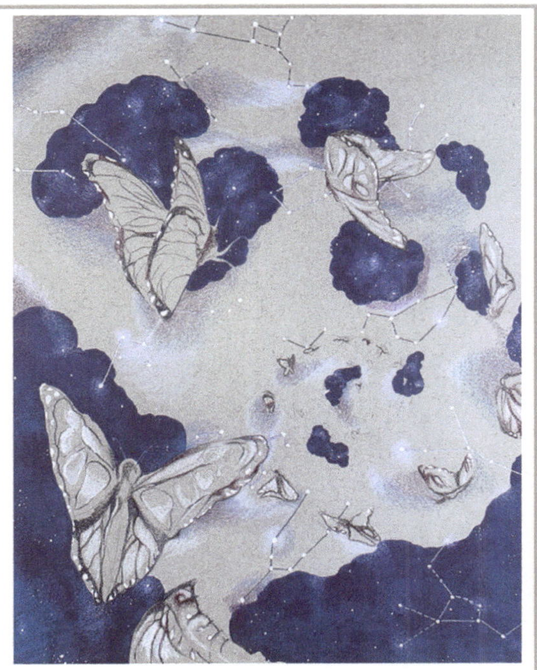

Flying, Floating, Falling

11" x 14"

Ink, marker and colored pencils

www.Andreaprince.com

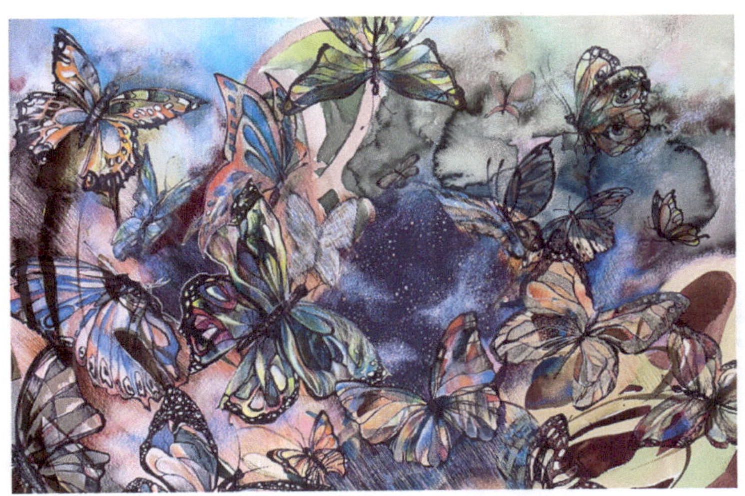

Into Being

14" x 20"

Ink, gouache and colored pencil

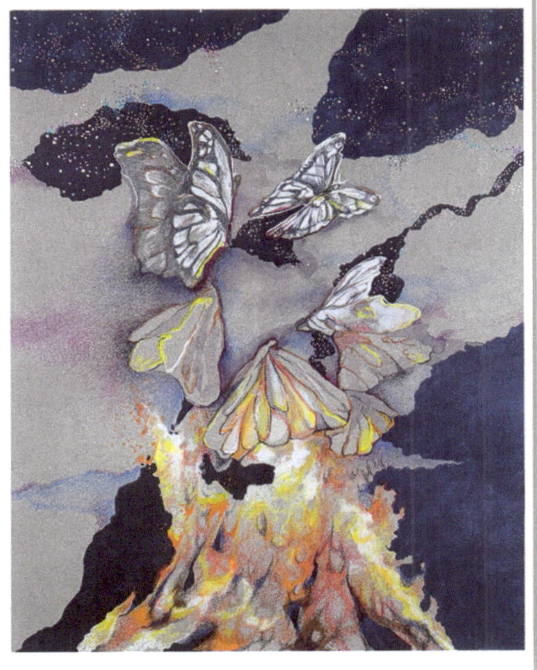

Desire

11" x 14"

Ink, marker and colored pencil

Statement

Images of butterflies immediately inspire thoughts of metamorphosis. The development from caterpillar to butterfly is learned at a young age. However, the process to achieve transformation isn't easy. Reflecting on what can make it difficult for people to reach their potential is what inspired this work. Places and things are used to communicate the resistance people face as they grow and change.

The butterflies represent the potential for transformation. The spaces I've chosen to place them in are either celestial spaces, earthly spaces or somewhere in between; each is chosen to represent different levels of transcendence. The anchoring objects like the ropes and the stone are stand ins for the conflicts and challenges of life.

ZARA GARZA

zaragarza.com
IG: @zara_garza

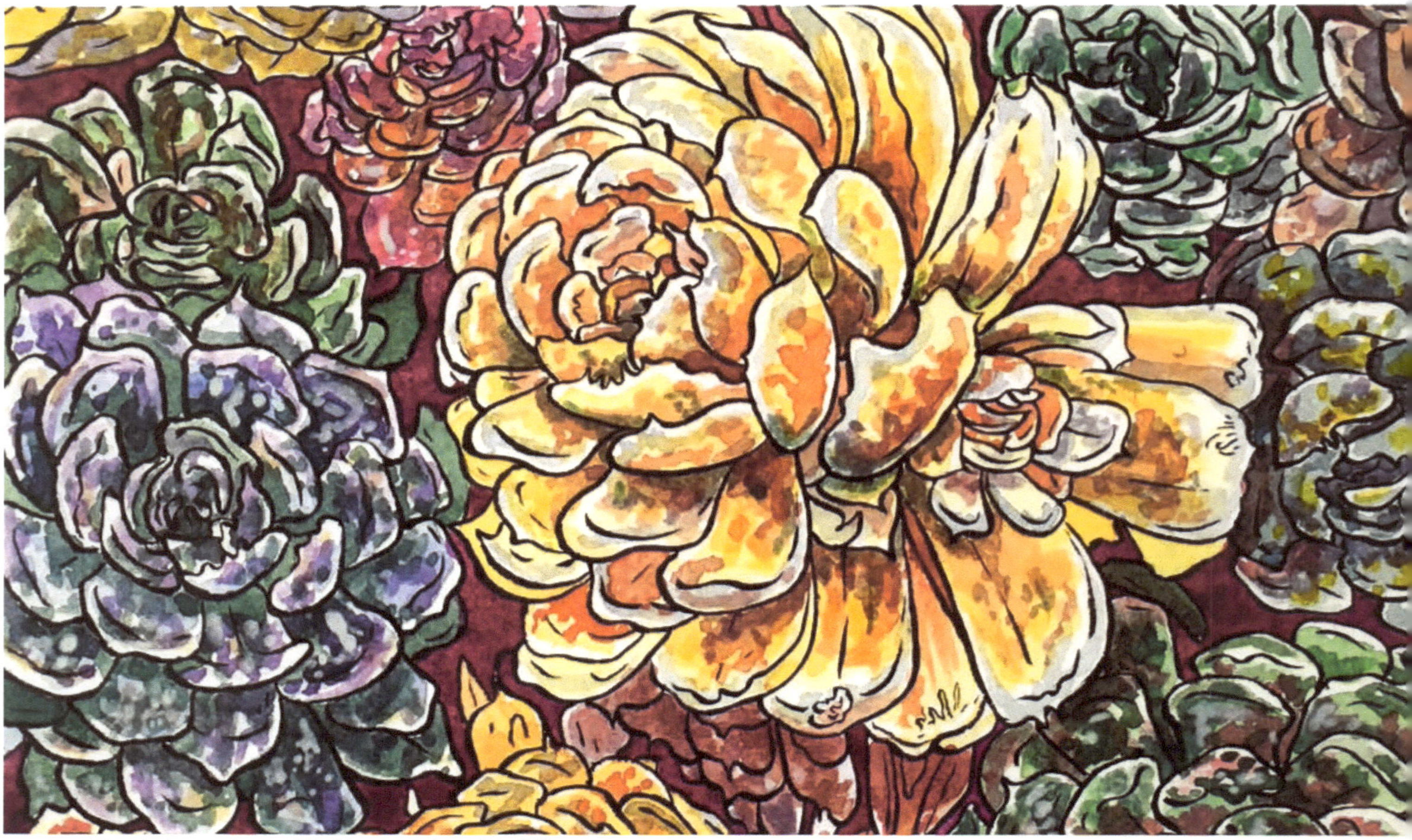

"Succulent watercolor study" 5 x 6 in., watercolor and ink, 2018

MEMPHIS COLLEGE OF ART
BACHELOR OF DESIGN ARTS IN ILLUSTRATION
MINOR IN ART HISTORY
2015

I find a lot of my inspiration comes from nature, wherever I can see clusters of flora gathered together with bright and vivid color schemes. While I try to diversify my portfolio with both traditional and digital artforms, I tend to stay consistent with watercolor and ink. Currently I'm working on a story about two sandwich pirates, with the lore and illustrations being created from a project I began at Memphis College of Art. It has always been a goal of mine to become a book or editorial illustrator, and I hope to collaborate with children's book authors to help tell their stories through visually captivating imagery.

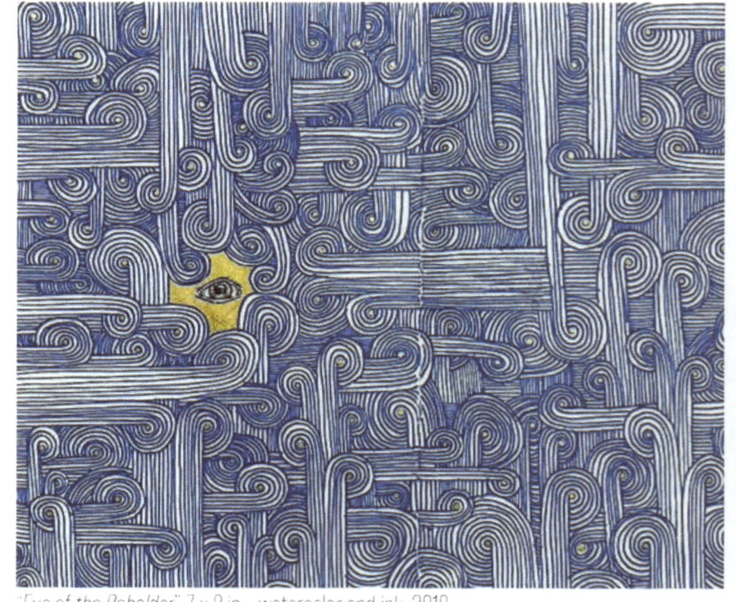

"Eye of the Beholder" 7 x 8 in., watercolor and ink, 2019

ZARA GARZA

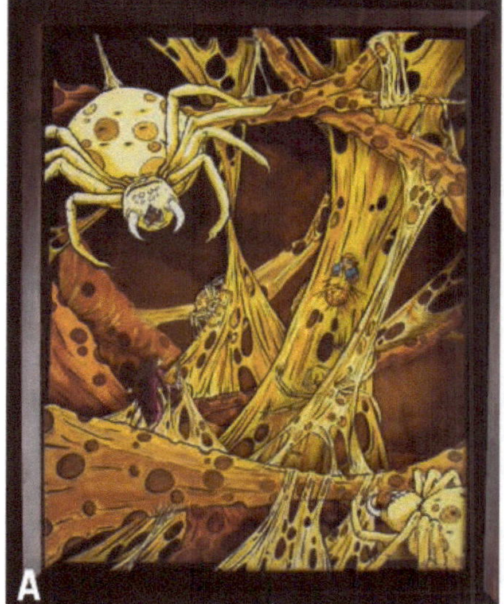

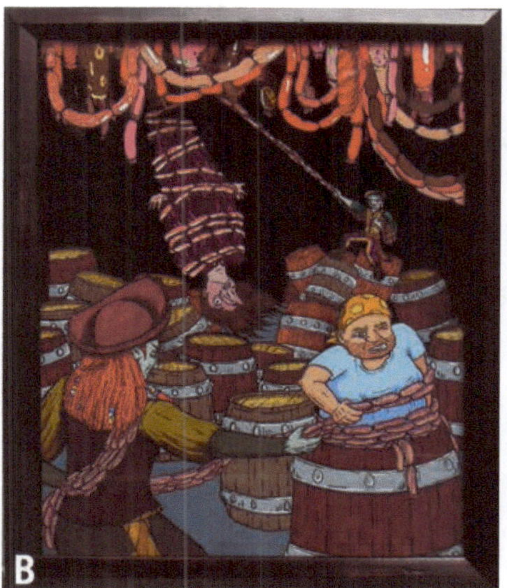

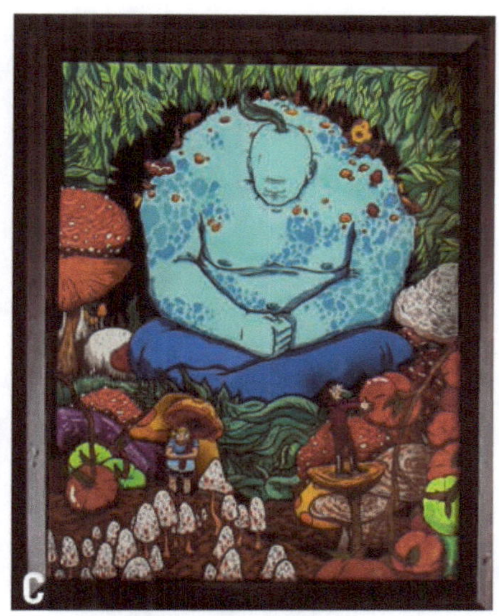

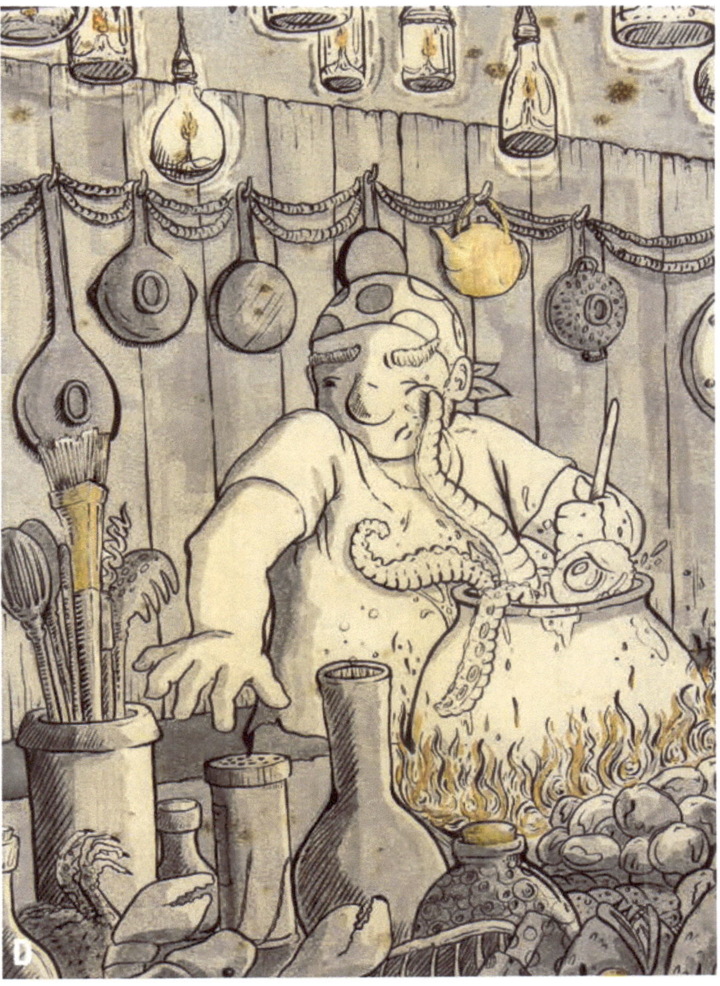

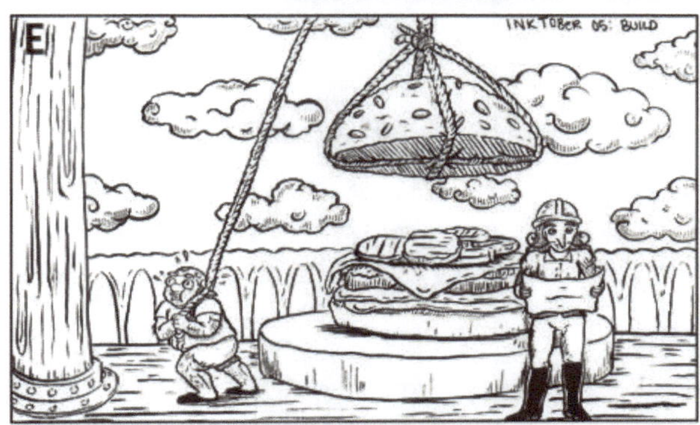

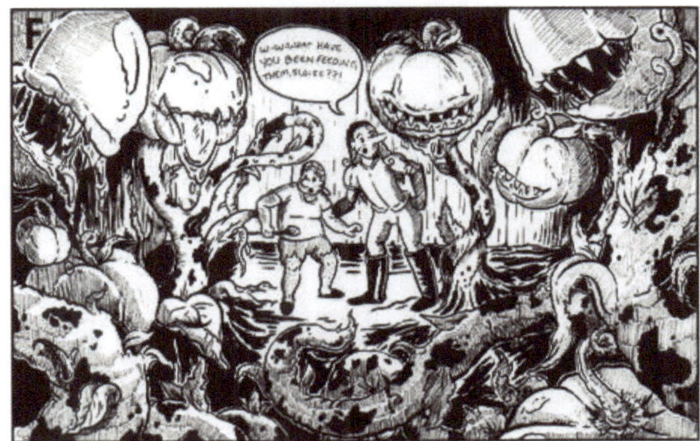

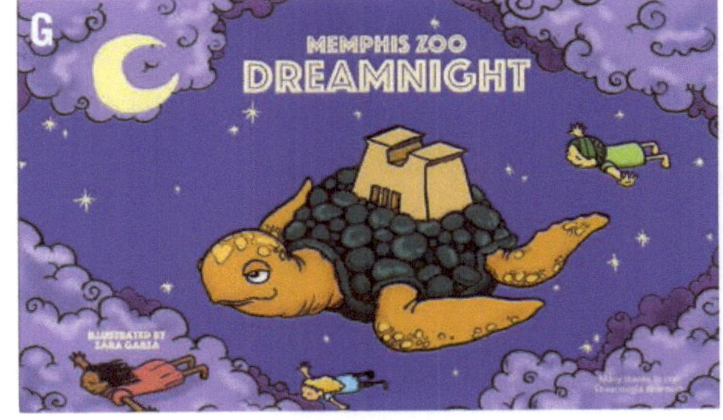

A: *"Attack of the Asiago Arachnids!"* 12 x 14 in., mixed media, 2015
B: *"Strung Up by the Salami Sisters"* 12 x 14 in., mixed media, 2015
C: *"Enter the Cyclops Garden"* 12 x 14 in., mixed media, 2015
D: *"Swiss' Strange Brew"* 11 x 14 in., mixed media, 2015
E: *"Inktober Day 05: Build (Your Own Burger)"* 5 x 8 in., ink brush and pen, 2019
F: *"Inktober Day 14: Overgrown"* 5 x 8 in., ink brush and pen, 2019
G: *"Memphis Zoo: DREAMNIGHT"* 11 x 17 in., digital media, 2019

MICHAEL LOREFICE

www.Michaellorefice.com

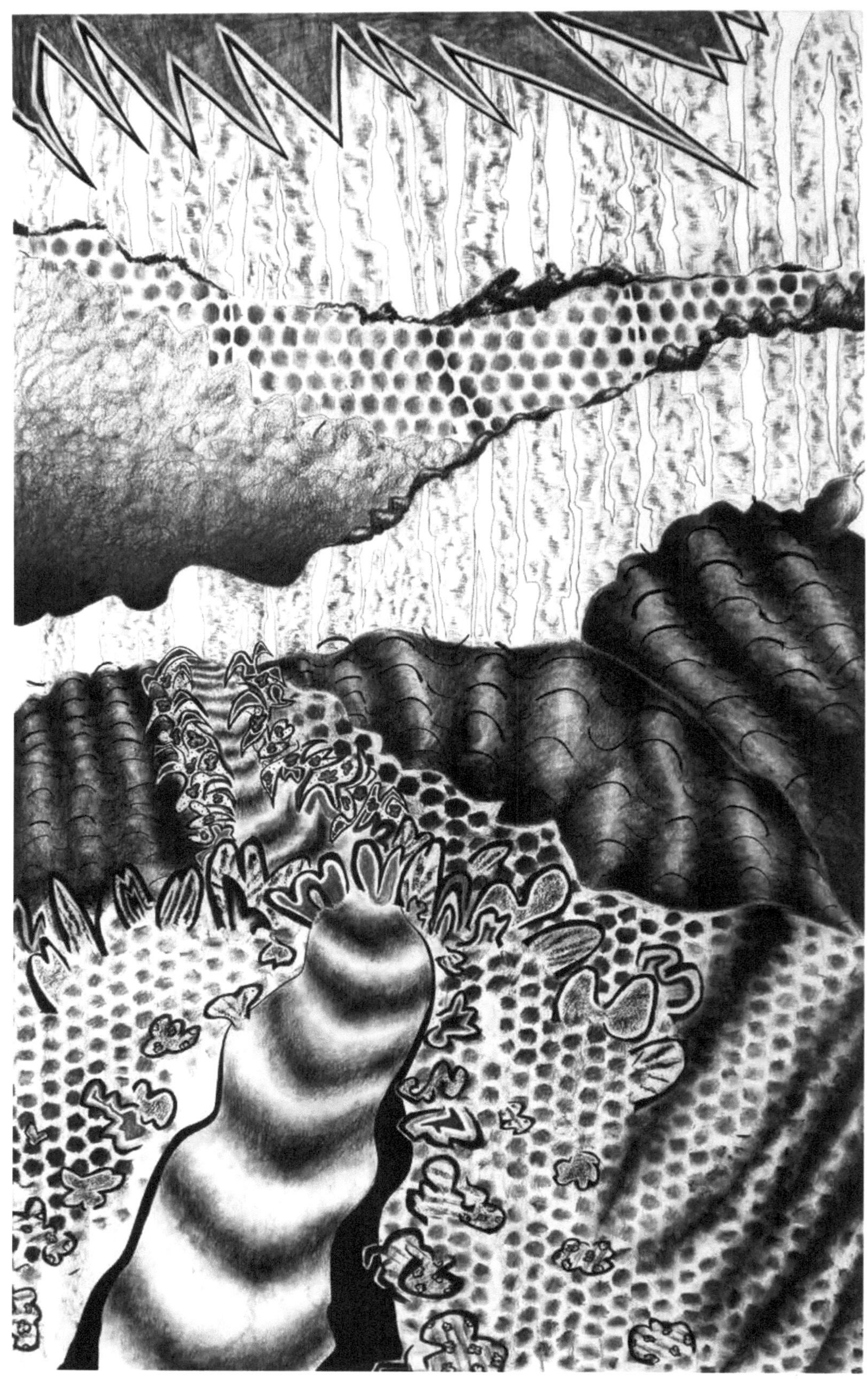

Untitled (Oaxacan landscape, #5), 2017
Charcoal on Arches paper, 70 x 42 inches

MICHAEL LOREFICE

www.Michaellorefice.com

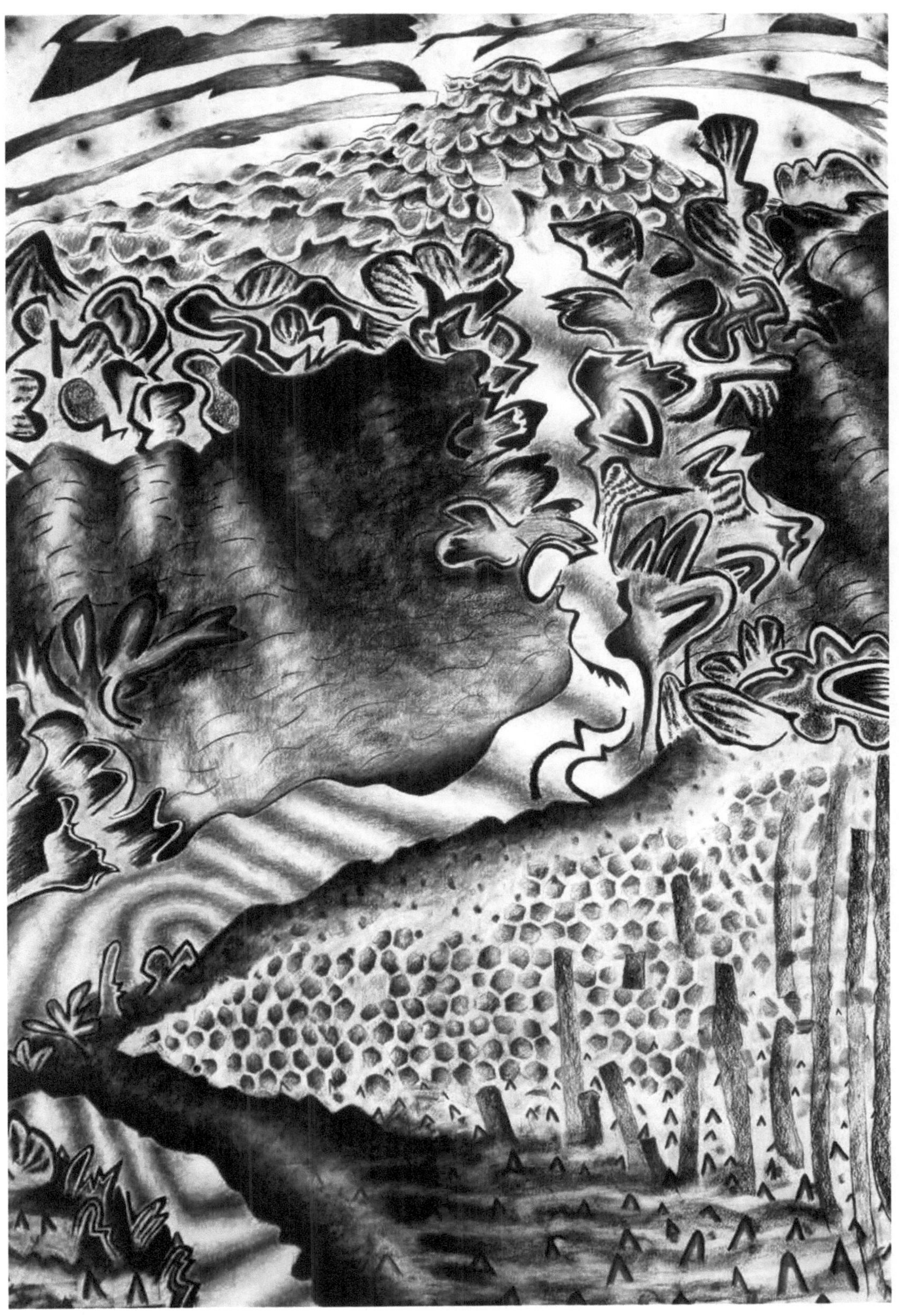

Untitled (Oaxacan andscape, #7), 2017
Charcoal on Arches paper, 64 x 42 inches

Meda Rae Rives Smith
Veda Mae Rives Aukerman

As artists and identical twin sisters, we established Mirror Image Press as our studio to pursue interests in printmaking, handmade paper, artists' books, and BookEnvirons. We create artworks both independently and collaboratively which have been exhibited nationally and internationally. We met many wonderful people at Memphis College of Art thanks to Maritza Dávila inviting us to be visiting artists.

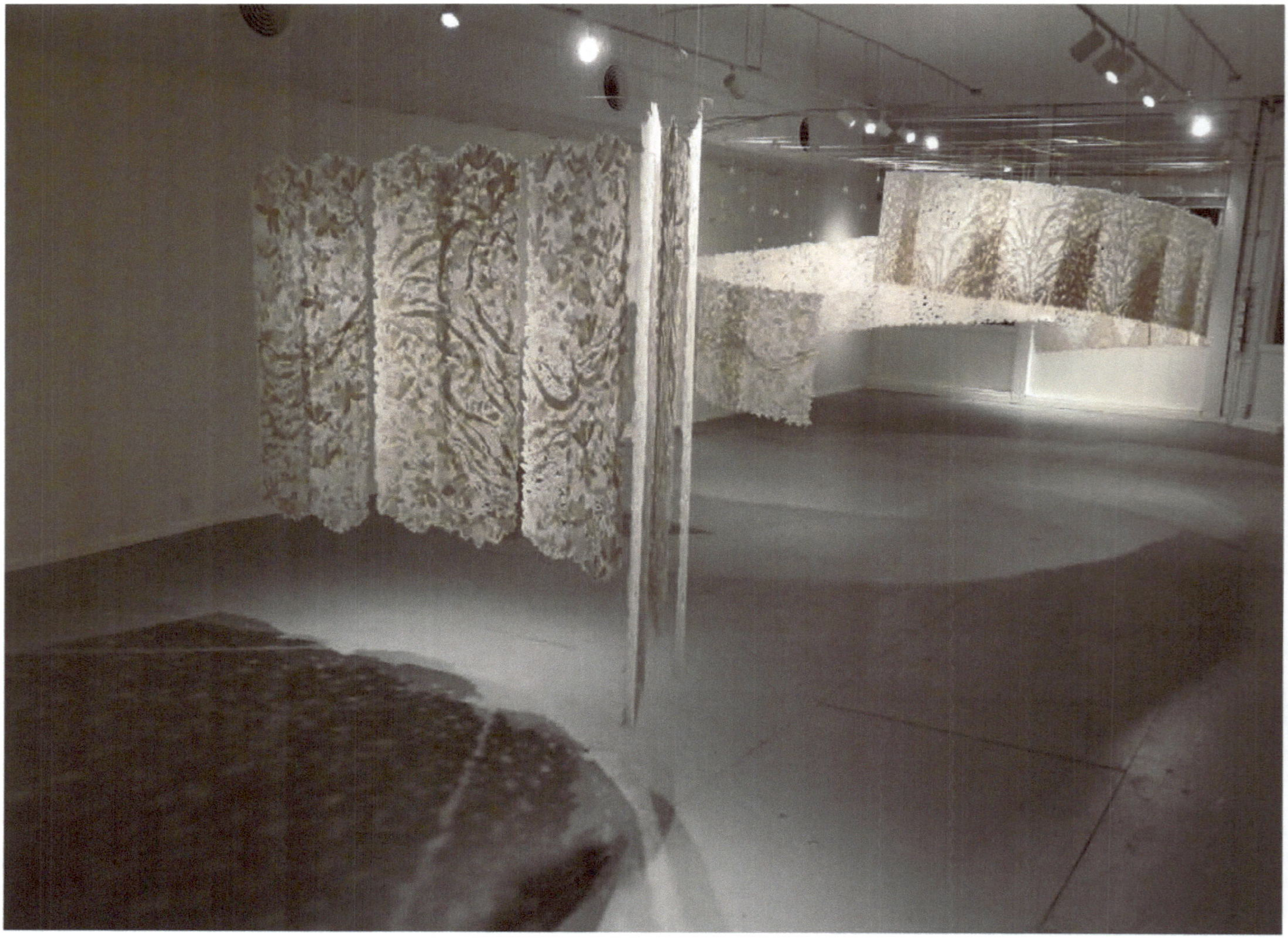

BookEnvirons: Memphis
Artists Books as Shelter, Escape, Epiphany; Shaping Our Space, Our Thoughts, and Our Aspirations
On the Street Gallery, Memphis College of Art, Memphis, TN, handmade paper, threads, branches, 2009
Memphis Magnolia, 10' x 14' x 5', foreground; ***TwinPath***, 10' x 14' x 20', background

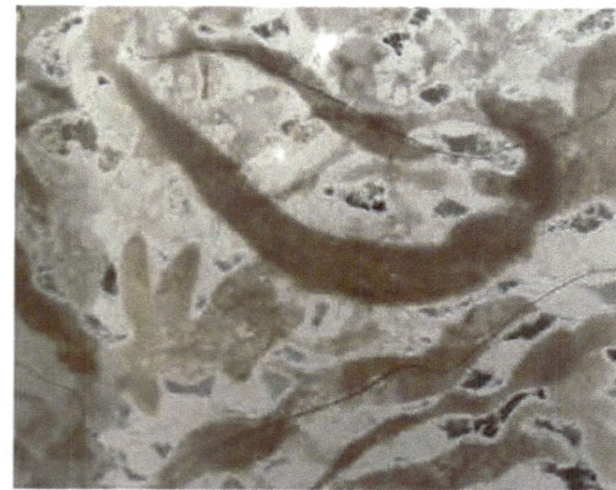

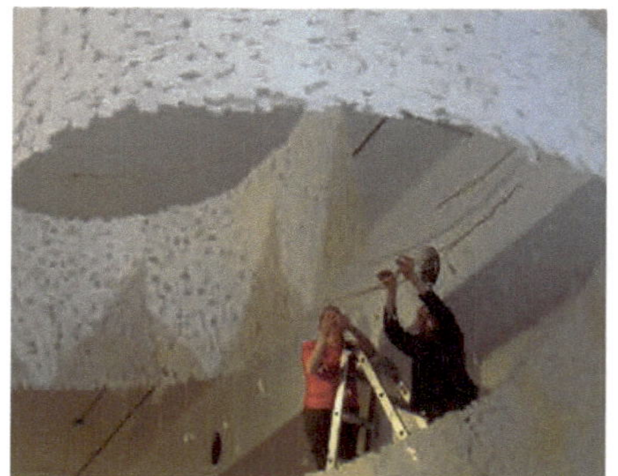

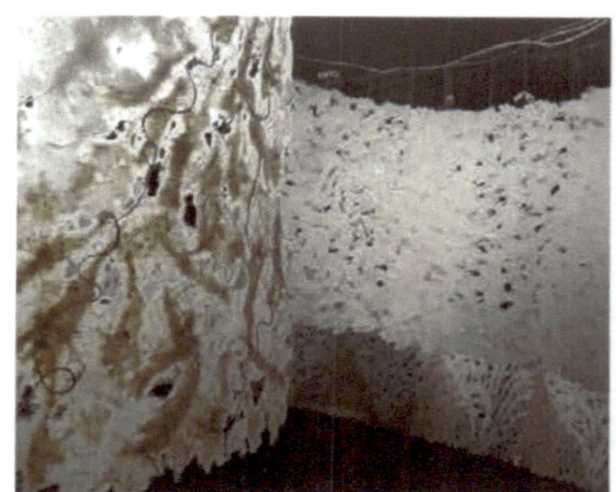

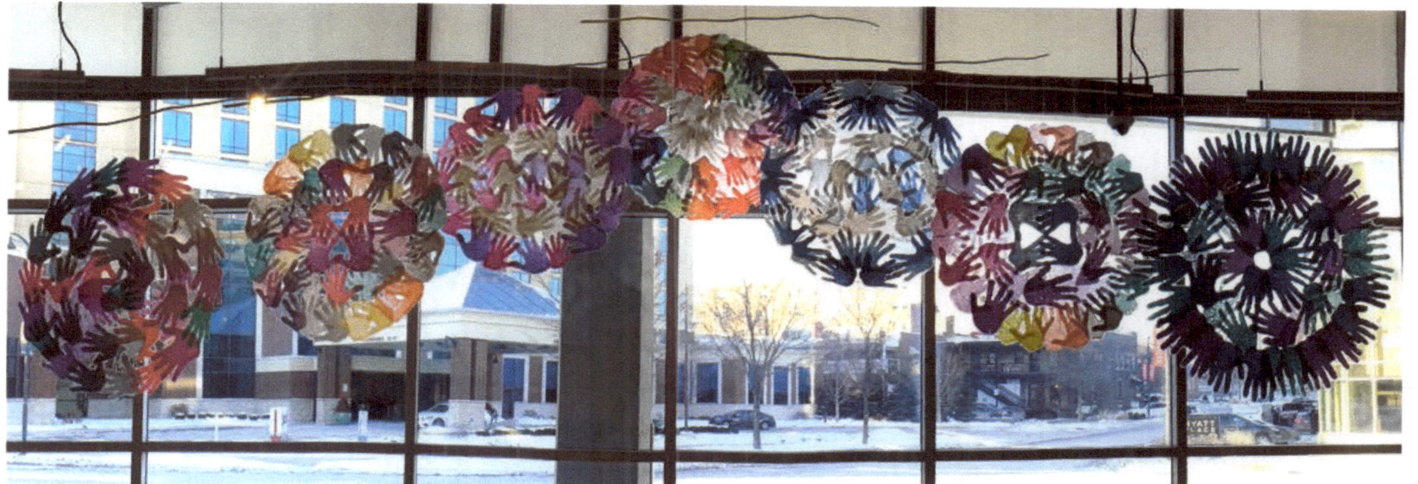

Inner Circles, University Galleries, Illinois State University, Normal, IL, pigmented handmade paper, threads, branches, 5' x 20' x 4', 2018

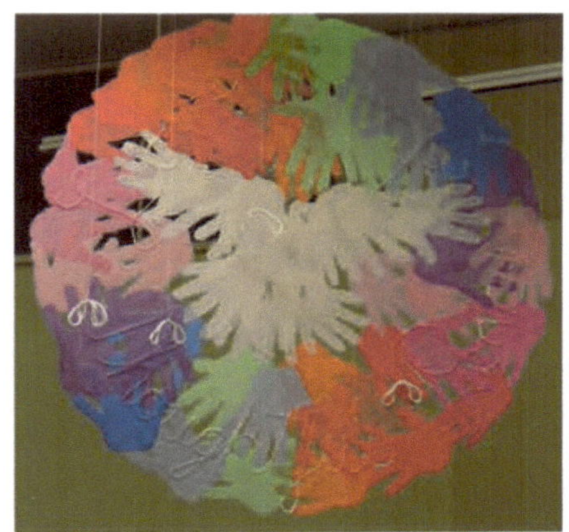

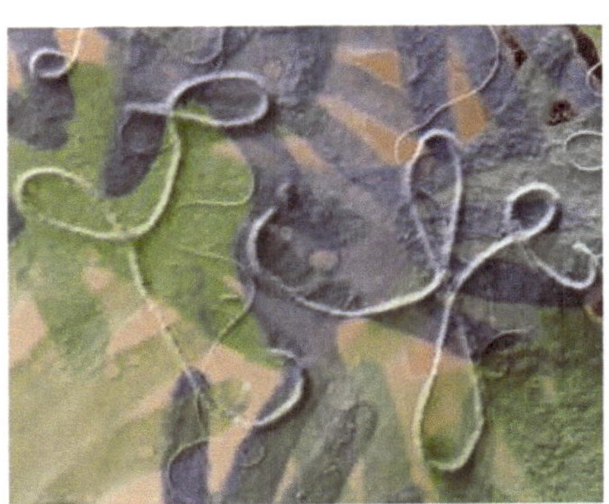

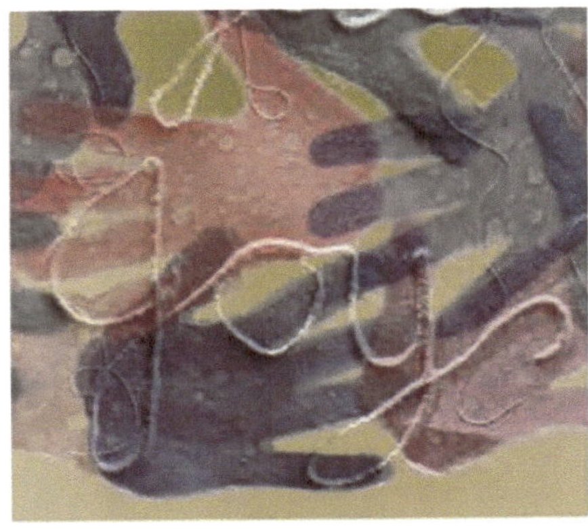

We create large-scale viewer interactive installations of handmade paper for which we coined the term "BookEnviron" to call attention to their status as large artists' books with a relationship to the environment. By concept and scale, BookEnvirons create immersion experiences for viewers who enter and explore the space shaped by the pages. Inspired by nature, seeking the sublime, BookEnvirons define actual spaces; pathways, arches, doors, which are metaphors for personal inner spaces that have no tangible structure. We intend our BookEnvirons to encourage viewers along mental and spiritual journeys, contemplating aspects of their own individual existence, beliefs, and destinations.

The term "inner circle" refers to the closest of friends and family — where we are truly known and unconditionally loved. Inside an inner circle the burdens of life's fiercest challenges are divided to conquer, joys are celebrated, and laughter is understanding. It is within these exceptional bonds that the *Inner Circle* series originates. At special occasions we ask attendees to trace the outline of their hands, suggest a color, and select a word that would serve as inspiration for random word poems. These unique verses are embedded with yarn in the handmade paper.

Awards and honors include: "Best of Show" *Liturgical and Sacred Art*, a national juried exhibition, Springfield, Illinois; "Honorable Mention" *Amateras Annual Paper Art*, an international group show, Sofia, Bulgaria; *Turning the Page: Contemporary Artists' Books*, a curated eight-artist exhibition at the Swope Art Museum, Terra Haute, Indiana; solo exhibitions at Judson University, Elgin, Illinois; Wentworth Institute of Technology, Boston, Massachusetts; and Georgetown College, Georgetown, Kentucky. Veda is Interim Director of Normal Editions Workshop in the School of Art at Illinois State University, Normal, Illinois. Meda has been a member of the art faculty at Heartland Community College in Normal, Illinois and Eureka College, Eureka, Illinois.

Meda Rae Rives Smith
Veda Mae Rives Aukerman
www.mirrorimagepress.com
info@mirrorimagepress.com

Follow me /JohnTorinaGallery

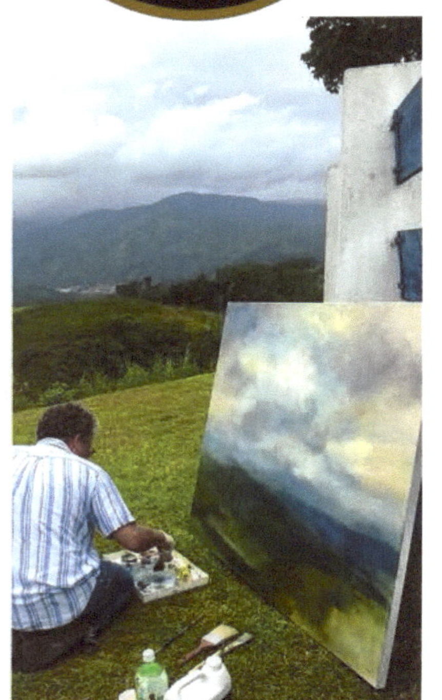

Working directly from life, wrestling wild forces, I find the challenge in painting is to materialize a state of intense pantheistic awareness. With raw attention to nature, painting is a physical, mental, and spiritual struggle that leads to a deep level of contemplation.

Rapid response to the ever-changing vista engages a certain automatism which endows the work with an energy conjured up from the depths of the unconscious. Beyond the immediate optical decisions are invisible elemental powers that give rise to abstract impulses.

The process of life, death, and rebirth is imprinted on all of the universe and is reflected in the silent witness of my work. To extrapolate from the words of Saint Paul: "Now we see in a glass darkly, but when we see face to face the function of iconography will cease".[Artist Statement]

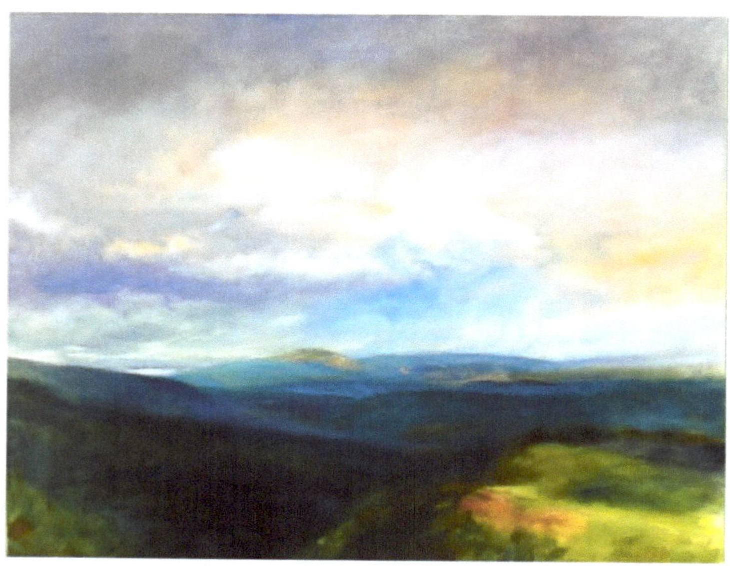

Sunrise in the Mountains | 48"x60"

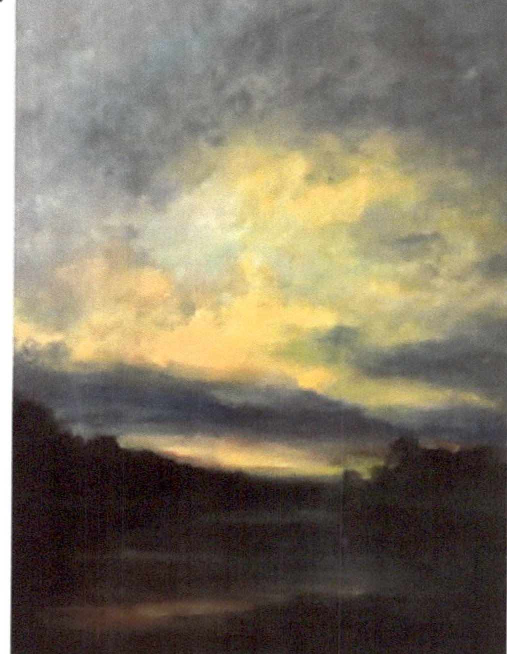

Mississippi River Channel | 36"x48"

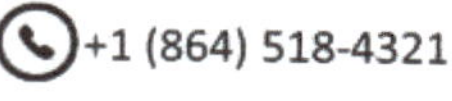
+1 (864) 518-4321

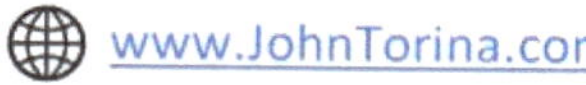
www.JohnTorina.com

johntorina.fineart@gmail.com

Follow me /JohnTorinaGallery

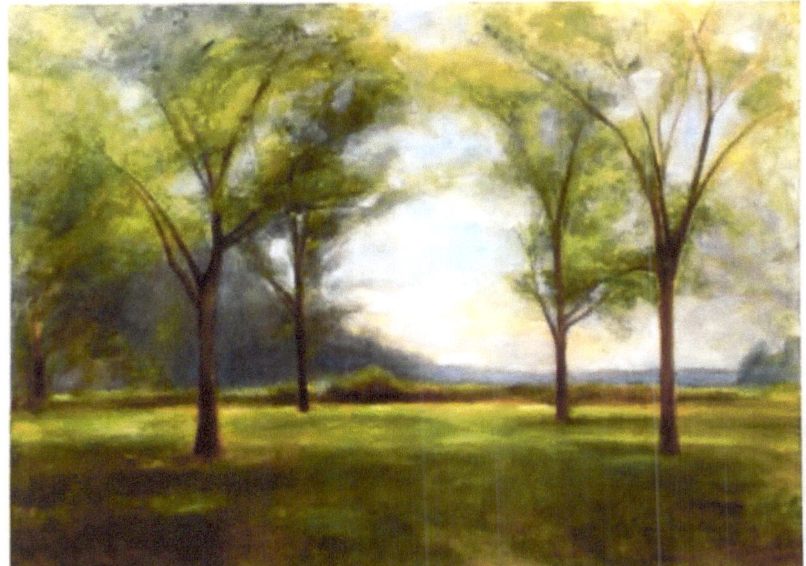

Pecan Grove | 5'x 6'

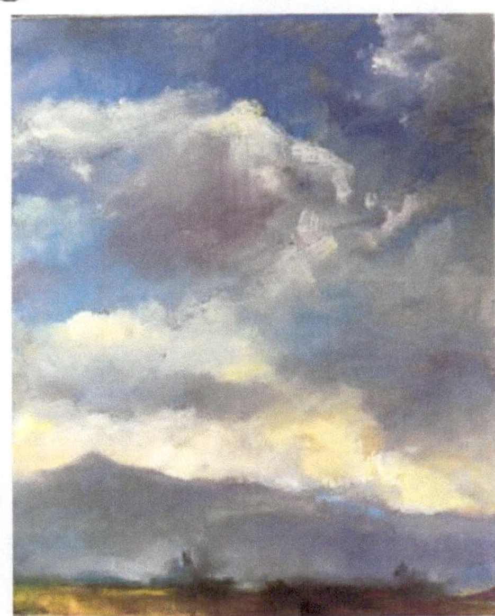

Moving Clouds over the Mountains | 48"x36"

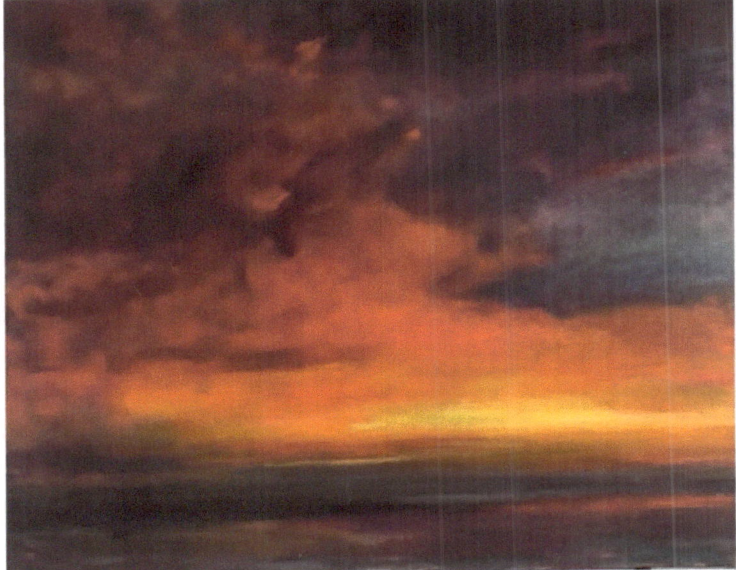

The Fire and The Water | 48" x 60"

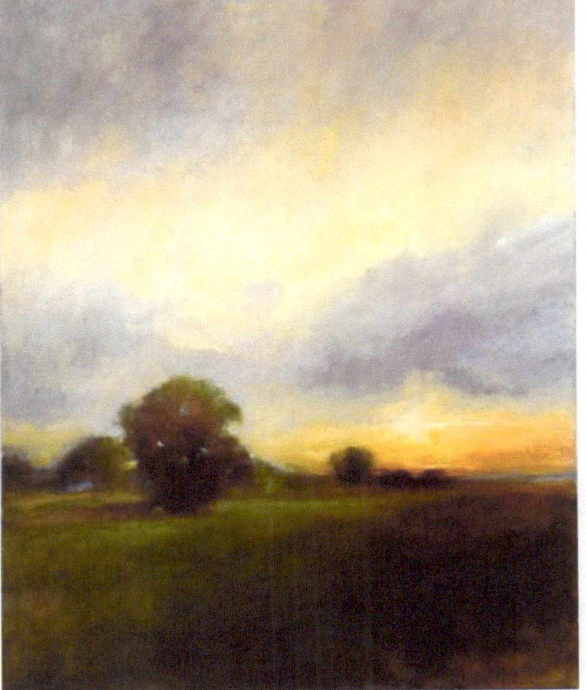

Shelby Farms | 60"x48"

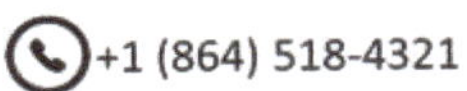
+1 (864) 518-4321

www.JohnTorina.com

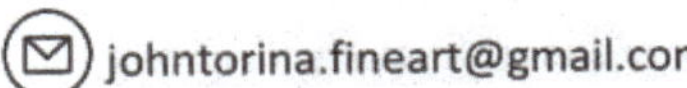
johntorina.fineart@gmail.com

April Ford Beasley

Having been interested in Art and Photography from a young age, I began shooting photos with my Barbie film camera. From there, I majored in Imaging Arts. While in college, I focused on working with Black and White film. I began to try different types of film and eventually found myself shooting with a Polaroid One Step. Being from the South and having a love for nostalgia, I began to focus on the Southern landscape such as vintage signage, advertising, old buildings, and typography. I would describe my work as Southern Documentary. One of my favorite things about shooting with a Polaroid is the viewer usually questions if the photo is present day or from the 70's or 80's.

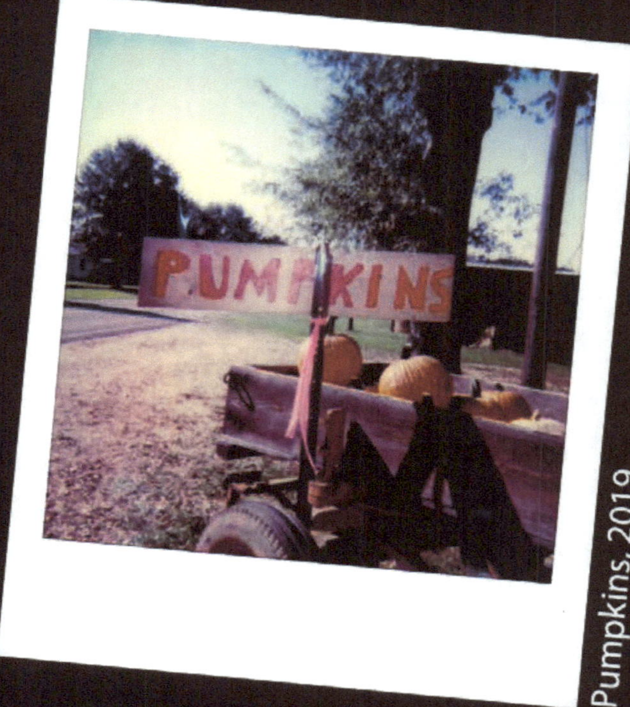

Pumpkins, 2019

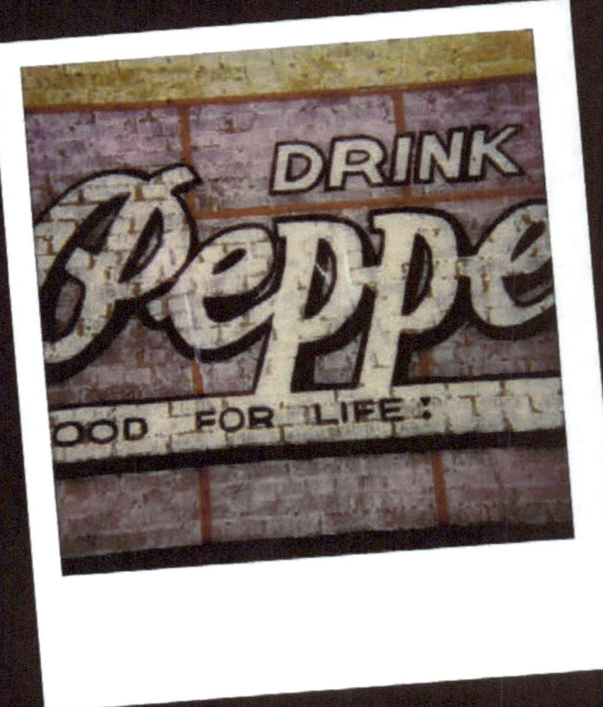

Dr Pepper, 2018

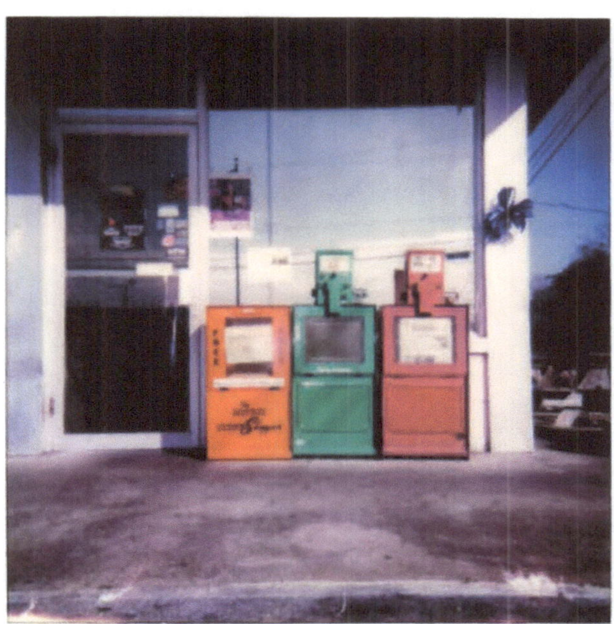

Dairy Kream, 2017

Oshkosh, 2018

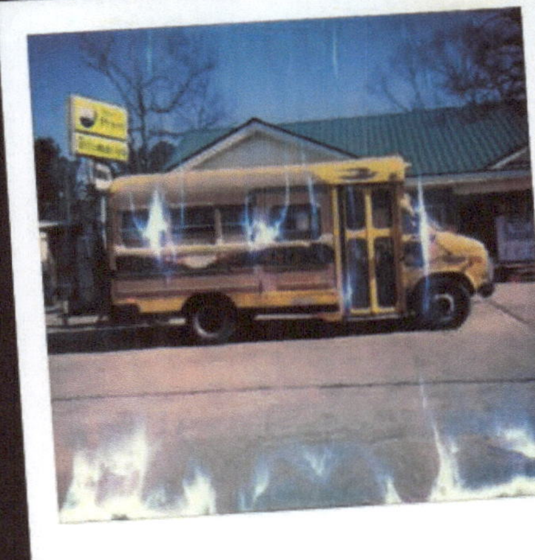

Short Bus, 2018

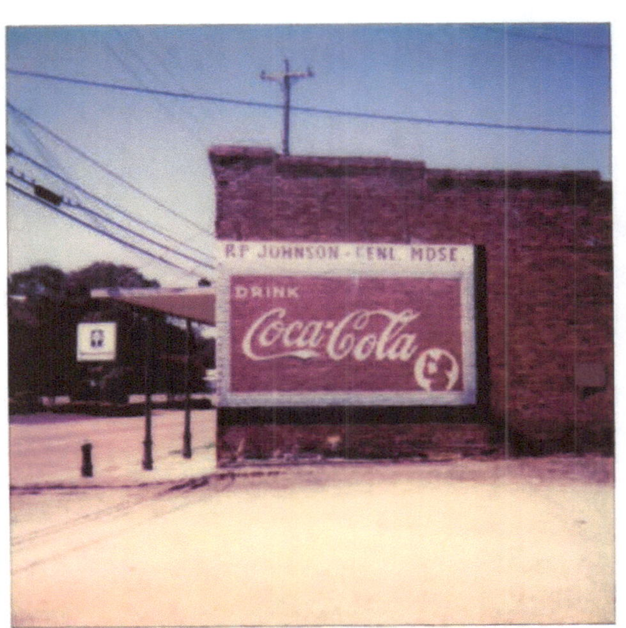

Coke, 2017

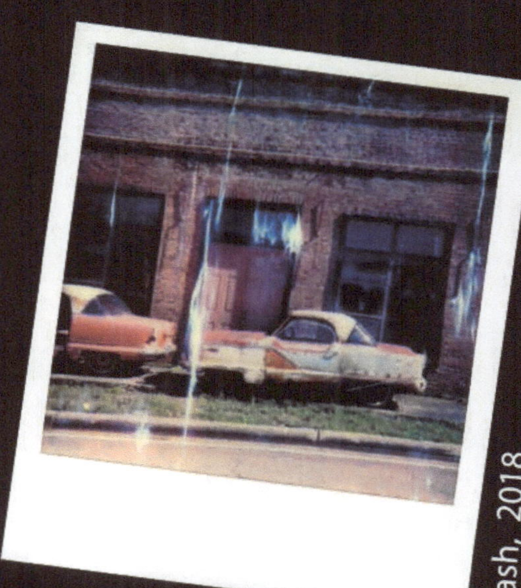

Nash, 2018

Patrick McMillan

Metalsmith Jeweler
Rhode Island, USA

www.mcmillanmetals.com
www.thebenchri.com
@mcmillanmetals
@thebenchri

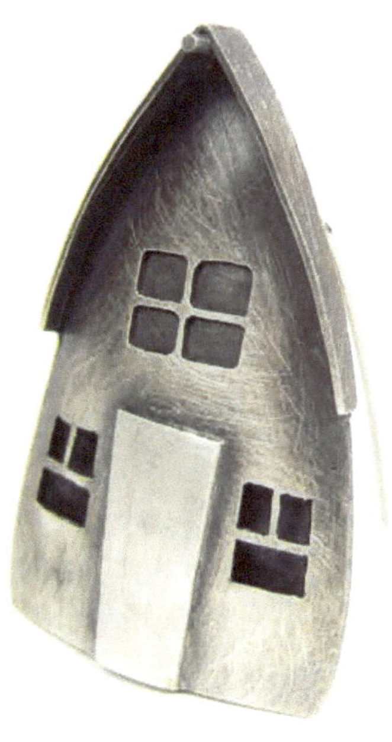

"LIttle Bird House"
Sterling Silver

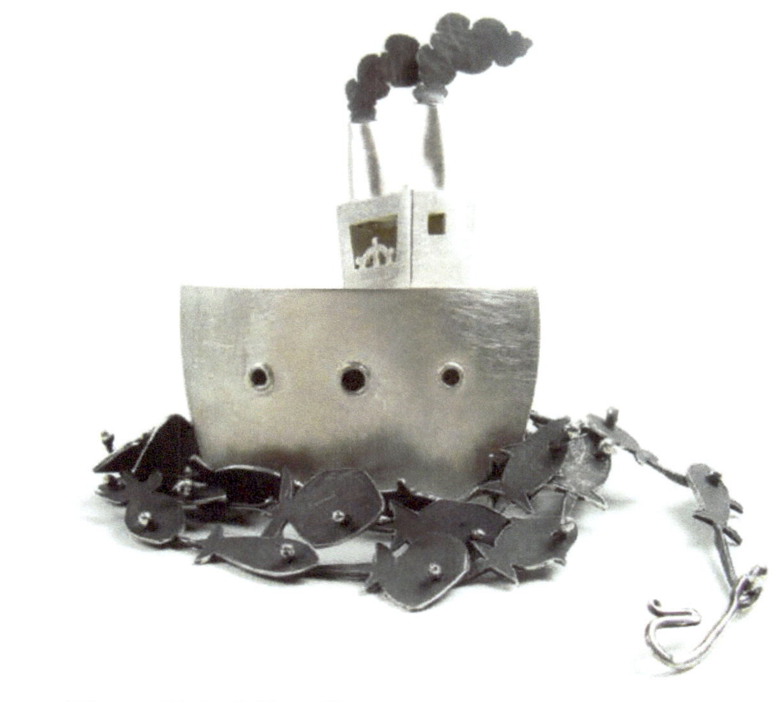

"Sea Side View"
Sterling Silver

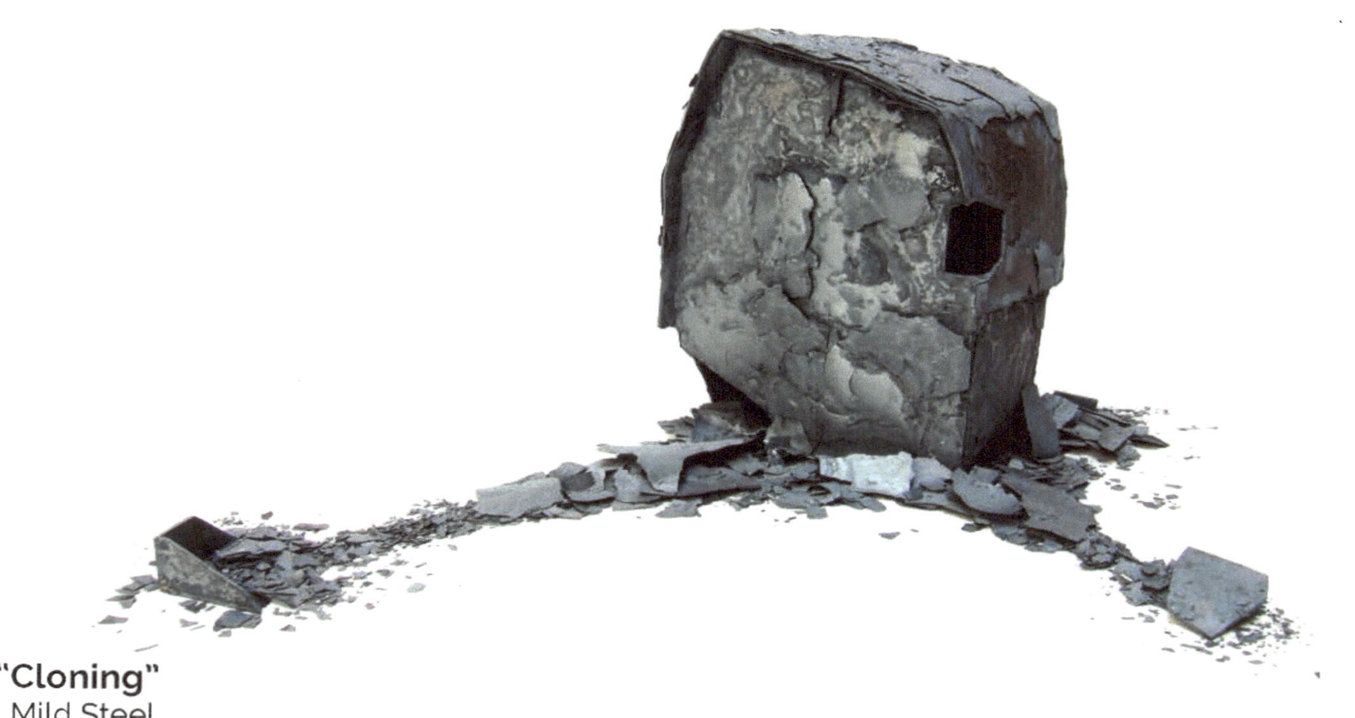

"Cloning"
Mild Steel

Patrick McMillan

Metalsmith Jeweler
Rhode Island, USA

www.mcmillanmetals.com
www.thebenchri.com
@mcmillanmetals
@thebenchri

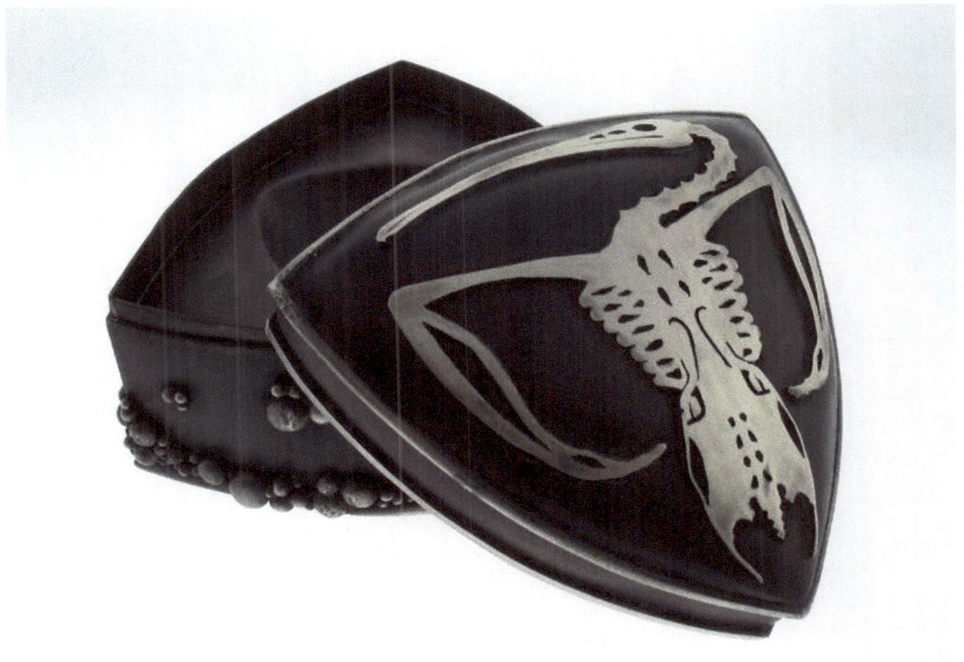

"Reliquary"
Sterling Silver, Copper

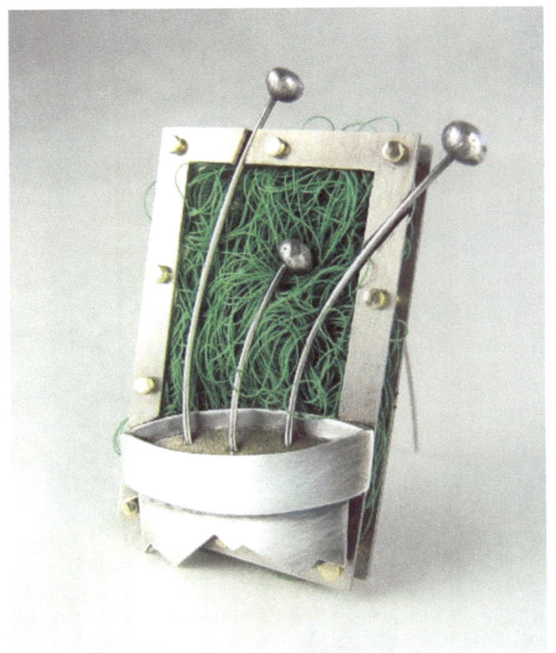

"A Garden View"
Sterling Silver, Brass, Nickel, Green Thread

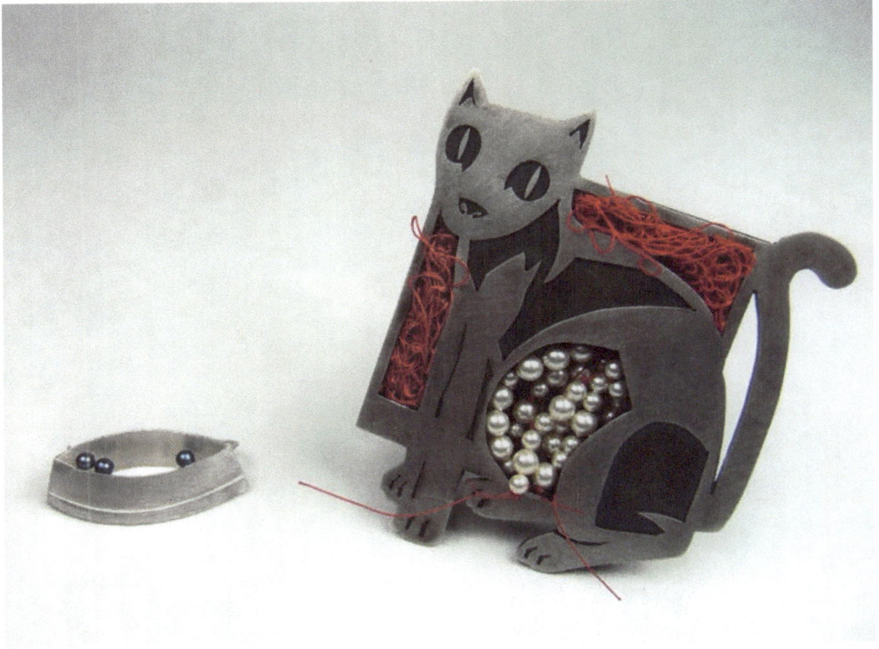

"The Pearl Thief"
Sterling Silver, Nickel, Pearls, Red Thread

ROBB DENNEY

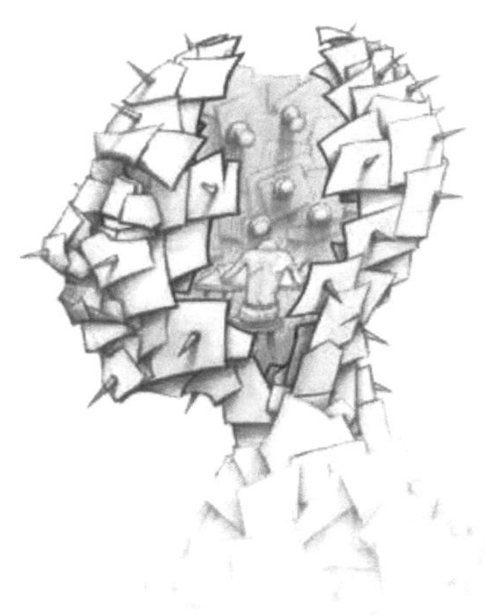

"My Memory Decor", 2003, graphite

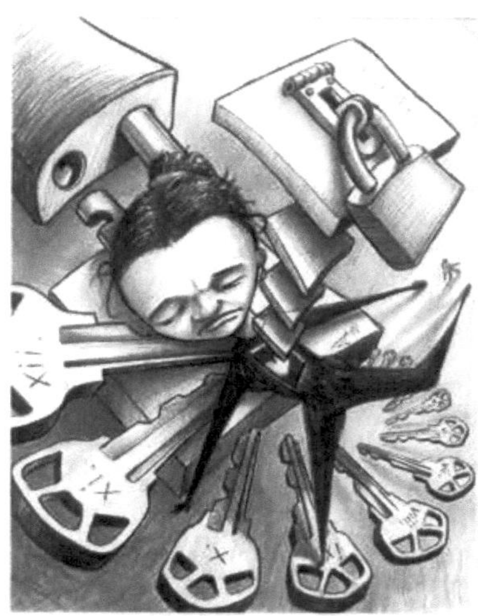

"Key Heart", 2003, graphite

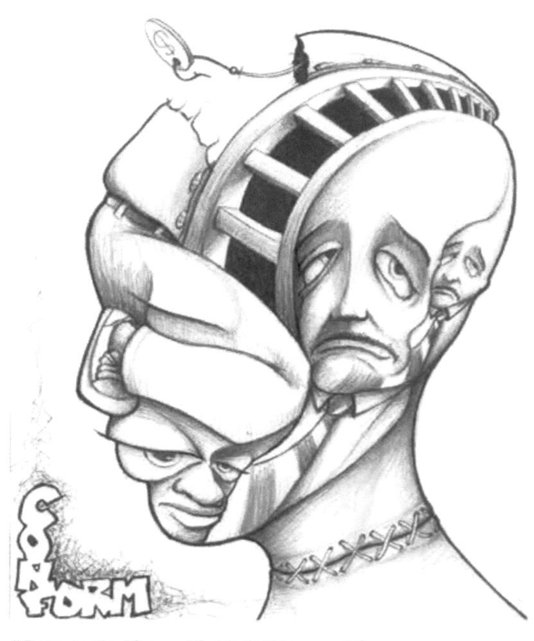

"Corporate Masochist", 2003, graphite

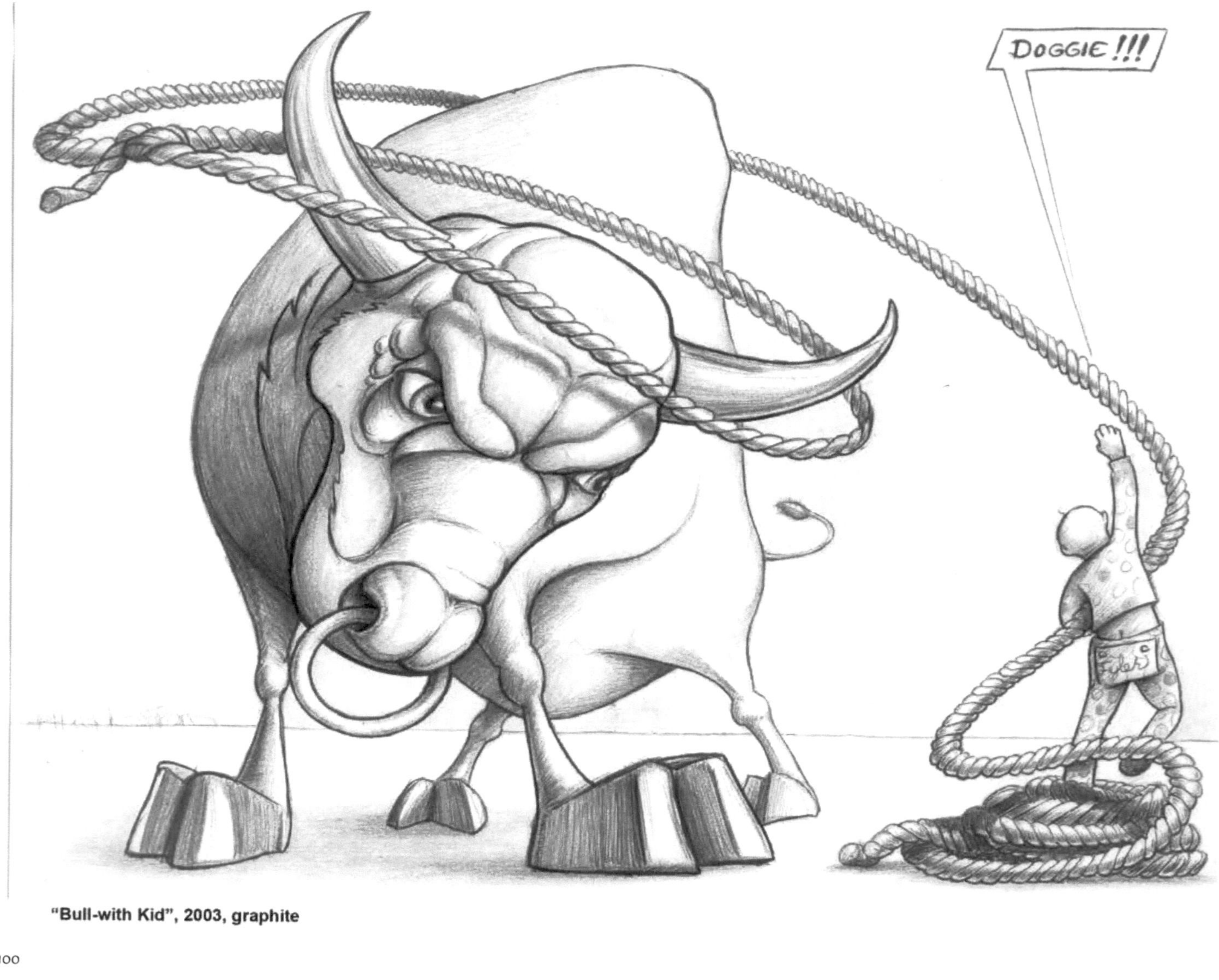

"Bull-with Kid", 2003, graphite

ROBB DENNEY

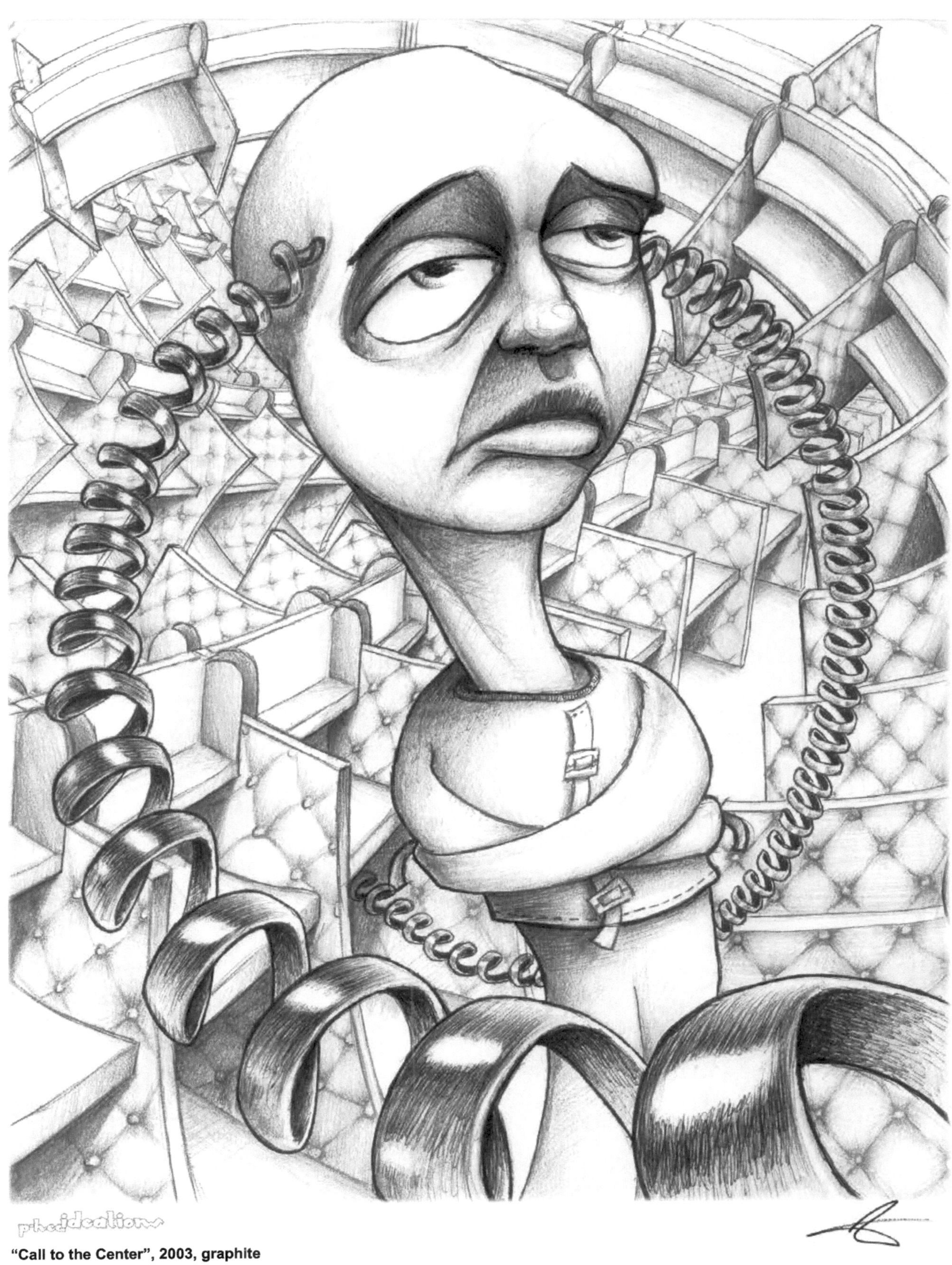

"Call to the Center", 2003, graphite

HELEN STUBBLEFIELD

www.helenofmemphis.com

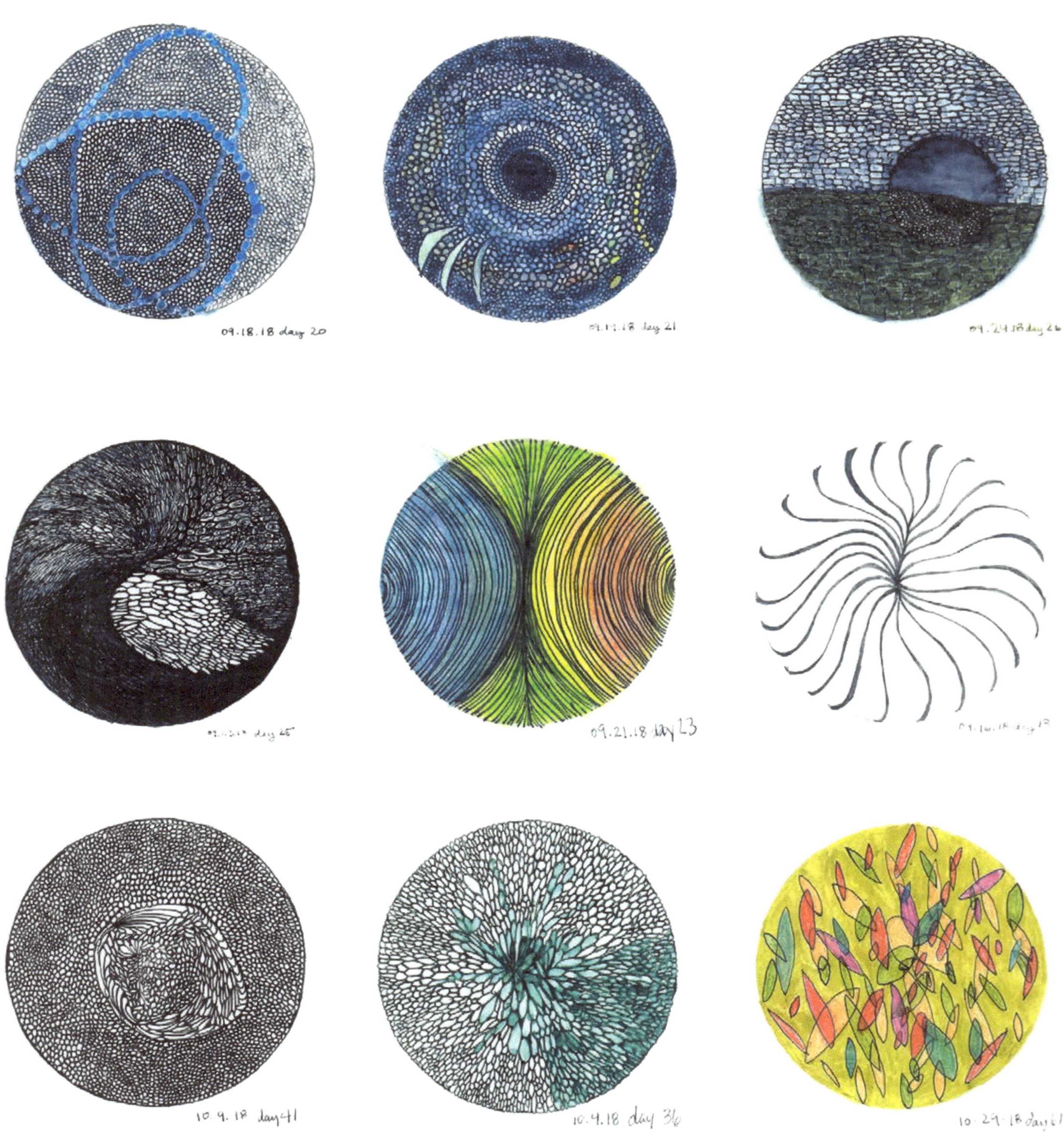

Pen and ink on Tomoe River paper 3 1/2" circumference Part of a series of 250 daily drawings

HELEN STUBBLEFIELD

www.helenofmemphis.com

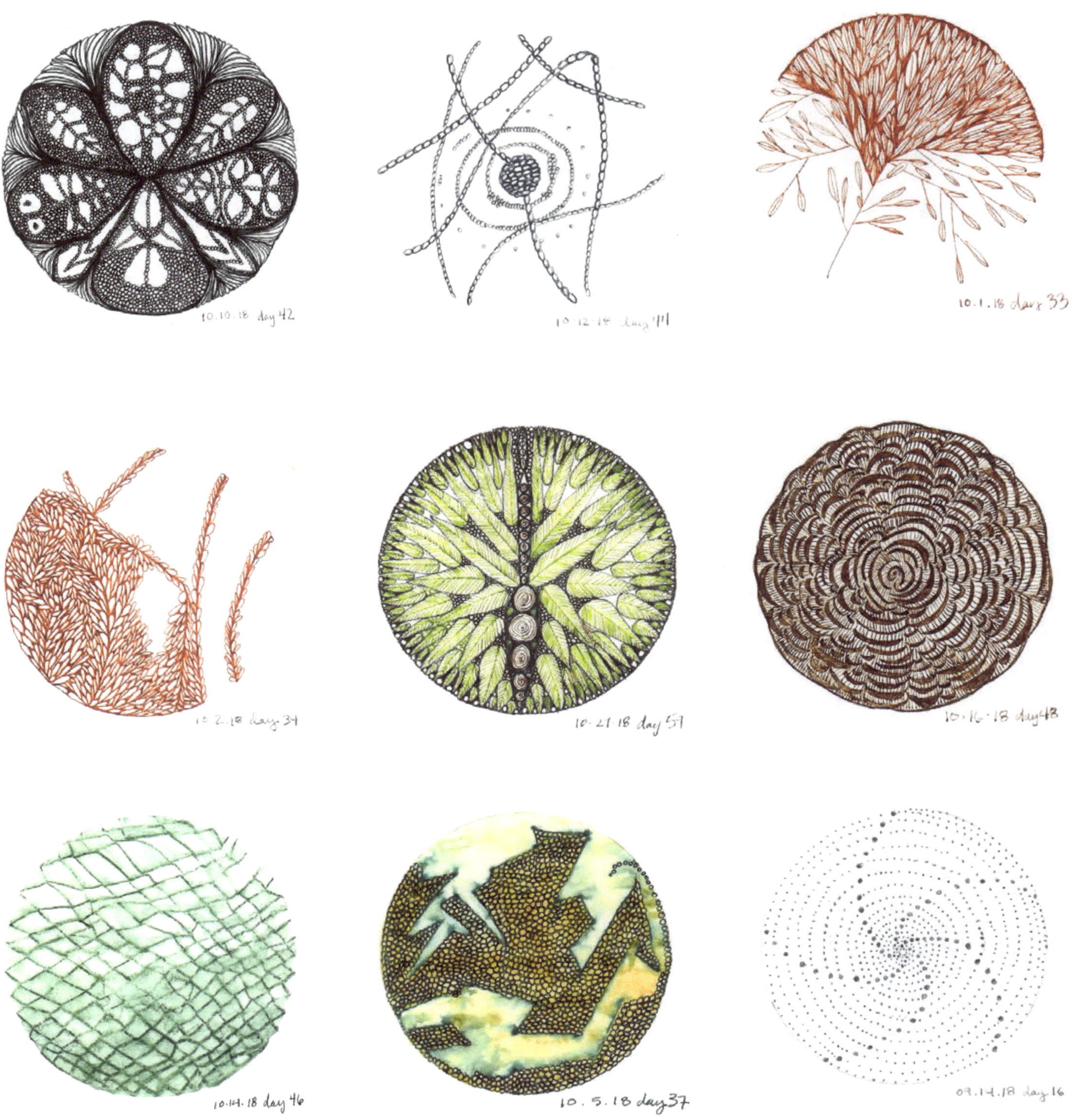

Pen and ink on Tomoe River paper 3 1/2" circumference Part of a series of 250 daily drawings

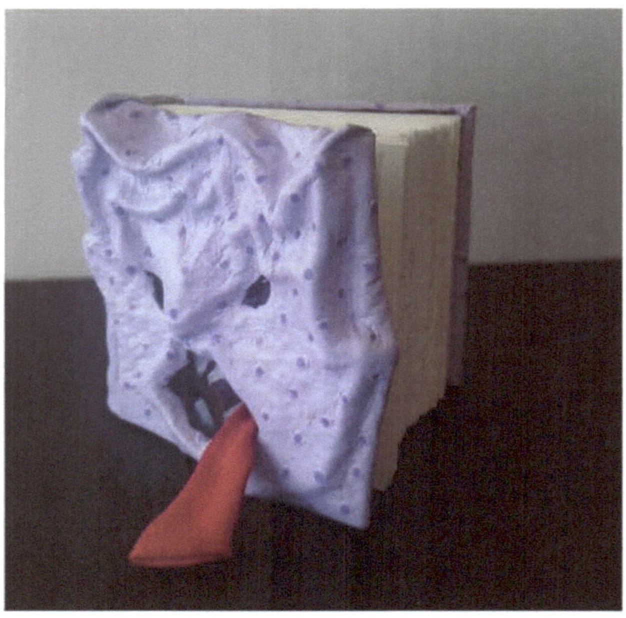

"MINE. But if you dare...." 2017 Le Monster Part Boo! A reimagination of a drawing by Le Bonheur patient Jay'Von Ross age 4

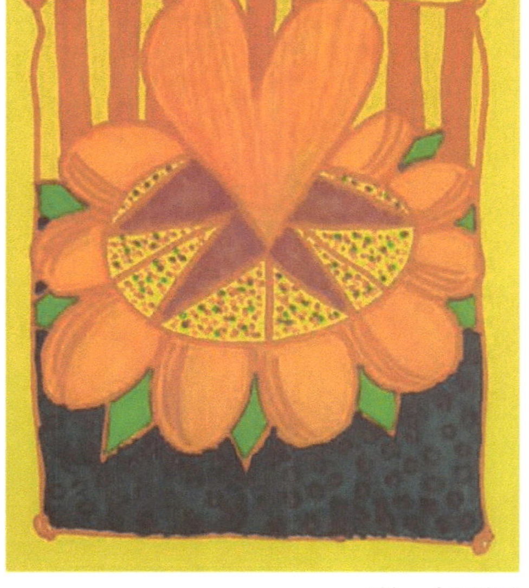

"Sketch" 2017

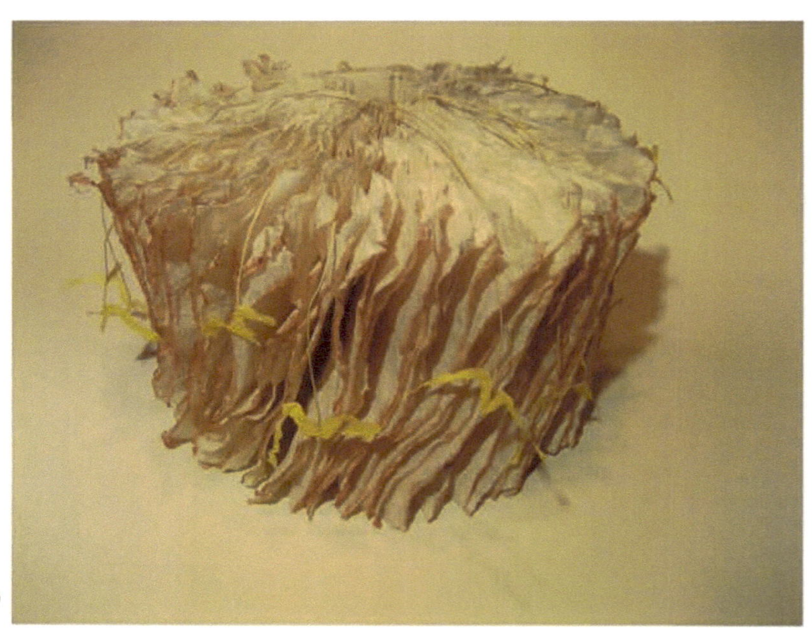

"Ghost River Book" 2010

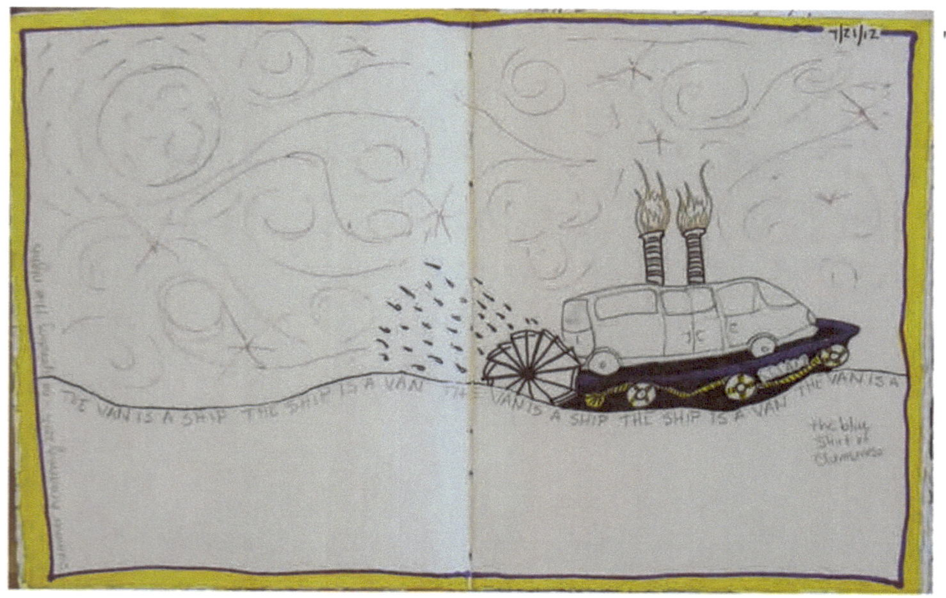

"Sketch Summer Academy" 2012

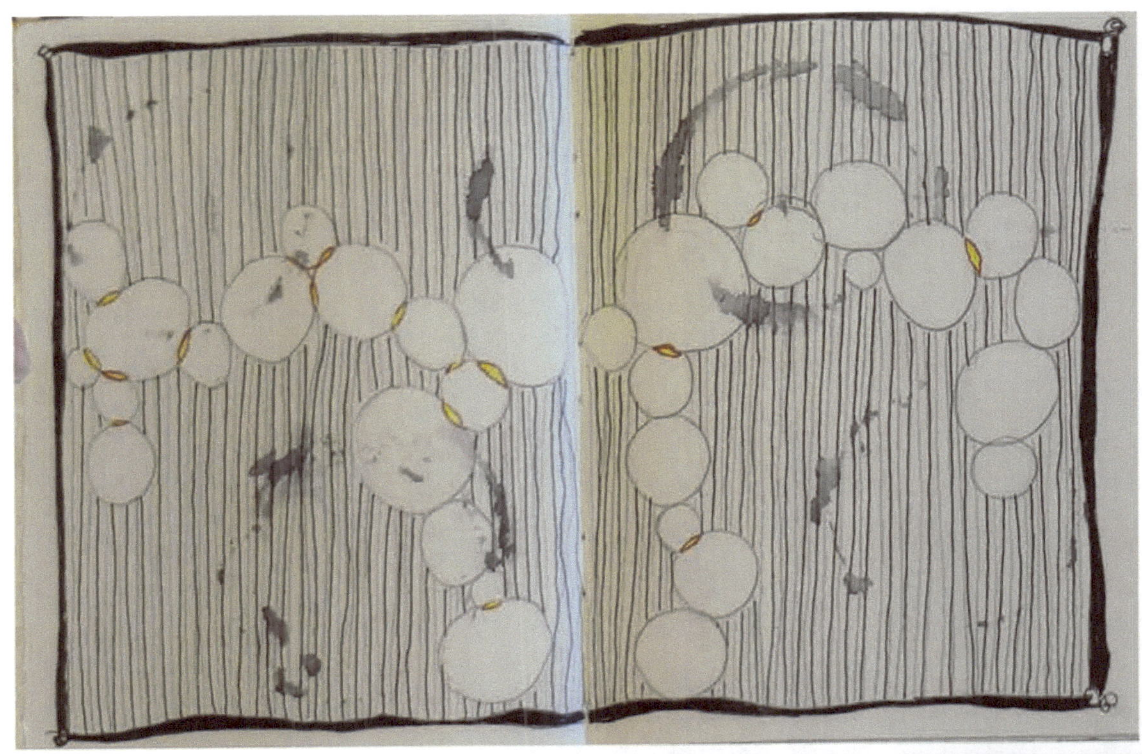

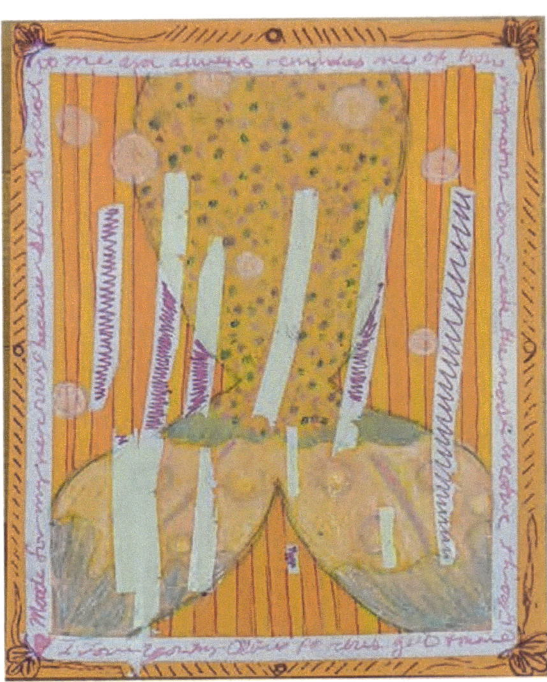

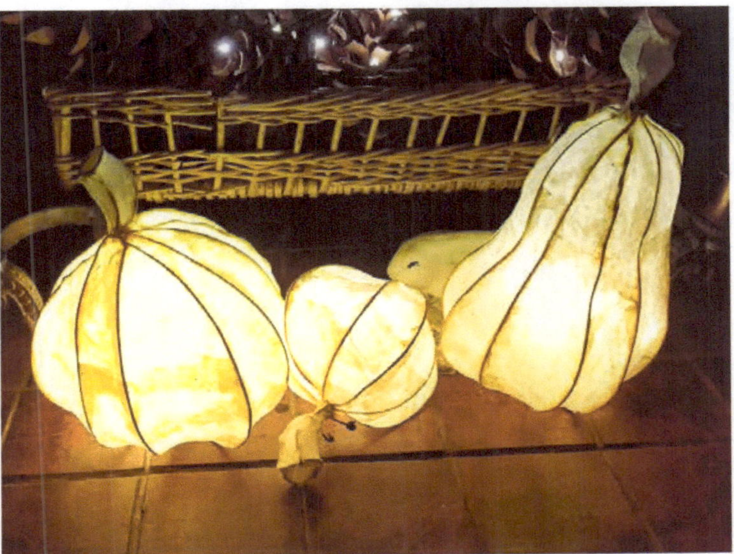

"Sketch 7:13" 2013; "Olive is a Mermaid Tale" 2019; "Tres Calabaza Resplandor" 2019

I adore making handmade paper and books. There is a comforting rhythm to the process with opportunities to this way of making lending themselves to recording memory, still hidden secrets, wishes, and incantations. The creation becomes a vessel for future imaginations while, perhaps unknowingly, carrying already stowed information. This way of working is echoed using memory, color, and form in patternmaking. These pieces explore perceived memories, moments in time, and decoration.

Katey Henriksen Gardner, MCA class of 1997. Double Major in Fine (Print & Papermaking) and Design Arts (Graphic Design) MCA Admissions 1999-2017
It has been a great honor to be responsible for ushering in artists to the MCA family I have always loved. My heart is full.

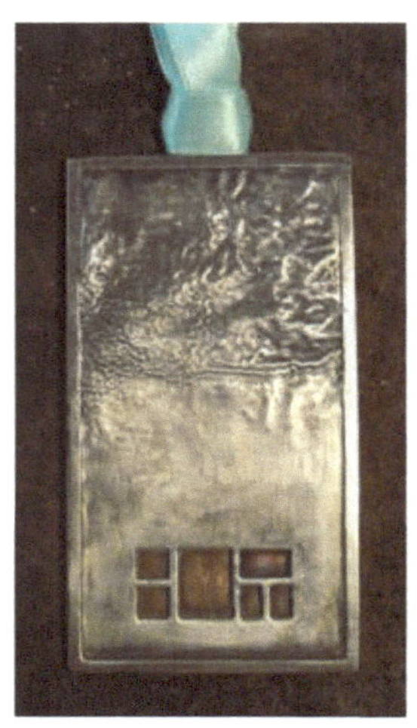
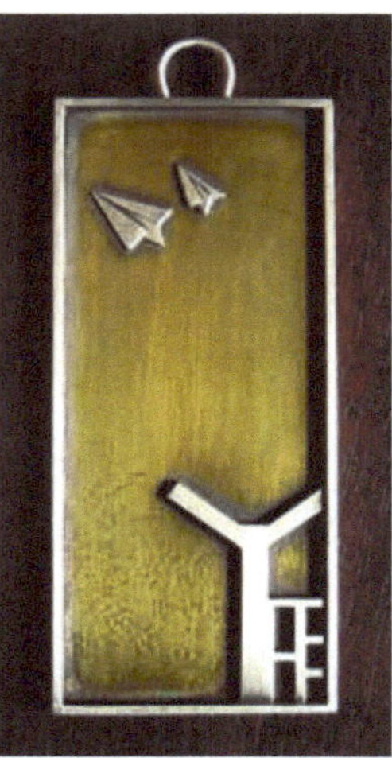
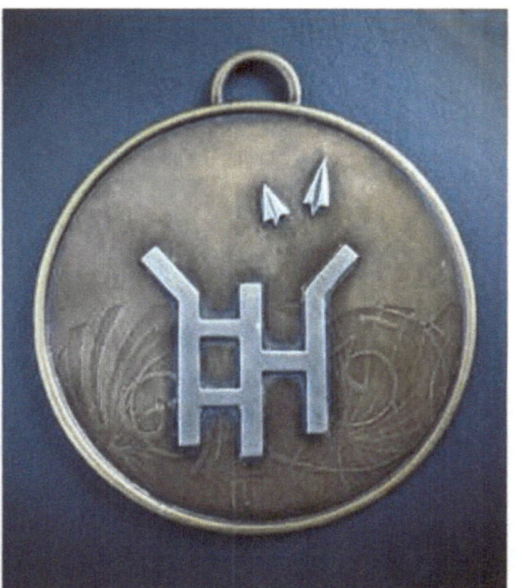
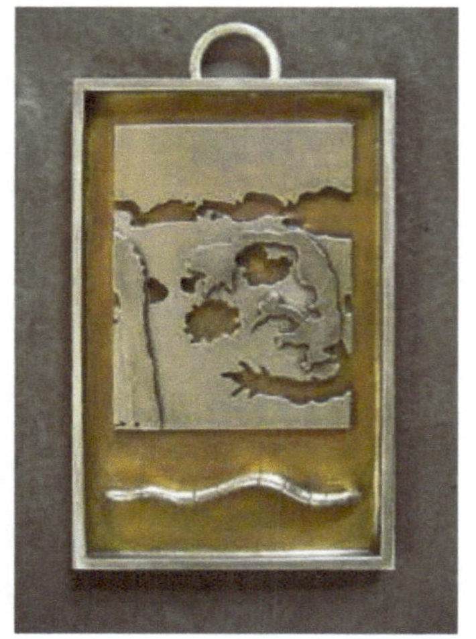
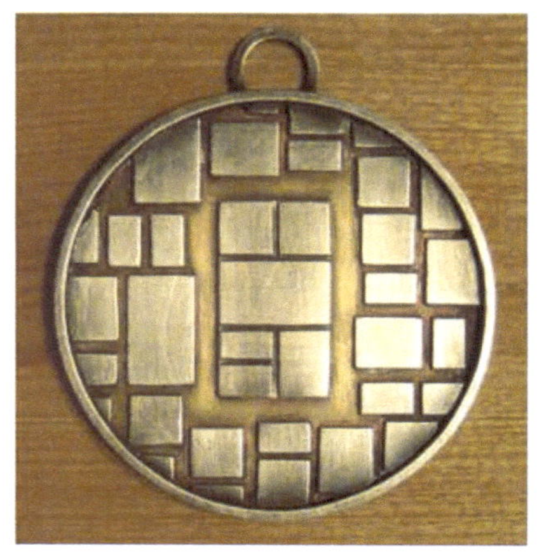
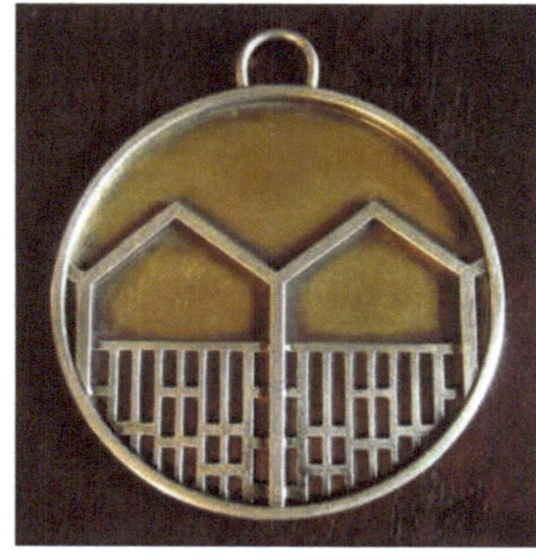
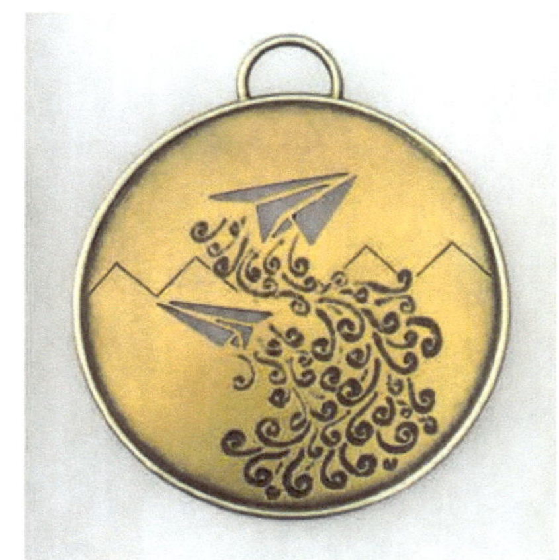
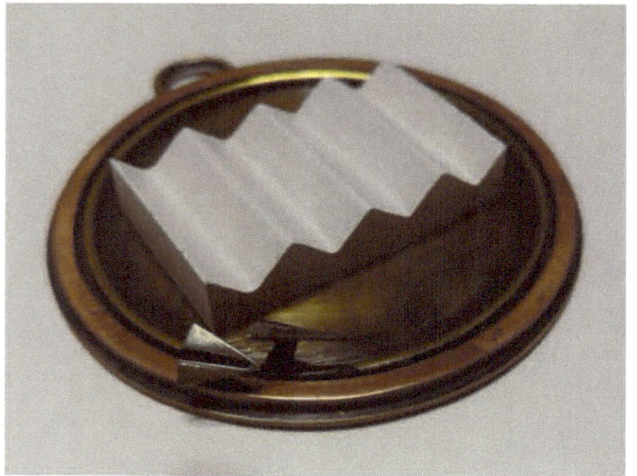
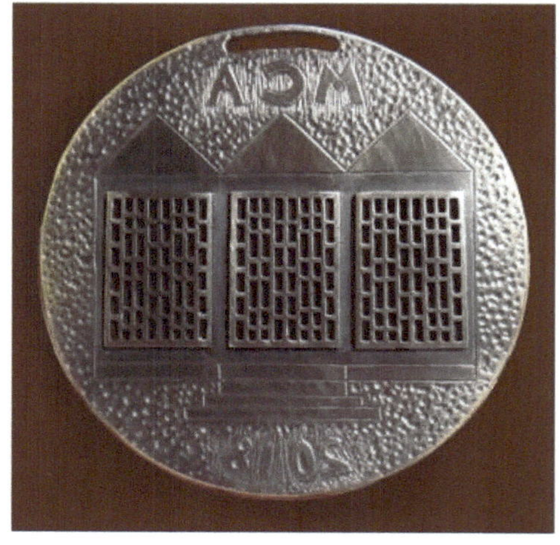

Jason Gardner

Awards for Memphis College of Art

2008 - 2020

Metal and Wood

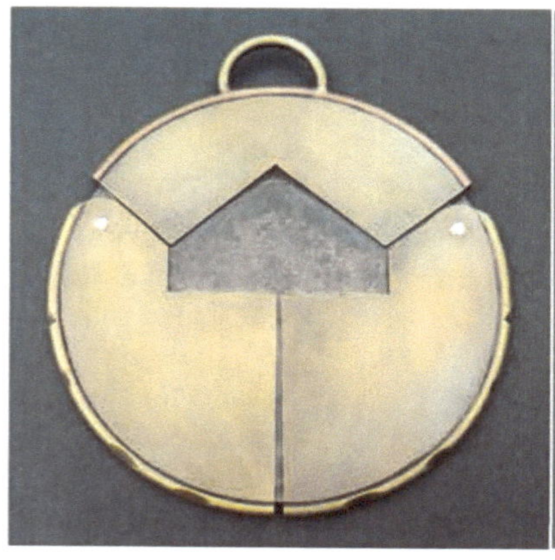
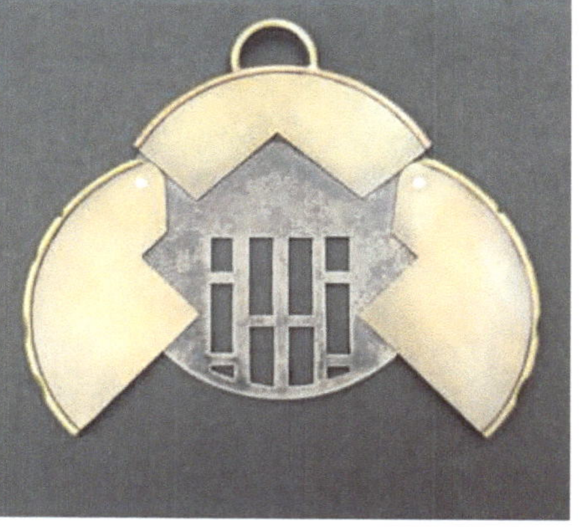
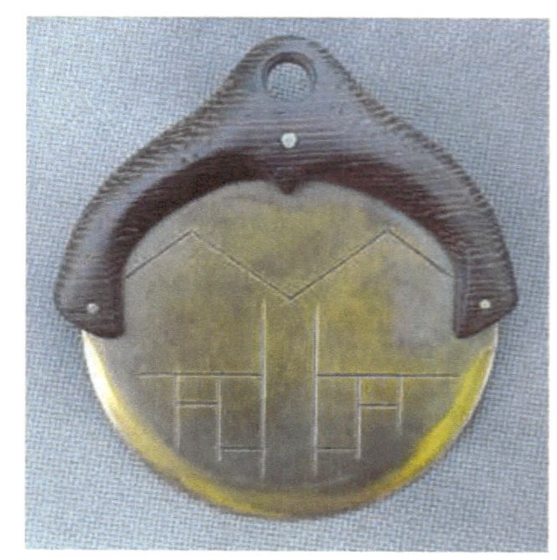

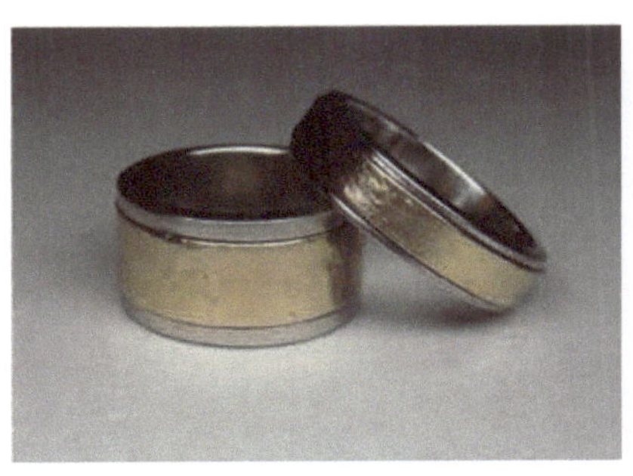
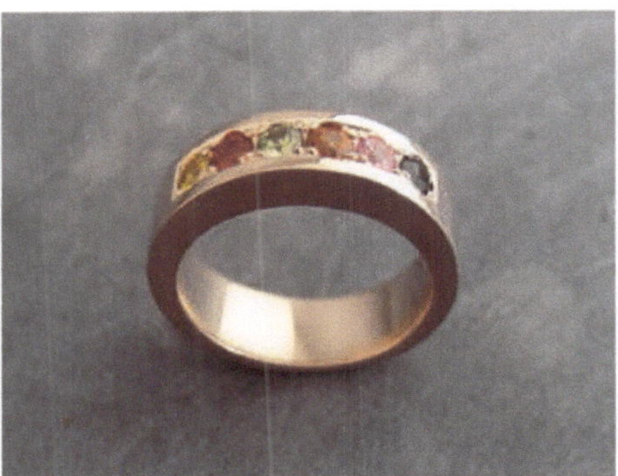
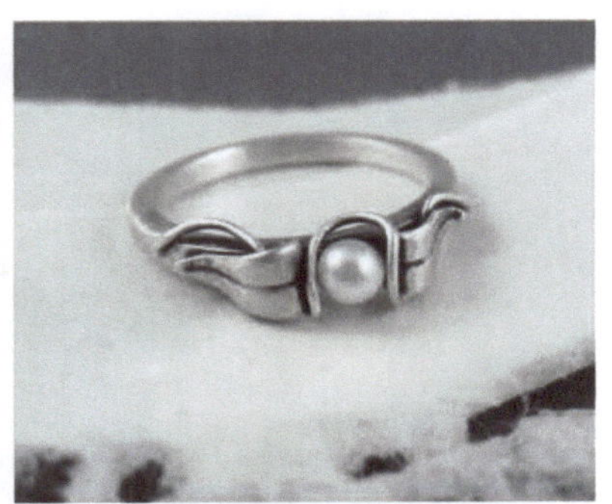
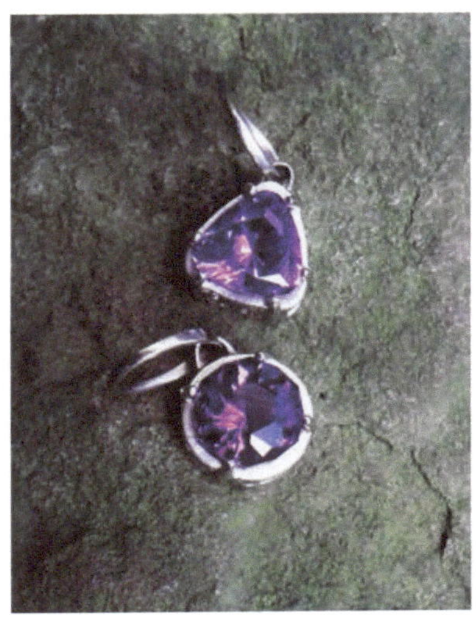
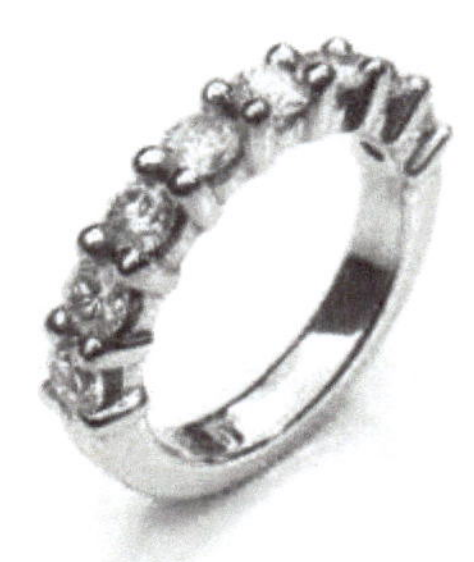
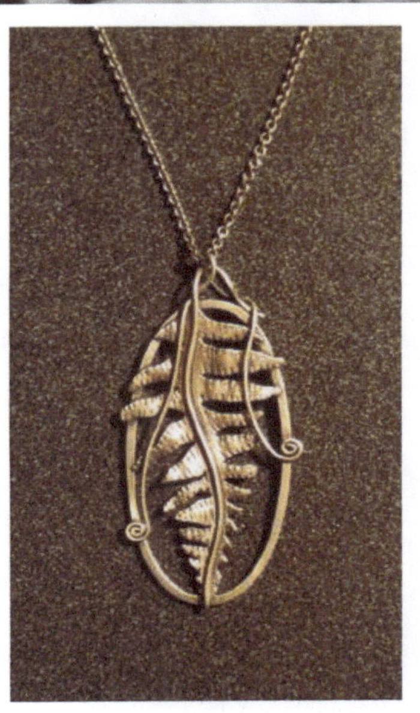
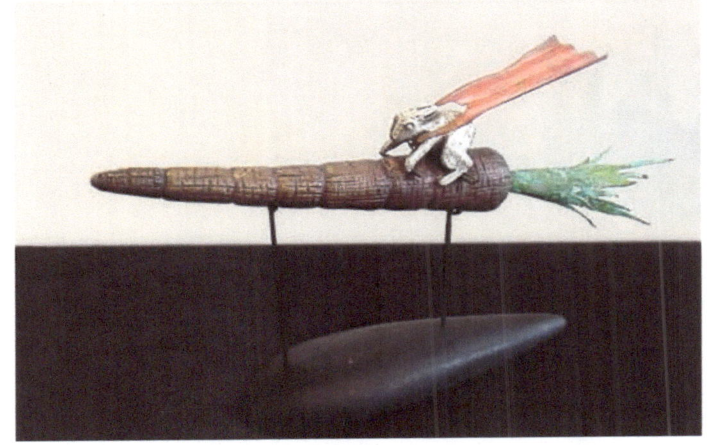
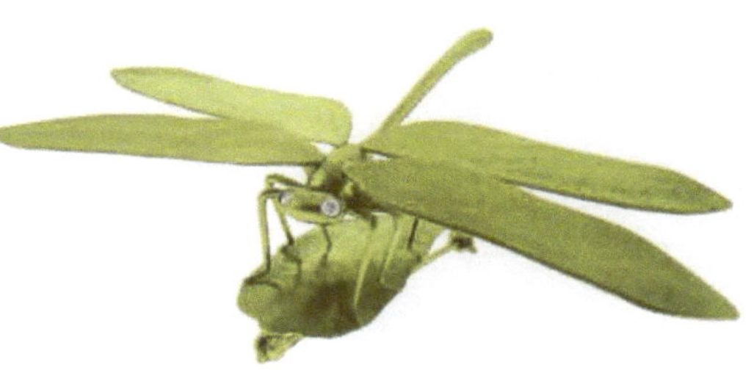
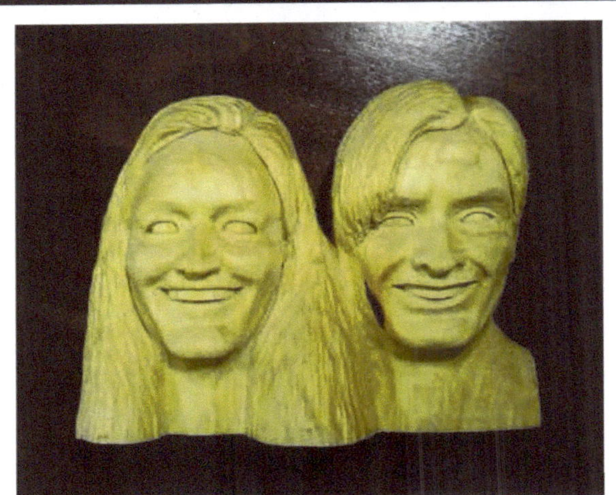

Jason Gardner

BFA Metal Sculpture
1995 - 2000

Various Works in Metal and Wood

TARA BULLINGTON, FLORENCE, ALABAMA

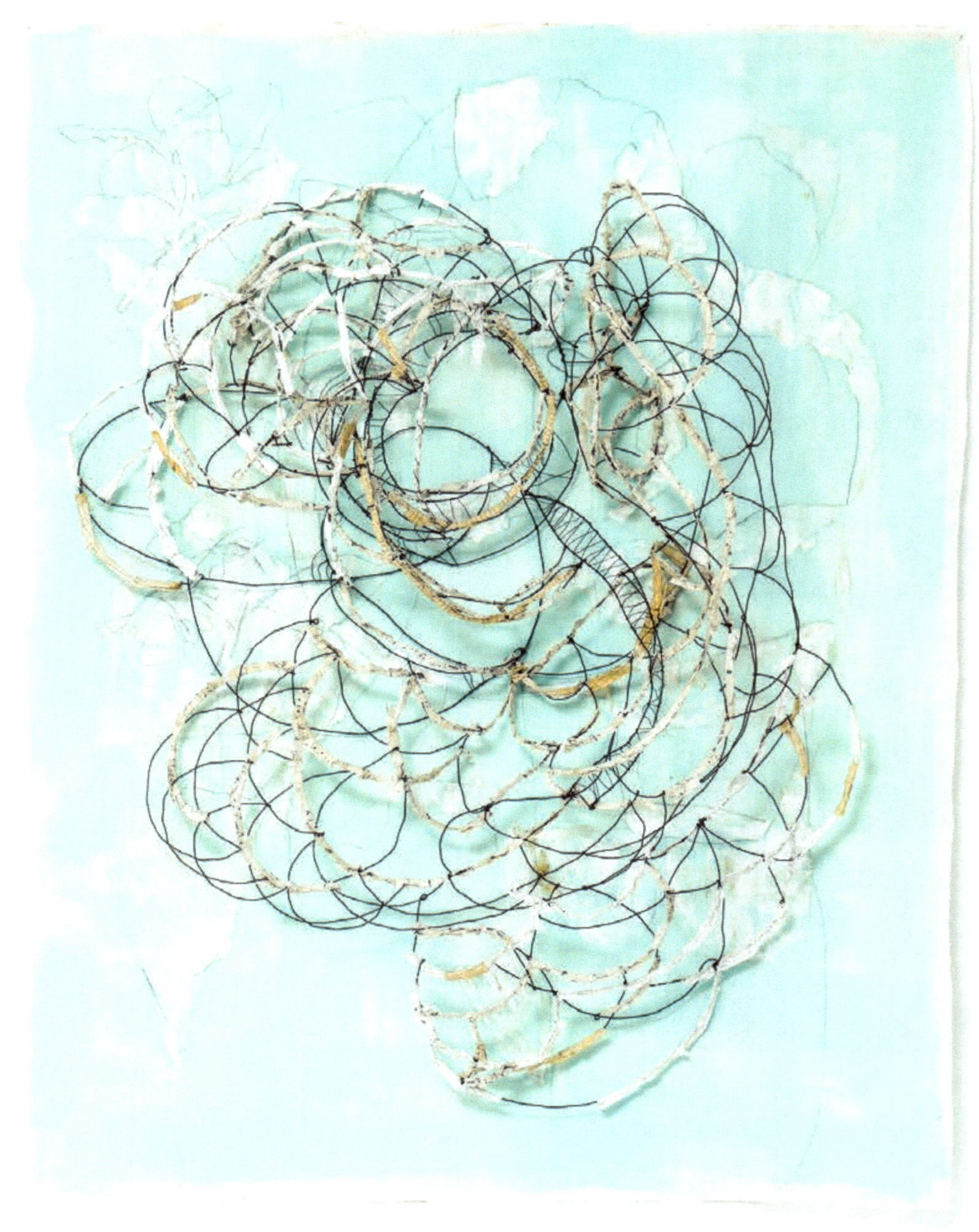

WINTER'S SONG / WIRE, PAINT, PAPER / 4'x6'x1'

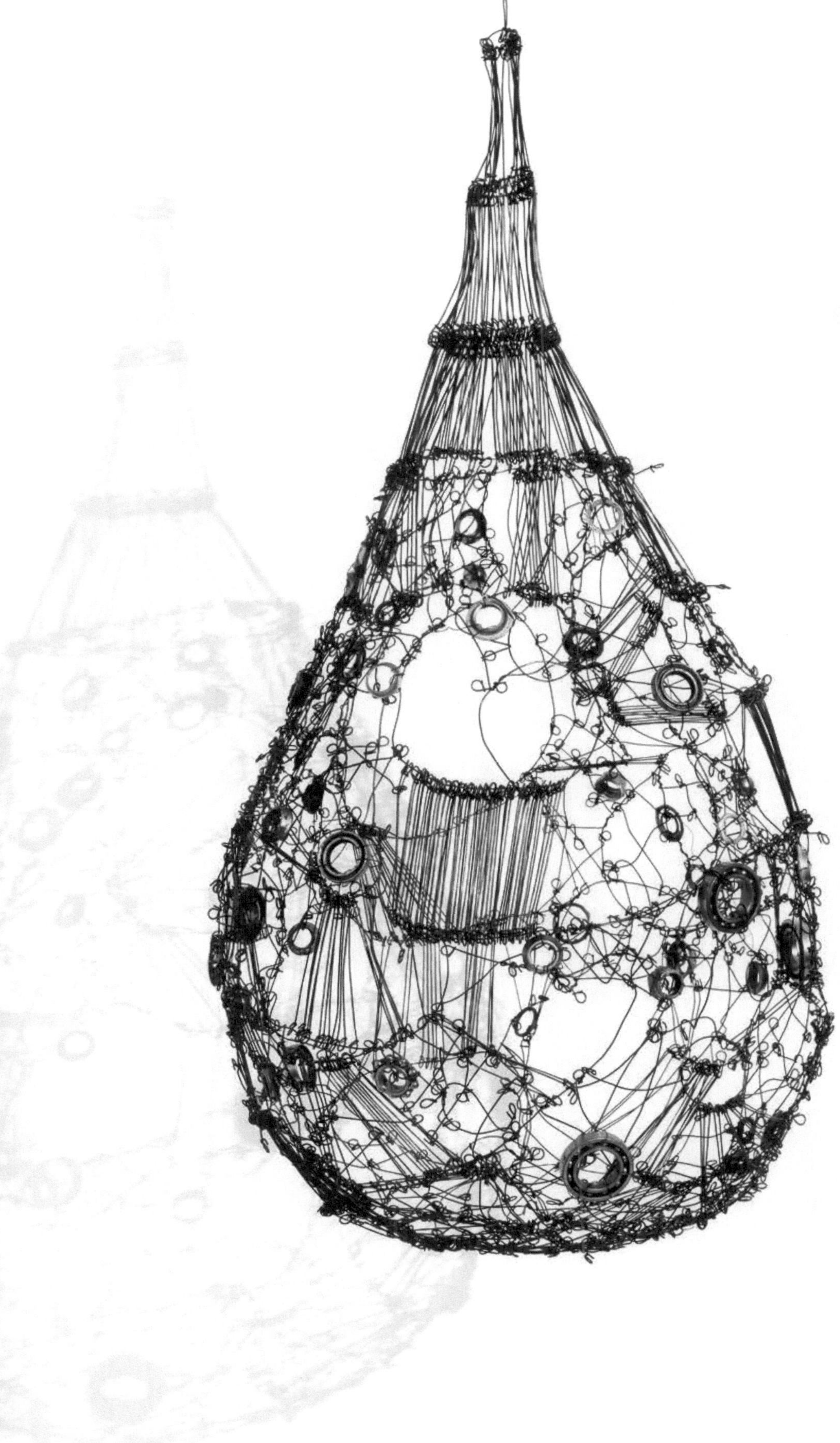

TARA BULLINGTON

SUBCONTEXTUAL / WIRE / 5'x 3.5'x 3.5'

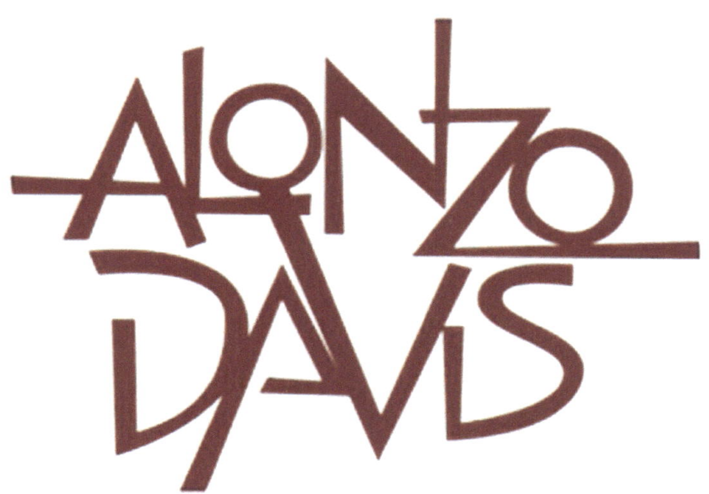

"NOW IS THE TIME"
BY ALONZO DAVIS

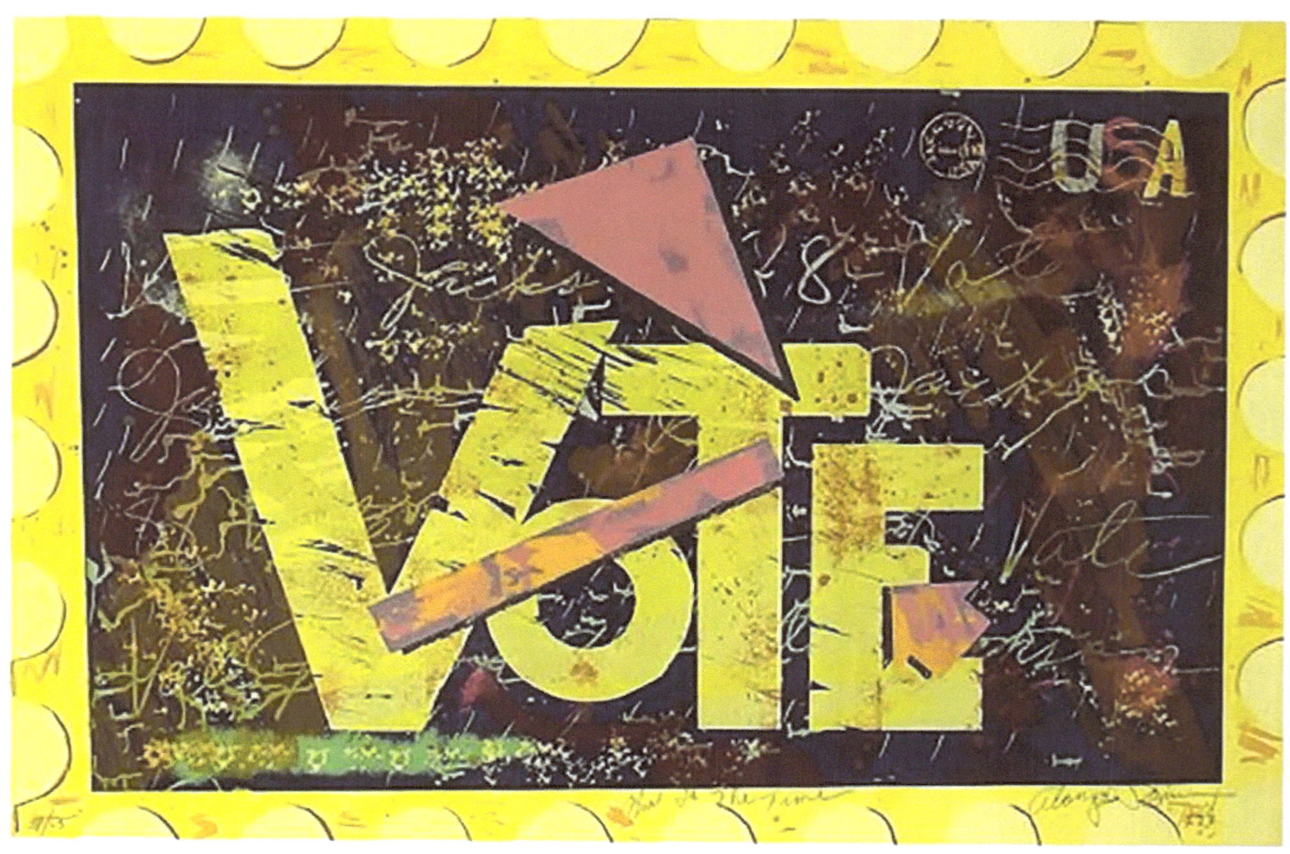

SILKSCREEN 1988
EDITION 3/55

EACH WORK OF ART IN THIS COLLECTION WAS OBTAINED WITH PERMISSION FROM THE ARTIST.

PAGE 58
"self-portrait on wacom tablet"
©2010
Jina Anne
www.sushiandrobots.com
Instagram: @jina
Twitter: @jina

PAGE 59
"photo manipulation"
©2012
Jina Anne
www.sushiandrobots.com
Instagram: @jina
Twitter: @jina

PAGE 97
"Dairy Kream"
©2017
April Ford Beasley
Instagram: @applefork

PAGE 97
"Coke"
©2017
April Ford Beasley
Instagram: @applefork

PAGE 97
"Oshkosh"
©2018
April Ford Beasley
Instagram: @applefork

PAGE 97
"Short Bus"
©2018
April Ford Beasley
Instagram: @applefork

PAGE 97
"Nash"
©2018
April Ford Beasley
Instagram: @applefork

PAGE 96
"Pumpkins"
©2019
April Ford Beasley
Instagram: @applefork

PAGE 96
"Dr Pepper"
©2018
April Ford Beasley
Instagram: @applefork

PAGE 32
"Heavier Than Expected"
©2019
Kelli Black
www.kelliblackprojects.com

PAGE 32
"It Went Real Good:
Self-Portrait in Childhood Home"
©2018
Kelli Black
www.kelliblackprojects.com

PAGE 33
"Untitled"
©2020
Kelli Black
www.kelliblackprojects.com

PAGE 48
"alone together"
©2011
Nikki Briggs
Instagram: @paper_wire_art

PAGE 49
"SunflowerMoon"
©2019
Nikki Briggs
Instagram: @paper_wire_art

PAGE 49
"Family"
©2011
Nikki Briggs
Instagram: @paper_wire_art

PAGE 49
"General Sherman"
©2004
Nikki Briggs
Instagram: @paper_wire_art

PAGE 49
"Bunny Rabbit"
©2009
Nikki Briggs
Instagram: @paper_wire_art

PAGE 28
"Mazurka"
©2019
Nona Bolin

PAGE 29
"Buddist Drive-In"
©2019
Nona Bolin

PAGE 108
"Winter's Song"
©2020
Tara Bullington
www.tarabullington.com

PAGE 109
"Subcontextual"
©2020
Tara Bullington
www.tarabullington.com

PAGE 24
"Goldfish on fire"
©2020
Heiming Chan
Instagram: heiming

PAGE 25
"Goldfish under firework"
©2020
Heiming Chan
Instagram: heiming

PAGE 80
"Self-Portait"
©2012
Rebecca Coleman
Instagram: @hoticer

PAGE 80
"Memory Field: The Bridge"
©2013
Rebecca Coleman
Instagram: @hoticer

PAGE 80
"Ancestor"
©2019
Rebecca Coleman
Instagram: @hoticer

PAGE 81
"Home"
©2012
Rebecca Coleman
Instagram: @hoticer

PAGE 81
"Impressions"
©2012
Rebecca Coleman
Instagram: @hoticer

PAGE 44
"The Appropriation"
©2018
Michael Coppage
www.MichaelCoppage.com
Instagram: prosper_jones_

PAGE 45
"Three/Fifths"
©2018
Michael Coppage
www.MichaelCoppage.com
Instagram: prosper_jones_

PAGE 45
"American Elephant"
©2018
Michael Coppage
www.MichaelCoppage.com
Instagram: prosper_jones_

PAGE 14
"Capilla Ancestral
(Ancestral Chapel)"
©2013
Maritza Dávila-Irizarry
www.atabeira.com

PAGE 14
"Lenguajes (languages)"
©2013
Maritza Dávila-Irizarry
www.atabeira.com

PAGES 14 and 15
"Manos en búsqueda de un idioma
(Hands in search of a language)"
©2011
Maritza Dávila-Irizarry
www.atabeira.com

PAGE 14
"Yagrumo"
©2020
Maritza Dávila-Irizarry
www.atabeira.com

PAGE 14
"Hola! (Hello!)"
©2011
Maritza Dávila-Irizarry
www.atabeira.com

PAGE 14
"Milagros (Miracles)"
©2019
Maritza Dávila-Irizarry
www.atabeira.com

PAGE 110
"NOW IS THE TIME"
©1988
Alonzo Davis
www.alonzodavis.com

PAGE 100
"My Memory Decor"
©2003
Robb Denney

PAGE 100
"Key Heart"
©2003
Robb Denney

PAGE 100
"Corporate Masochist"
©2003
Robb Denney

PAGE 100
"Bull-with Kid"
©2003
Robb Denney

PAGE 101
"Call to the Center"
©2003
Robb Denney

PAGE 30
"Almost"
©2010
Killean Evans
www.Killeanevans.com
Instagram: @killeanevansmetalsmith

PAGE 31
"Untitled"
©2009
Killean Evans
www.Killeanevans.com
Instagram: @killeanevansmetalsmith

PAGE 31
"Built Upon 1"
©2010
Killean Evans
www.Killeanevans.com
Instagram: @killeanevansmetalsmith

EACH WORK OF ART IN THIS COLLECTION WAS OBTAINED WITH PERMISSION FROM THE ARTIST.

PAGE 31
"Built Upon 2"
©2010
Killean Evans
www.Killeanevans.com
Instagram: @killeanevansmetalsmith

PAGE 31
"Built Upon 3"
©2010
Killean Evans
www.Killeanevans.com
Instagram: @killeanevansmetalsmith

PAGE 31
"Detail"
©2018
Killean Evans
www.Killeanevans.com
Instagram: killeanevansmetalsmith

PAGE 104
"Sketch"
©2013
Katey Henriksen Gardner

PAGE 105
"Olive is a Mermaid Tale"
©2019
Katey Henriksen Gardner

PAGE 105
"Tres Calabaza Resplandor"
©2019
Katey Henriksen Gardner

PAGE 104
"MINE. But if you dare...."
©2017
Katey Henriksen Gardner

PAGE 104
"Sketch"
©2017
Katey Henriksen Gardner

PAGE 104
"Ghost River Book"
©2010
Katey Henriksen Gardner

PAGE 104
"Sketch Summer Academy"
©2012
Katey Henriksen Gardner

PAGE 106
"Various Works in Metal and Wood"
©1995 - 2000
Jason Gardner
www.gardnerfinejewelry.com
jason@gardnerfinejewelry.com

PAGE 107
"Awards for Memphis College of Art"
©2008 - 2020
Jason Gardner
www.gardnerfinejewelry.com
jason@gardnerfinejewelry.com

PAGE 88
"Succulent watercolor study"
©2018
Zara Garza
www.zaragarza.com

PAGE 88
"Eye of the Beholder"
©2019
Zara Garza
www.zaragarza.com

PAGE 89
"Attack of the Asiago Arachrids!"
©2015
Zara Garza
www.zaragarza.com

PAGE 89
"Strung Up by the Salami Sisters"
©2015
Zara Garza
www.zaragarza.com

PAGE 89
"Enter the Cyclops Garden"
©2015
Zara Garza
www.zaragarza.com

PAGE 89
"Swiss Strange Brew"
©2016
Zara Garza
www.zaragarza.com

PAGE 89
"Inktober Day 05: Build (Your Own Burger)"
©2019
Zara Garza
www.zaragarza.com

PAGE 89
"Inktober Day 04: Overgrown"
©2019
Zara Garza
www.zaragarza.com

PAGE 89
"Memphis Zoo DREAMNIGHT"
©2019
Zara Garza
www.zaragarza.com

PAGE 72
"Catrina"
©2015
Vanessa Gonzalez
www.vanessagonzalezart.com

PAGE 72
"No Child Left Behind"
©2019
Vanessa Gonzalez
www.vanessagonzalezart.com

PAGE 72
"Abuelita Antonia"
©2020
Vanessa Gonzalez
www.vanessagonzalezart.com

PAGE 73
"Orgullo #1"
©2020
Vanessa Gonzalez
www.vanessagonzalezart.com

PAGE 73
"Orgullo #2"
©2015
Vanessa Gonzalez
www.vanessagonzalezart.com

PAGE 73
"Valadores"
©2018
Vanessa Gonzalez
www.vanessagonzalezart.com

PAGE 73
"Loss of Identidad"
©2015
Vanessa Gonzalez
www.vanessagonzalezart.com

PAGE 60
"Illusory Dancer"
©2020
David Hall
www.jayetkingallery.com

PAGE 61
"A Braid Unravelled"
©2020
David Hall
www.jayetkingallery.com

PAGE 38
"Moon Journals"
©2015-20017
Amanda Michael Harris
Instagram: @ _a_harris

PAGE 38
"Bajulate"
©2017
Amanda Michael Harris
Instagram: @ _a_harris

PAGE 38
"Commendaces"
©2017
Amanda Michael Harris
Instagram: @ _a_harris

PAGE 39
"Moosh Bokhoradet"
©2018
Amanda Michael Harris
Instagram: @ _a_harris

PAGE 39
"Pang"
©2019
Amanda Michael Harris
Instagram: @ _a_harris

PAGE 39
"Tosh"
©2018
Amanda Michael Harris
Instagram: @ _a_harris

PAGE 39
"My Little Round Thing"
©2018
Amanda Michael Harris
Instagram: @ _a_harris

PAGE 39
"Wring"
©2019
Amanda Michael Harris
Instagram: @ _a_harris

PAGE 39
"Trois (orange)"
©2019
Amanda Michael Harris
Instagram: @ _a_harris

PAGE 39
"Goad"
©2019
Amanda Michael Harris
Instagram: @ _a_harris

PAGE 7
"3DP5"
©2016
Adam Hawk
www.adamhawk.com
Instagram: adamhawk_

PAGE 7
"3DP5"
©2018
Adam Hawk
www.adamhawk.com
Instagram: adamhawk_

PAGE 7
"Nautilus #4"
©2018
Adam Hawk
www.adamhawk.com
Instagram: adamhawk_

PAGE 7
"White T-cube"
©2018
Adam Hawk
www.adamhawk.com
Instagram: adamhawk_

PAGE 7
"Nautilus #3"
©2018
Adam Hawk
www.adamhawk.com
Instagram: adamhawk_

PAGE 6
"Black on Green"
©2008
Adam Hawk
www.adamhawk.com
Instagram: adamhawk_

PAGE 6
"Black on White #2"
©2008
Adam Hawk
www.adamhawk.com
Instagram: adamhawk_

EACH WORK OF ART IN THIS COLLECTION WAS OBTAINED WITH PERMISSION FROM THE ARTIST.

PAGE 6
"Ellipse"
©2018
Adam Hawk
www.adamhawk.com
Instagram: adamhawk_

PAGE 6
"Black on Orange"
©2008
Adam Hawk
www.adamhawk.com
Instagram: adamhawk_

PAGE 6
"Black on Black #1"
©2008
Adam Hawk
www.adamhawk.com
Instagram: adamhawk_

PAGE 42
"KenyonsArt"
©2000-2020
Kenyon Hawkins
FB: KenyonsArt
Instagram: @kenyonsart

PAGE 43
"KenyonsArt"
©2000-2020
Kenyon Hawkins
FB: KenyonsArt
Instagram: @kenyonsart

PAGE 18
"Solo"
©2003
C.S. Hubble
www.hubbleducks.com
Instagram: @artistcyn

PAGE 18
"Mother & Child"
©2002
C.S. Hubble
www.hubbleducks.com
Instagram: @artistcyn

PAGE 18
"Ancestors"
©2002
C.S. Hubble
www.hubbleducks.com
Instagram: @artistcyn

PAGE 18
"Melancholy"
©1989
C.S. Hubble
www.hubbleducks.com
Instagram: @artistcyn

PAGE 18
"Portrait"
©2018
C.S. Hubble
www.hubbleducks.com
Instagram: @artistcyn

PAGE 18
"City Impressions"
©2020
C.S. Hubble
www.hubbleducks.com
Instagram: @artistcyn

PAGE 19
"before the moment became legendary,
it was just another day in the studio"
©2018
C.S. Hubble
www.hubbleducks.com
Instagram: @artistcyn

PAGE 19
"Grandma Vivian"
©2018
C.S. Hubble
www.hubbleducks.com
Instagram: @artistcyn

PAGE 56
"Celestial Alchemy"
©2018
Art Hullender
www.fastercreature.com
Instagram: @fastercreature

PAGE 56
"Serpent in the Garden"
©2020
Art Hullender
www.fastercreature.com
Instagram: @fastercreature

PAGE 57
"Dragonflies in Isolation"
©2020
Art Hullender
www.fastercreature.com
Instagram: @fastercreature

PAGE 57
"Realities of Perpetual Wing Flutter"
©2020
Art Hullender
www.fastercreature.com
Instagram: @fastercreature

PAGE 57
"Dragon on the Wind"
©2019
Art Hullender
www.fastercreature.com
Instagram: @fastercreature

PAGE 40
"Out side"
©2016
Kohei Kato
www.koheikato.com
Instagram: kohei.kato

PAGE 40
"Shower"
©2010
Kohei Kato
www.koheikato.com
Instagram: kohei.kato

PAGE 40
"Daughter"
©2018
Kohei Kato
www.koheikato.com
Instagram: kohei.kato

PAGE 41
"Takao"
©2020
Kohei Kato
www.koheikato.com
Instagram: kohei.kato

PAGE 41
"unknown"
©2002
Kohei Kato
www.koheikato.com
Instagram: kohei.kato

PAGE 8
"Immersed"
©2019
Wendy Hailey Kim
Instagram: lemonlushie

PAGE 8
"Family Pool"
©2019
Wendy Hailey Kim
Instagram: lemonlushie

PAGE 8
"Bobbie"
©2019
Wendy Hailey Kim
Instagram: lemonlushie

PAGE 8
"SubMarina"
©2019
Wendy Hailey Kim
Instagram: lemonlushie

PAGE9
"Dylan 2"
©2019
Wendy Hailey Kim
Instagram: lemonlushie

PAGE 9
"Dylan 1"
©2019
Wendy Hailey Kim
Instagram: lemonlushie

PAGE 9
"Chrissy"
©2019
Wendy Hailey Kim
Instagram: lemonlushie

PAGE 9
"Dylan 2"
©2019
Wendy Hailey Kim
Instagram: lemonlushie

PAGE 62
"Blowout"
©2015
Mary Long
www.marylongart.com

PAGE 62
"Game Day"
©2019
Mary Long
www.marylongart.com

PAGE 63
"Carolina 2"
©2017
Mary Long
www.marylongart.com

PAGE 63
"Carolina 3"
©2017
Mary Long
www.marylongart.com

PAGE 63
"Red River"
©2020
Mary Long
www.marylongart.com

PAGE 90
"Untitled (Oaxacan Landscape, #5"
©2017
Michael Lorefice
www.Michaellorefice.com

PAGE 91
"Untitled (Oaxacan Landscape, #7"
©2017
Michael Lorefice
www.Michaellorefice.com

PAGE 46
"Golden"
©2019
Susan Maakestad
www.susanmaakestad.com

PAGE 47
"Spring"
©2019
Susan Maakestad
www.susanmaakestad.com

PAGE 52
"The Stoned Barber"
©2015
Brian Madden
www.maddenbrian.wordpress.com

PAGE 53
"Blue Futures"
©2015
Brian Madden
www.maddenbrian.wordpress.com

PAGE 53
"A Man is a Cat is a Pig is a Turtle"
©2018
Brian Madden
www.maddenbrian.wordpress.com

EACH WORK OF ART IN THIS COLLECTION WAS OBTAINED WITH PERMISSION FROM THE ARTIST.

PAGE 53
"Straight to Video"
©2014
Brian Madden
www.maddenbrian.wordpress.com

PAGE 76
"Spirit Angel Doll"
©2015-2020
Aundra McCoy
Instagram: @mccoyaundra

PAGE 77
"various works"
©2015-2020
Aundra McCoy
Instagram: @mccoyaundra

PAGES 50
"murals with meaning"
©2008-2019
Joybella McCray

PAGES 51
"murals with meaning"
©2008-2019
Joybella McCray

PAGE 98
"Little Bird House"
©2015
Patrick McMillan
www.mcmillanmetals.com
www.thebenchri.com
Instagram: @mcmillanmetals
Instagram: @thebenchri

PAGE 98
"Sea Side View"
©2010
Patrick McMillan
www.mcmillanmetals.com
www.thebenchri.com
Instagram: @mcmillanmetals
Instagram: @thebenchri

PAGE 98
"Cloning"
©2007
Patrick McMillan
www.mcmillanmetals.com
www.thebenchri.com
Instagram: @mcmillanmetals
Instagram: @thebenchri

PAGE 99
"Reliquary"
©2003
Patrick McMillan
www.mcmillanmetals.com
www.thebenchri.com
Instagram: @mcmillanmetals
Instagram: @thebenchri

PAGE 99
"A Garden View"
©2011
Patrick McMillan
www.mcmillanmetals.com
www.thebenchri.com
Instagram: @mcmillanmetals
Instagram: @thebenchri

PAGE 99
"The Pearl Thief"
©2010
Patrick McMillan
www.mcmillanmetals.com
www.thebenchri.com
Instagram: @mcmillanmetals
Instagram: @thebenchri

PAGE 16
"Riches and Infamy"
©2018
Tommy Mavra
www.tmavra.com
Instagram: @tommymavra

PAGE 16
"the way things go"
©2018
Tommy Mavra
www.tmavra.com
Instagram: @tommymavra

PAGE 16
"Sunken Jeep"
©2018
Tommy Mavra
www.tmavra.com
Instagram: @tommymavra

PAGE 16
"Night Shift"
©2018
Tommy Mavra
www.tmavra.com
Instagram: @tommymavra

PAGE 17
"Alligator"
©2018
Tommy Mavra
www.tmavra.com
Instagram: @tommymavra

PAGE 17
"Pineapple Farms"
©2017
Tommy Mavra
www.tmavra.com
Instagram: @tommymavra

PAGE 17
"Dining Rats"
©2017
Tommy Mavra
www.tmavra.com
Instagram: @tommymavra

PAGE 68
"The Drinkers"
©2020
Robert Miller
Instagram: @yo_yogidog22

PAGE 68
"Jason and Wyatt"
©2011
Robert Miller
Instagram: @yo_yogidog22

PAGE 68
"Priscilla"
©2016
Robert Miller
Instagram: @yo_yogidog22

PAGE 69
"Strange Dreams"
©2016
Robert Miller
Instagram: @yo_yogidog22

PAGE 69
"Marlee"
©2020
Robert Miller
Instagram: @yo_yogidog22

PAGE 69
"Bobby and Josie"
©2016
Robert Miller
Instagram: @yo_yogidog22

PAGE 36
"Matthew Moss Illustrations"
©2000-2020
Matthew Moss
www.touchtouchstudio.com
Instagram: matthew_touchtouchstudio

PAGE 37
"Matthew Moss Illustrations"
©2000-2020
Matthew Moss
www.touchtouchstudio.com
Instagram: matthew_touchtouchstudio

PAGE 20
"Trickle Down"
©2017
David C. Mueller
www.muellerlowlife.com
Instagram: @muellerlowlife

PAGE 20
"Turtlehead"
©2019
David C. Mueller
www.muellerlowlife.com
Instagram: @muellerlowlife

PAGE 20
"Rabbit Season"
©2019
David C. Mueller
www.muellerlowlife.com
Instagram: @muellerlowlife

PAGE 20
"The Mashed Potato"
©2018
David C. Mueller
www.muellerlowlife.com
Instagram: @muellerlowlife

PAGE 21
"Leave a Mark"
©2019
David C. Mueller
www.muellerlowlife.com
Instagram: @muellerlowlife

PAGE 21
"Witness to a Murder"
©2017
David C. Mueller
www.muellerlowlife.com
Instagram: @muellerlowlife

PAGE 26
"untitled"
©2020
Amber Palecek
www.Palechickstudios.com
Instagram: @Palechickstudios

PAGE 26
"Gheera in the ferns"
©2018
Amber Palecek
www.Palechickstudios.com
Instagram: @Palechickstudios

PAGE 26
"Mine"
©2016
Amber Palecek
www.Palechickstudios.com
Instagram: @Palechickstudios

PAGE 26
"Tamlin"
©2016
Amber Palecek
www.Palechickstudios.com
Instagram: @Palechickstudios

PAGE 27
"Cleo"
©2015
Amber Palecek
www.Palechickstudios.com
Instagram: @Palechickstudios

PAGE 27
"Gia"
©2018
Amber Palecek
www.Palechickstudios.com
Instagram: @Palechickstudios

PAGE 27
"Little Artist"
©2015
Amber Palecek
www.Palechickstudios.com
Instagram: @Palechickstudios

PAGE 27
"Tamlin in a teacup"
©2016
Amber Palecek
www.Palechickstudios.com
Instagram: @Palechickstudios

PAGE 27
"Extroverted Introvert"
©2016
Amber Palecek
www.Palechickstudios.com
Instagram: @Palechickstudios

EACH WORK OF ART IN THIS COLLECTION WAS OBTAINED WITH PERMISSION FROM THE ARTIST.

PAGE 27
"Manatee"
©2016
Amber Palecek
www.Palechickstudios.com
Instagram: @Palechickstudios

PAGE 64
"Sweet Beef"
©2018
Thomas Matthew Pierson
www.mattpiersonart.com
Instagram: @mattpiersonart

PAGE 65
"Amoeba Fractal 9"
©2020
Thomas Matthew Pierson
www.mattpiersonart.com
Instagram: @mattpiersonart

PAGE 86
"Twilight"
©2019-2020
Andrea Prince
www.Andreaprince.com

PAGE 86
"Patina Dream"
©2019-2020
Andrea Prince
www.Andreaprince.com

PAGE 86
"Reflect"
©2019-2020
Andrea Prince
www.Andreaprince.com

PAGE 86
"Weather the Storm"
©2019-2020
Andrea Prince
www.Andreaprince.com

PAGE 87
"Flying, Floating, Falling"
©2019-2020
Andrea Prince
www.Andreaprince.com

PAGE 87
"Into Being"
©2019-2020
Andrea Prince
www.Andreaprince.com

PAGE 87
"Desire"
©2019-2020
Andrea Prince
www.Andreaprince.comq

PAGE 87
"Reflect"
©2019-2020
Andrea Prince
www.Andreaprince.com

PAGE 87
"Weather the Storm"
©2019-2020
Andrea Prince
www.Andreaprince.com

PAGE 87
"Flying, Floating, Falling"
©2019-2020
Andrea Prince
www.Andreaprince.com

PAGE 87
"Into Being"
©2019-2020
Andrea Prince
www.Andreaprince.com

PAGE 66
"Gold"
©2020
Erica Quinn
Instagram: @butiluvhim

PAGE 67
"Flower Girl"
©2020
Erica Quinn
Instagram: @butiluvhim

PAGE 92
"Artist Books as Shelter, Escape, Epiphany;
Shaping Our Space, Our Thoughts, and Our Aspirations"
©2009
Meda Rae Rives Smith, Veda Mae Rives Aukerman
www.mirrorimagepress.com

PAGE 92
"Memphis Magnolia"
©2009
Meda Rae Rives Smith, Veda Mae Rives Aukerman
www.mirrorimagepress.com

PAGE 93
"TwinPath"
©2009
Meda Rae Rives Smith, Veda Mae Rives Aukerman
www.mirrorimagepress.com

PAGE 93
"Inner Circles"
©2018
Meda Rae Rives Smith, Veda Mae Rives Aukerman
www.mirrorimagepress.com

PAGE 84
"Atlas Reckoning"
©2009
r salant
rslant.com

PAGE 85
"Aliyah"
©2010
r salant
rslant.com

PAGE 12
"Pit-Fired Boxes with Wild Clay"
©2020
Bronco Sloan
Facebook: Bronco Sloan Creations

PAGE 13
"A Bird with the Head of a Bird-Headed Boy Dancing the Dance of His People"
©2015
Bronco Sloan
Facebook: Bronco Sloan Creations

PAGE 10
"Baba Yaga"
©2019
Corey Michael Smithson
www.coreymichaelsmithson.com

PAGE 10
"Lush Fish"
©2000
Corey Michael Smithson
www.coreymichaelsmithson.com

PAGE 10
"Quixote"
©2014
Corey Michael Smithson
www.coreymichaelsmithson.com

PAGE 10
"The Tower"
©2014
Corey Michael Smithson
www.coreymichaelsmithson.com

PAGE 10
"Prong"
©2009
Corey Michael Smithson
www.coreymichaelsmithson.com

PAGE 10
"Knight"
©2007
Corey Michael Smithson
www.coreymichaelsmithson.com

PAGE 10
"Snake Oil"
©2017
Corey Michael Smithson
www.coreymichaelsmithson.com

PAGE 10
"Underground"
©2008
Corey Michael Smithson
www.coreymichaelsmithson.com

PAGE 10
"2018_6_9748"
©2018
Corey Michael Smithson
www.coreymichaelsmithson.com

PAGE 11
"2018_6_8282"
©2018
Corey Michael Smithson
www.coreymichaelsmithson.com

PAGE 11
"2011_3_9733"
©2011
Corey Michael Smithson
www.coreymichaelsmithson.com

PAGE 11
"2011_5_1522"
©2011
Corey Michael Smithson
www.coreymichaelsmithson.com

PAGE 11
"2014_8_2796"
©2014
Corey Michael Smithson
www.coreymichaelsmithson.com

PAGE 11
"2011_3_1327"
©2011
Corey Michael Smithson
www.coreymichaelsmithson.com

PAGE 11
"2012_3_3386"
©2012
Corey Michael Smithson
www.coreymichaelsmithson.com

PAGE 11
"2012_1-2447"
©2012
Corey Michael Smithson
www.coreymichaelsmithson.com

PAGE 11
"2018_6_9249"
©2018
Corey Michael Smithson
www.coreymichaelsmithson.com

PAGE 11
"Mona"
©1992
Corey Michael Smithson
www.coreymichaelsmithson.com

PAGE 11
"Meat"
©1992
Corey Michael Smithson
www.coreymichaelsmithson.com

PAGE 11
"Dunce"
©1993
Corey Michael Smithson
www.coreymichaelsmithson.com

PAGE 102
"Part of a Series of 250 Daily Drawings"
©2020
Helen Stubblefield
www.helenofmemphis.com

EACH WORK OF ART IN THIS COLLECTION WAS OBTAINED WITH PERMISSION FROM THE ARTIST.

PAGE 103
"Part of a Series of 250 Daily Drawings"
©2020
Helen Stubblefield
www.helenofmemphis.com

PAGE 70
"Long's Laundry"
©2000
Laura Summerford
tomyrislaura@gmail.com

PAGE 70
"A.J. Mattox"
©2018
Laura Summerford
tomyrislaura@gmail.com

PAGE 71
"Walker Radiator Works"
©2018
Laura Summerford
tomyrislaura@gmail.com

PAGE 71
"Fill 'er Up"
©2018
Laura Summerford
tomyrislaura@gmail.com

PAGE 71
"The Sun Sets on Fulton"
©2018
Laura Summerford
tomyrislaura@gmail.com

PAGE 71
"Mr. Theo's Turnip Greens"
©2017
Laura Summerford
tomyrislaura@gmail.com

PAGE 71
"Dress Me Up"
©2018
Laura Summerford
tomyrislaura@gmail.com

PAGE 71
"Kermit's Bakery"
©2020
Laura Summerford
tomyrislaura@gmail.com

PAGE 34
"Can't Stop Won't Stop"
©2018
Anna Tillett
www.annatillett.com
Instagram: @annatrobot

PAGE 34
"Dole Whip It Good"
©2017
Anna Tillett
www.annatillett.com
Instagram: @annatrobot

PAGE 34
"Jon Snow Cone"
©2019
Anna Tillett
www.annatillett.com
Instagram: @annatrobot

PAGE 34
"Nerdicorn"
©2018
Anna Tillett
www.annatillett.com
Instagram: @annatrobot

PAGE 35
"Astronaut Ice Cream-Major Tom"
©2019
Anna Tillett
www.annatillett.com
Instagram: @annatrobot

PAGE 35
"Ill Humored Ice Cream-Rocket Science"
©2019
Anna Tillett
www.annatillett.com
Instagram: @annatrobot

PAGE 35
"Devil's Food Cake"
©2019
Anna Tillett
www.annatillett.com
Instagram: @annatrobot

PAGE 35
"Glazed and Confused with Sprinkles"
©2019
Anna Tillett
www.annatillett.com
Instagram: @annatrobot

PAGE 22
"Gato Silvestre"
©2017
Justin Tolentino
www.studiotolentino.com
Instagram: @studiotolentino

PAGE 23
"Gato colorido"
©2018
Justin Tolentino
www.studiotolentino.com
Instagram: @studiotolentino

PAGE 23
"Serpentine"
©2018
Justin Tolentino
www.studiotolentino.com
Instagram: @studiotolentino

PAGE 23
"Gato colorido"
©2018
Justin Tolentino
www.studiotolentino.com
Instagram: @studiotolentino

PAGE 23
"Untitled"
©2018
Justin Tolentino
www.studiotolentino.com
Instagram: @studiotolentino

PAGE 95
"Pecan Grove"
©2005
John Torina
www.JohnTorina.com

PAGE 95
"Moving Clouds over the Mountains"
©2016
John Torina
www.JohnTorina.com

PAGE 95
"The Fire and The Water"
©2014
John Torina
www.JohnTorina.com

PAGE 95
"Shelby Farms"
©2003
John Torina
www.JohnTorina.com

PAGE 94
"Sunrise in the Mountains"
©2015
John Torina
www.JohnTorina.com

PAGE 94
"Mississippi River Channel"
©2005
John Torina
www.JohnTorina.com

PAGE 5
"Portraits of Students"
©1995-2018
Lisa Tribo

PAGE 78
"Details of 'The Night Garden'"
©2018
Lisa Tribo

PAGE 79
"Details of 'The Night Garden'"
©2018
Lisa Tribo

PAGE 54
"Growth"
©2010
Tamika D. Williams
www.tdwms.com
www.wmsstudios.com
Instagram: @tdwms

PAGE 54
"Soft Dreams"
©2007
Tamika D. Williams
www.tdwms.com
www.wmsstudios.com
Instagram: @tdwms

PAGE 55
"Green Mountain Trail"
©2019
Tamika D. Williams
www.tdwms.com
www.wmsstudios.com
Instagram: @tdwms

PAGE 55
"Arc de Triomphe Detail"
©2019
Tamika D. Williams
www.tdwms.com
www.wmsstudios.com
Instagram: @tdwms

PAGE 55
"Ditto Landing"
©2019
Tamika D. Williams
www.tdwms.com
www.wmsstudios.com
Instagram: @tdwms

PAGE 55
"Binary Motions"
©2009
Tamika D. Williams
www.tdwms.com
www.wmsstudios.com
Instagram: @tdwms

PAGE 74
"A Masterpiece of
Introspective Nostalgia"
©2019
Tad Lauritzen Wright
www.tadlauritzenwright.com

PAGE 75
"Everything I Remember About You"
©2019
Tad Lauritzen Wright
www.tadlauritzenwright.com

www.ingramcontent.com/pod-product-compliance
Lightning Source LLC
LaVergne TN
LVHW070128110826
845147LV00002B/213

9781934740996